W9-CHI-760

Japanese Family and Society

Words from Tongo Takebe, A Meiji Era Sociologist

Haworth Series in Marriage & Family Studies
Suzanne K. Steinmetz, PhD, MSW
Editor

Japanese Family and Society
Words from Tongo Takebe,
A Meiji Era Sociologist

Teruhito Sako, PhD
Suzanne K. Steinmetz, PhD, MSW
Editors

The Haworth Press
New York

For more information on this book or to order, visit
http://www.haworthpress.com/store/product.asp?sku=5840

or call 1-800-HAWORTH (800-429-6784) in the United States and Canada
or (607) 722-5857 outside the United States and Canada
or contact orders@HaworthPress.com

© 2007 by The Haworth Press, Inc. All rights reserved. No part of this work may be reproduced or utilized in any form or by any means, electronic or mechanical, including photocopying, microfilm, and recording, or by any information storage and retrieval system, without permission in writing from the publisher. Printed in the United States of America.

The Haworth Press, Inc., 10 Alice Street, Binghamton, NY 13904-1580.

PUBLISHER'S NOTE
The development, preparation, and publication of this work has been undertaken with great care. However, the Publisher, employees, editors, and agents of The Haworth Press are not responsible for any errors contained herein or for consequences that may ensue from use of materials or information contained in this work. The Haworth Press is committed to the dissemination of ideas and information according to the highest standards of intellectual freedom and the free exchange of ideas. Statements made and opinions expressed in this publication do not necessarily reflect the views of the Publisher, Directors, management, or staff of The Haworth Press, Inc., or an endorsement by them.

Frontispiece from *The 75 Years History of Faculty of Sociology* by Seikichi Imai and Keikai Hayashi (1954, Department of Letters, University of Tokyo, Tokyo: Private Printing).

Library of Congress Cataloging-in-Publication Data

Takebe, Tongo, 1871-1945.
 Japanese family and society : words from Tongo Takebe, a Meiji era sociologist / Teruhito Sako, Suzanne K. Steinmetz, editors.
  p. cm.
 Includes bibliographical references.
 ISBN: 978-0-7890-3260-7 (hard : alk. paper)
 ISBN: 978-0-7890-3261-4 (soft : alk. paper)
 1. Sociology—Japan. 2. Sociology—Japan—History. 3. Family—Japan. 4. Sociology. 5. Family.
I. Sako, Teruhito, 1968-. II. Steinmetz, Suzanne K. III. Title.

HM477.J3T35 2007
306.850952—dc22

                                                                    2007000473

建部遯吾博士

Tongo Takebe
March 21, 1871-February 18, 1945

NOTES FOR PROFESSIONAL LIBRARIANS AND LIBRARY USERS

This is an original book title published by The Haworth Press, Inc. Unless otherwise noted in specific chapters with attribution, materials in this book have not been previously published elsewhere in any format or language.

CONSERVATION AND PRESERVATION NOTES

All books published by The Haworth Press, Inc., and its imprints are printed on certified pH neutral, acid-free book grade paper. This paper meets the minimum requirements of American National Standard for Information Sciences-Permanence of Paper for Printed Material, ANSI Z39.48-1984.

DIGITAL OBJECT IDENTIFIER (DOI) LINKING

The Haworth Press is participating in reference linking for elements of our original books. (For more information on reference linking initiatives, please consult the CrossRef Web site at www.crossref.org.) When citing an element of this book such as a chapter, include the element's Digital Object Identifier (DOI) as the last item of the reference. A Digital Object Identifier is a persistent, authoritative, and unique identifier that a publisher assigns to each element of a book. Because of its persistence, DOIs will enable The Haworth Press and other publishers to link to the element referenced, and the link will not break over time. This will be a great resource in scholarly research.

CONTENTS

ABOUT THE EDITORS

Dr. Teruhito Sako, PhD, received his undergraduate degree from Meiji Gakuin University in 1992 and his Doctorate from Hosei University in 1998. He is currently a lecturer in the Department of Sociology, Hosei University, Tokyo, Japan. Dr. Sako was a Research Fellow of Japan Society for the Promotion of Science from 2001-2004. He has published "Two different Aspects of Social Order: From the Participant's View" and "Confucianism and Sociology: A Reevaluation of Tongo Takebe's Early Works," both published in the *Japanese Sociological Review,* "The Concepts of Action Reconsidered," published in *Sociology,* and the book *Clarifying the Problem of Order.*

Dr. Suzanne K. Steinmetz, PhD, MSW, received her PhD in 1975 from Case Western Reserve University and her MSW in 1994 from Indiana University. She is Professor and former Chair of the Department of Sociology at Indiana University—Purdue University at Indianapolis. She is author/editor or co-author/editor of fourteen books, including: *Parent-Youth Relations: Cultural and Cross-Cultural Perspectives; Pioneering Paths in the Study of Families: The Lives and Careers of Family Scholars; Fatherhood: Research, Interventions and Policies; Concepts and Definitions of Family for the 21st Century; Sourcebook of Family Theory and Methods: A Contextual Approach; Marriage and Family Reality: Historical and Contemporary Analysis; Duty Bound: Elder Abuse and Family Care; Family and Support Systems Across the Life Span; Handbook of Marriage and the Family* (1st & 2nd Ed.); and *Violence in the Family.* She has also authored more than 100 additional publications and has produced a curriculum for reducing conflict and violence in the school, and two videos on elder abuse. Dr. Steinmetz is Editor of *Marriage & Family Review.*

Japanese Family and Society
© 2007 by The Haworth Press, Inc. All rights reserved.
doi:10.1300/5840_a

Foreword

Since the end of the last century, so many researchers, practitioners, and educators of social sciences have advocated the necessity of incorporating multiculturalism or cultural pluralism in research, practice, and education. Thanks to the ongoing efforts on the part of the advocators of multicultural and pluralistic perspectives, not only students but also faculty and staff members of the institutions of higher education have more opportunities to learn about and actually receive the benefit of such perspectives.

Despite our collective efforts to understand and appreciate differences among humankind, some of the most tragic terrorist attacks have already occurred in the beginning of this century. In 2001, the tragic incident of 9/11 terrorized the entire nation. While the conflicts among different racial and ethnic groups are growing at the macroscale, conflicts among individuals in family or at work and violence against other members of the community have resulted in serious social problems that are eroding the basic trust among the members of our society at the microlevel. The irony that the social scientists can see in all these conflicts is that we mostly already know why they are happening: Simply stated, they are happening over the distribution of resources, because of different interests, due to lack of understanding, tolerance, or respect for people with different backgrounds.

Unlike the time of sociology's conception, no one in today's society would dispute the status of sociology as an already established academic discipline that ought to be responsible for finding solutions to all those conflicts and advancing multiculturalism or cultural pluralism at the same time. As a matter of fact, sociology teaches us the mechanism of conflicts at both macro- and microlevels, and preaches to us the importance of *empathetic/interpretive understanding, role taking, positive exchange of rewards,* and so forth. If one takes a look

Japanese Family and Society
© 2007 by The Haworth Press, Inc. All rights reserved.
doi:10.1300/5840_b

at the table of contents of any sociology textbook, she or he will notice a chapter or two incorporating multiculturalism or cultural pluralism.

However, what concerns us as sociologists and as educators is the fact that most students in social theory courses (including my own) are not really exposed to perspectives and social philosophies other than those offered by European theorists or theorists of European descent with a Judeo-Christian background such as Auguste Comte, Herbert Spencer, Karl Marx, Emile Durkheim, Max Weber, George Simmel, George Herbert Mead, and other modern theorists with Judeo-Christian backgrounds. For this reason, I am excited about this new book by Drs. Teruhito Sako and Suzanne K. Steinmetz, *Japanese Family and Society: Words from Tongo Takabe, a Meiji Era Sociologist,* and am also honored to be a part of the collective effort to introduce a social theory of one of the finest Japanese Sociologists of the nineteenth century.

Tongo Takebe (1871-1945), a former Professor of Sociology at Tokyo University, was one of the earliest sociologists in Japan. Takebe was born in 1871, just three years after the Meiji Restoration, when the rule of the *samurai* class officially ended. As a sociologist and also a politician, Takebe worked through the eras of the Russo-Japanese War, World War I, and World War II. During his tenure at Tokyo University, Takebe established Japan's first academic program in sociology and published numerous articles and many books, the most famous of which is his four volume book *General Sociology* (1904-1918). In this book Takebe successfully constructed a rather distinctive sociological paradigm that integrates Western social thoughts and Eastern philosophy. Indeed Takebe's *General Sociology* was a cornerstone that went far beyond a mere commentary on Spencerian social evolutionism, but it successfully integrated European social thoughts of the West and Chinese Confucianism of the East in a rigidly pluralistic manner while examining the strengths and weaknesses of both (Sako, 1999).

Despite his tremendous contributions to the development of pluralistic sociology and numerous publications, Takebe's social theory and his insights have largely been neglected in both the English-speaking world and post–World War II Japan. In the English-speaking world, Takebe's works, which were written in semiclassical Japanese, were simply not available because they have never been fully translated into English. In Japan, Takebe's work on neo-social evolutionism has largely been neglected because of his support of the past wars, especially after he became a member of the Japanese Diet in 1923.

The effort of Drs. Teruhito Sako and Suzanne K. Steinmetz in introducing to the English speaking world the work of Takebe, particularly his pluralistic social thought of Japan and unique conceptualization of the family as embedded in Asian culture and tradition, is something that I have personally been waiting for in theoretical sociology. Both authors are established sociologists with different theoretical and methodological backgrounds but with similar interests in a multicultural approach. In this book, the authors have successfully combined their expertise in Japanese social philosophy and in the family to develop a concise yet comprehensive review of the evolution of Japanese history and the major parts of Takebe's important work. I believe this book would be an ideal addition for those who are interested in or seeking social thought of non-Judeo-Christian origin. For instructors and students of courses in classic social theory, I also believe that this book would be a perfect addition to an ordinary textbook.

S. Alexander Takeuchi, PhD
Department of Sociology
University of North Alabama

REFERENCE

Sako, Teruhito. (1999). Takebe, Tongo no shakai-shinnkaron wo sai-hyoka suru. [Reevaluating the social evolution theory of Tongo Takebe.] Paper presented at the 72nd annual meeting of the Japanese Sociological Society. Tokyo, Japan.

Preface

Japanese Family and Society: Words from Tongo Takebe, a Meiji Era Sociologist, is an interesting and informative book. Drs. Teruhito Sako and Suzanne K. Steinmetz should be commended for their decision to introduce to the English-speaking world the thoughts and social theory of Takebe (1871-1945), a unique social thinker and researcher of his generation. As is shown in the book, Takebe was one of the leading figures among the sociologists who contributed greatly to the development of modern sociology during the Meiji and Taisho periods. Takebe was particularly active in his research and writing from 1901 (when he returned from his three years of study in Germany and France and touring in Europe, Russia, and the United States, to assume his role as a professor of sociology at Tokyo Imperial University) to 1922 (when he suddenly resigned from his position at the University and returned to his hometown in the Niigata Prefecture). During these twenty-one years, Takebe was credited with many accomplishments, including the 1913 establishment and the subsequent administration of the Japan Sociological Academy [Nihon Shakaigakuin], which had served as the predecessor for the Japan Sociological Society [Nihon Shakai Gakkai] established in 1924. Takebe conducted a large number of research projects in sociology, and wrote many technical reports, articles, and books, including his well-known four-volume *General Sociology,* which took him a total of fourteen years to complete. There is no question that Takebe was one of the most influential Japanese sociologists during his time.

Despite his great accomplishments in sociology, Takebe remains relatively unknown by contemporary Japanese sociologists and unknown by contemporary sociologists in the United States. After accepting the assignment of writing the preface for this book, I talked with several members of the faculty at our university's sociology

Japanese Family and Society
© 2007 by The Haworth Press, Inc. All rights reserved.
doi:10.1300/5840_c

department concerning what I should know about Tongo Takebe. I was totally puzzled to find out that they knew very little about him. One of them brought up the fact that Takebe had successfully run for the House of Representatives from his hometown in Niigata Prefecture in 1924 and served as an elected member of the legislative branch of national government for two terms until 1928, when he retired from politics. However, Takebe was appointed to the House of Peers in 1938, and served in that capacity throughout the war years until February 1945, when he died. Indeed, Takebe was a sociologist who later became a politician. Or, must we say that Takebe was a politician who earlier was a sociologist? Whichever was Takebe's case, I do not recall ever seeing or hearing about a person like him in my life.

Another colleague of mine related that Takebe was a proud man who was reported to have said "There was no Tongo before Tongo. Nor was there Tongo after Tongo." My colleague remembered reading somewhere another statement attributed to Takebe was that "sociology was started by Auguste Comte but was completed with greatness by Takebe." After discovering these types of anecdotes about Takebe, I could not help becoming more intrigued by him as a person and by his social theory as well. Thus, I decided to take a look at one of the Japanese books on the development of modern Japanese sociology that my colleague had suggested. There I have discovered a great deal of very interesting information about Takebe, and I have a lot to talk about concerning his social theory now. However, because my assignment here is not to assess Takebe's sociology, I will try to refrain from discussing anything that is extraneous to my purposes. The author of the Japanese book (who happened to be an expert on Takebe) recognizes that despite Takebe's strong influence in the field of sociology during his time, the extent of inquiry about his social theory by contemporary sociologists has been indeed limited (Kawai, 2003, p. 206). He also identifies the criticisms of Takebe's social theory that were made by his contemporaries and by social theorists of subsequent generations. For example, one critic suggested that Takebe's theoretical constructs were more like philosophical speculations and were deficient in scientific rigor. Furthermore, there was a criticism that his social theory was completed and fixed so quickly that it became inflexible and incapable of adapting to new social developments in a new era. Thus, another critic stated that Takebe's sociology already was a thing of the past at the end of the Taisho period, and another one yet observed that although Takebe had trained a large number of sociologists during his days at Tokyo Imperial University, there were hardly any formal followers of his sociology at the end (Kawai, 2003, pp. 205-207).

All of these discoveries of mine about Takebe are great for my purposes and would portray him as the interesting and unconventional person that he was. I also must say that all of the information about Takebe I described previously, and a great deal more, are used by Sako and Steinmetz to show the significance of Takebe's social theory in the history of Japanese sociology. Furthermore, Takebe's merging of Eastern and Western social thought, especially in his discussions of societal development, greatly enhances the traditional Eurocentric perspective assumed in contemporary sociological theory. It is evident that these two authors have done extensive research on the history of Japanese sociology, in addition to Japanese history, family, and culture. Finally, it is great that a young and hard-working Japanese scholar, Sako, has teamed up with an accomplished United States researcher, Steinmetz, whom I have known for more than twenty years and worked with in the past, for good purposes. This team has produced a remarkable product. I sincerely hope that others will follow the example of these outstanding people.

Toshio Tatara, PhD
College and Graduate School
of Integrated Human
and Social Welfare Studies
Shukutoku University
Chiba, Japan

REFERENCE

Kawai, T. (2003) *The Development of Modern Japanese Sociology—Scholastic Movement Is As the Systematization of Sociology (Kindai Nihon Shakaigaku no Tenkai—Gakumon Undo to Shiteno Shakaigaku no Seidoka),* Kouseisha Kouseikaku, Tokyo.

Collaboration and Acknowledgments

This book is the result of a five-year collaboration. It began when Suzanne Steinmetz, in an attempt to broaden the material included in her classical theory course beyond the purely Western perspective, was searching for work by early Asian sociologists. Teruhito Sako's work on Takebe was found on his Web site, but it was in Japanese with an English description. A few e-mails later, this project was born. Teruhito Sako was responsible for translating Tongo Takebe's work from Japanese to English. This was more problematic because the Japanese written language was simplified in the 1940s. Suzanne Steinmetz assumed the role of editing the translation, making sure that the essence would be clear while retaining the accuracy of Takebe's words. Sako wrote the chapter on "Founding Fathers"; Steinmetz wrote the chapter on "The History of Japan." Technology enabled us to work efficiently via e-mails, although this was often difficult because of the struggle to maintain a balance between Takebe's exact words and conveying the meanings in a more readable fashion. There were also a number of visits to Indianapolis to enable us to work on this project.

Takebe felt strongly that knowledge should be used for the betterment of society, not just for one's own intellectual development. Thus, following Takebe directives, we hope this book, by introducing Takebe's blending of Eastern and Western sociological perspectives, will enrich the knowledge of future scholars.

* * *

Teruhito Sako: I wish to acknowledge the support by the Grant-in-Aid for Scientific Research provided by the Japanese Government which supported my research and travel. A few days after my first visit to Indianapolis, on September 11, 2001, my wife, Yumiko, and I were in New York City, where we witnessed the worst aspect and the best aspect of human life together. Under such a panicked situation, Yumiko calmly looked for how to survive, and found the right way. As always she stands by me. I wish to dedicate this book to my master Hideaki Hirano, Professor Emeritus, Hosei University.

Suzanne K. Steinmetz: I wish to acknowledge the tremendous support provided by The Haworth Press and its president, Bill Cohen. This publication would not be possible without them. I would also like to thank Alexander Takeuchi for his patient teaching and extensive help in the preparation of the history chapter, and Xiaorong Han, Butler University, for translating the Chinese Hong-fan general system of categories. I wish to dedicate this book to my husband, Tom Pickett, a calming influence in my life.

PART I:
OVERVIEW OF JAPANESE HISTORY
AND SOCIOLOGY

I.1

Society and Family:
A Brief Overview
of the History of Japan

Suzanne K. Steinmetz

Theories of social development cannot be separated from the historical, political, social, and family influences that the theorist experienced.[1] As such, it is necessary to have some understanding of the forces that shaped Japanese thought, not just during the specific era during which the theorist lived, but also those events that became part of the psychic fabric of Japanese citizens prior to this era.

Although most American students and scholars have some background in western European history, our knowledge of Asian history and philosophy is woefully lacking. The Judeo-Christian belief system not only underlies European civilization, history, culture, and

Japanese Family and Society
© 2007 by The Haworth Press, Inc. All rights reserved.
doi:10.1300/5840_01

political views, it also shapes how Asian and other non-European history and culture are evaluated. Our Judeo-Christian background is so ingrained that it influences our ideas of societal development, modernization, values, and beliefs. Takebe, in his discussion of family, notes

> . . . the basic historical assumption of Christian creation theory has been penetrating the Westerner's mind, even the scholar's mind. Their sociological theories of family reflect it . . . it is not acceptable for me that they look down on polygamy and polytheism as uncivilized customs, regardless of the fact that the ancient Grecian, their spiritual spiritual ancestor, practiced those. (Part IV: Family Organization, p. 169 of this book)

Regardless of one's particular religious background or degree of religiosity, this perspective is part of the way that we view the world often without even realizing it.

For example, BC (before Christ) and AD (after Christ's birth) are used worldwide to designate historical time. More recently, BCE (before common era) and CE (common era) for dates have been used. While this renaming adheres to political correctness, the dates still revolve around Christ's birth. In Western societies, an indicator of modernization is the evolution from the family/clan as the primary unit to the nuclear family as the primary unit. The family as a unit of economic production becomes the family as a unit of consumption. However, this is not true in Japan where industrialization and modernization were not equated with a change in the primacy of the family lineage in all matters. This is best summarized by Kawamura's discussion of an article by Kōzō Tsuda written in 1934. This quote emphasized the close connection between the emperor and the family system. In the article, "The Present State of Japanese Fascism," Tsuda wrote

> In the family-system principle of Japan, the keynote of society is not the demand for individual rights, as in the modern countries of the West, but service to the family as a whole. Socially, each family is an independent animate body, a complete cell. Our nationalism should be the extension and enlargement of this family-system principle. This is because our nationalism is

nothing but the union of these families at the national level. The Emperor is the sovereign, family head, center, and general representative of the state as a united body. (Kawamura, 1994, p. 9)

Because Takebe (1871-1945) lived and wrote his study of society during the Meiji era which informed and influenced his most prolific period, this history also concludes with this period (about 1912). Later events such as World War I and II did inform his writing and changed his views, but these events had not yet transpired.

PALEOLITHIC JAPAN

Geology, Geography, and Archeology

The area that is now Japan was first mentioned in the chapter on the Japanese in *Chinese Chronicles of Wei* written during the Han dynasty in the third century CE.[2] The chronicles report that more than thirty Japanese states had been united under a queen and had established relations with China in 239 BCE (Churchill, 2005; Kasahara, 1988). The Japanese, however, did not write their own history until two expansive works appeared, *Kojiki* [The Record of Ancient Matters] written in 712 CE and *Nihon-shoki* [Chronicles of Japan] written in 720 CE.

However, the geological and archeological records tell us much about Paleolithic Japan, which was generally considered to be inhabited between 20,000 and 30,000 BCE (Schirokauer, 1993).[3] During the last Ice Age, the islands which comprise the geographic area known as Japan looked very different. Because of the lowered sea level, the four main islands of Japan, Hokkaidō (the northernmost island), Honshu (the largest island where Tokyo, Kōyoto, and Ōsaka are located), Shikoku (located off the southeast coast of Honshu), and Kyushu (the southernmost island) were connected. Likewise, many of the over 3,000 small islands surrounding Japan, of which 600 are currently inhabited, were part of these land masses. Furthermore, the southernmost island, Kyushu, was connected to the Korean peninsula, and the northernmost island, Hokkaido, was connected to Siberia. Thus, Stone Age humans as well as plants, birds, and mammals crossed these land bridges, and their flint tools, remains of animals, and covered pits provide evidence of their habitation (Hooker, 1996; Schirokauer, 1993; Yamasa Institute, 2005).

Keally (1991) has suggested that Early Paleolithic in Japan is defined as human artifacts that are older than 30,000 years. This *"Pre-Ceramic"* period experienced immigration from the Eurasian continent about 20,000 years ago (Schirokauer, 1993; Yamasa Institute, 2005). Tools and the remains of prehistoric animals that were similar to those found on mainland Asia have been found in archeological sites. Cooking stones and fishing traps such as the *"Yana"* have been dated to the Paleolithic period (Diamond, 1998; Yamasa Institute, 2005).

Roughly 10,000 to 13,000 years ago, sea levels began to rise as the average temperatures around the world increased, heralding the end of the last Ice Age. This resulted in the land bridges submerging, and eventually the land bridge to Korea became submerged making it impossible to reach Japan via land. Contact with other lands ceased because Japan was now 110 miles from South Korea, 190 miles from mainland Russia, and 480 miles from mainland China.

During the earliest times, the inhabitants of Japan were hunters and gatherers. However, as a result of the availability of rich resources in the sea and on land these inhabitants were a sedentary rather than a nomadic people. The early development of pottery is one indication of a sedentary people because carrying large pots would not be practical among nomadic people. The gradual warming of this area resulted in migration to coastal areas.

MESOLITHIC JAPAN

Who Are the Japanese?

Identification of the ethnic lineage of the contemporary inhabitants of Japan and their language has been controversial and the subject of considerable investigation. Anthropological evidence suggests that based on structural characteristics, the Yayoi (immigrants from southern Korea) were a different ethnicity from the earliest Jomon inhabitants. Advances in technology, such as DNA analysis, and archeological evidence support the belief that the early stone-age inhabitants called the Ainu and described as proto-Caucasian with long beards,

were distinct from contemporary Japanese who share genetic characteristics with the inhabitants of the Yayoi period (Diamond, 1998;
Schirokauer, 1993; Yamasa Institute, 2005).

It appears that Jomon period inhabitants spoke an Austronesian
(Papuan, Malayan, and Pacific Island) language. During the Yayoi
period, roughly 900 BCE to 250 BCE, the language of the South
Koreans (an Altaic language group spoken by Koreans, Mongolians,
and Turkish) was merged with the indigenous Austronesian language.
Research indicates that the Austronesian language spoken by the
Jomon was markedly changed after contact and introduction of the
Altaic language (Diamond, 1998; Hooker, 1996).

As a result of this fairly intense contact between the South Koreans
and Jomon inhabitants not only does the contemporary Japanese language contain remnants of both cultures, but DNA analysis also indicates a sharing of genetic traits. However, the Ainu who lived on
Hokkaido, the northernmost island of Japan, remained isolated until
relatively recently, and they have a distinct genetic makeup and language (Diamond, 1998; Schirokauer, 1993).

The Jomon Period: The Earliest Inhabitants

Around 15,000-11,000 BCE and lasting until about 300 BCE,
these Mesolithic or Middle Stone Age people, developed a culture
that was named after the pattern on their pottery, the oldest known
pottery in existence. Discovered by Edward Morse, a nineteenth century American zoologist, the pottery was named *jomon* ("cord marks")
to describe the patterns pressed into the clay (Yamasa Institute,
2005). Although these Mesolithic hunters and gatherers were living
in small tribal groups, they engaged in Neolithic practices such as
making pots and figurines suggesting ancient goddess worship. Although the Jomon period produced pottery without the potter's wheel
(MetroMuseum, 2005) unlike most other world cultures during the
Neolithic period, there is no evidence of weaving technology or mon-
ument building (Hooker, 1996). The pottery fragments that were discovered in Kyushu were highly decorated and considerably older
than known fragments found in China. Totem related to fertility, safe
childbirth, and religious rituals dating from the middle Jomon period
were also found (Schirokauer, 1993).

What was most unique was that the pottery predated the development of agriculture, which is contrary to the accepted beliefs that pottery making is associated with sedentary cultures, not with with hunters and gatherers. Evidence of large pottery, heavy stone tools, and the remains of substantial houses in villages of fifty or more dwellings clearly documents that Jomon inhabitants had a sedentary culture. The access to rich food resources as a result of an extensive coastline and fertile lands covered with a variety of natural foodstuff resulted in the inhabitants being called "affluent foragers" (Pearson as cited by Schirokauer, 1993). Although there was no need for the development of agriculture, pots for cooking the food (increasing the variety of foods which could be eaten) and storing the food were needed. The Jomon period has been divided into six eras described below.

Incipient (15,000-8000 BCE) and Initial Jomon (8000-5000 BCE). Pottery fragments from this earliest period in Japan indicate that these represent the first ceramics in human history, predating Mesopotamian ceramics by over two thousand years. Initial Jomon is distinguished from the earlier period by the availability of nearly complete pots, instead of just fragments.

Early Jamon (5000-2500 BCE) and Middle Jomon (2500-1500 BCE). Global warming at the end of the last Ice Age played a role in the development of agriculture during the Early Jomon period. Not only were the land bridges connecting Japan to Siberia, China, and southern Korea submerged, the coastline expanded and fertile lands were increased. These rich resources enabled the growth of settlements into larger villages and cities. This period is identified with the building of large pit-houses (the floor is built about a foot below ground level), and the production of large clay figurines representing the first Japanese sculptures. Middle Jomon is characterized by increasing sophistication of the clay statuary depicting animals and stylized figurines of humans, known as *dogu*.

Late Jamon (1500-1000 BCE) and Final Jomon (1000-300 BCE). These periods were characterized by the neoglaciation stage in modern climatic history—it got colder! In the third century BCE inhabitants from northern China migrated to Korea and from south Korea they migrated to the more temperate southern areas of Japan. This increased contact resulted in the intermingling of the people (primarily of South Korea, with some Chinese influence) and their languages with the inhabitants of Japan. The immigrants from the Korean peninsula introduced metal working into the culture. In about 660 BCE, the production of heavy female figurines suggests that they practiced a goddess religion. According to Japanese mythology, Jinmu (divine warrior), the first legendary emperor of the Yamato Court of Japan, was seen as descending from the sun goddess Amaterasu Omikami, who is credited with establishing the empire (Kasahara, 2001; Reischauer, 1970).

NEOLITHIC JAPAN: CROSS-CULTURAL CONTACT AND A WRITTEN LANGUAGE

Mesolithic Jomon culture thrived in Japan from the eleventh century BCE to the third century BCE, when it underwent an extensive cultural transformation as a result of waves of immigrants from the Asian mainland, primarily South Korea. The Yayoi had come from northern China, which had experienced a lack of rainfall resulting in the once rich forests and streams becoming the Gobi desert. The original inhabitants of this area immigrated into Korea displacing the indigenous population, and later waves of immigrants from northern China arrived on the Japanese islands.

The Yayoi Period: Contact with China and Korea (300 BCE-250 CE)

The name of this period, Yayoi, is the name of the area in Tokyo where wheel-turned pottery, evidence of habitation by Chinese and Koreans, was discovered. Rice cultivation and bronze and iron metal working was further evidence of increased contact. The *Wei Chih* [Chinese Chronicles] (220-264 CE) report that more than thirty Japanese states had been united into a federation known as Yamatai under Queen Himiko, after a period of civil conflict (Kasahara, 1988; Schirokauer, 1993). In 1999, excavations on Tsushima Island (midway between the Korean peninsula and Kyushu Island) discovered the remains of the capitol of the Tsushima-koku kingdom which was noted in the Wei Chronicles during the Yayoi Period (Yamasa Institute, 2005). Schirokauer (1993, p. 10) noted "The most profound change that occurred during the Yayoi period was the development of wet-field rice cultivation," because it increased economic resources and encouraged population growth and geographic expansion. A Chinese colony established by the Han dynasty began to exert its cultural influence on Japan. Excavations discovered glass beads, bracelets, bronze tools, iron tools, and decorated bronze bells that were produced during this period (Schirokauer, 1993).

An early religion, which later developed into Shintoism, emerged. In this religion, each clan was associated with a god (*Kami*) who was responsible for all things that occurred in nature. The clans (*uji*), whose patriarchal head was both a priest and chief warrior, developed into small states that were engaged in conflict with other *uji*. During this period, Japan developed a centralized government based on the principles of Confucianism. It was also during this period that the importance of family and family lineage became strongly embedded in the culture and remained a critical component of political organization until the Meiji Restoration.

Yamato Period: Beginning of the Empire (250-710 CE)

This period is named after the fertile Yamato plains in the south of the island of Honshu where the first Japanese kingdom, the basis of future Japanese civilizations, arose. The Yamato kings located their capital at Naniwa (modern day Osaka). Increased contact with Korea and China resulted in wars and led to the Yamato subjugating the Koreans and forcing them to pay tribute. The existence of weapons and *Kangou shuuraku* [settlements surrounded by moats], suggest that this was a period of internal conflict (JAANUS, 2005). Impressed with the accomplishment of China, Japan began to redefine itself as an empire with the clan leaders being considered as kings on an equal footing with China. Reischauer (1970, pp. 21-22) reported that "Prince Shotoku even dared to phrase a letter to the Chinese Emperor Yangdi as coming from the Emperor of the Rising Sun to the Emperor of the Setting Sun."

About 405 CE, the Japanese court officially adopted the Chinese writing system and calendar, followed by the official arrival of Buddhism from Korea in 538 CE. From this period on, Shintoism, Japan's original religion, and Buddhism, a newly imported foreign religion, coexisted in a unique manner.

Through wars and kinship ties resulting from marriage, the Yamato clan was able to increase their control over other clan leaders, thus increasing their wealth and political power. However, the Yamato court began to decline when it lost control of the Korean territories and the Chinese emperors refused to provide military assistance to help the Yamato regain this control.

The Kofun *(Tomb) period.* The name *Kofun* is given to this sub-period (250-538 CE) because the clan rulers were buried in large mounds called *Kofun,* similar to those found in Korea. Earlier tombs contained clay sculptures, jewels, and baubles, but beginning in 500 CE the tombs were filled with armor and weapons consistent with the family's wealth and reflecting the importance of the military in Japanese life.

Chinese Confucianism was introduced in 513 CE. In 603 CE Prince Shotoku Taishi, a regent under Empress Suiko, established the first national treasury and began to shape the Japanese government in a manner similar to China's government. Following the Confucian ethical and political model of values for government officials, Prince Shotoku centralized the government and developed a bureaucracy with twelve formal government ranks based on merit, not on family lineage and kinship relationship to the imperial family. His major contribution was the "Constitution of Seventeen Articles" written in 604 (Kasahara, 2001; Takinami, 2004).

Confucian philosophy reinforced the primacy of the family as it defined appropriate interactions for the five critical relationships in the family, community, and state. Most important of these five relationships was that between family and filiality, the obedience the child owes the parents. In Confucian philosophy, the obligation of the son toward his father is stronger than that owed to the state. The relationship between husband and wife and between older brother and younger brother described the appropriate relationship between other family members. Finally, the relationship between friends defined appropriate community level interaction and between the ruler and minister define state-level relationships (Schirokauer, 1993). Family relationships, which constituted three of the five critical relationships identified in Confucianism, provide some insights into family/clan behavior, especially the passionate loyalty to the family/clan, throughout Japan's development.

Asuka period. With the introduction of Buddhism, the Kofun period with its elaborate tombs was replaced by the Asuka period named after the *Asukadera* temple in Asuka, Nara. In 622, Prince Shotoku died and the Soga family regained power through a civil war in which the Soga family killed Shotoku's son and all his family (Kasahara, 1988, 2001).[4] New aristocratic families were formed and of these Fujiwara no Kamatari, who helped push the reforms, was most powerful.

ARISTOCRACY, BUDDHIST PRIESTS, AND SHOGUNS: THE STRUGGLE FOR CONTROL

In spite of attempts to strengthen the power of the emperor, from roughly 710 (the Nara period) until 1867 with the Meiji Restoration, the emperors of the Yamato dynasty were nominal rulers. However, except for a brief period (897-930) when Emperor Daigo suspended the Fujiwara regency and ruled directly, the actual power was held by court nobles, regents, the military governors (shoguns), or local warlords (*daiymō*). The Taika code, introduced in 645, was influenced by the Chinese government systems. The peasants were organized at the village level with land redistributed into equal sizes but redistributed every six years based on the number of children over five in each household. Taxes were collected from the peasants via a portion of the grains or textiles, or by providing labor. Military service was also required. However, following the example in China, the land owned by the aristocracy or that held by religious organizations was exempt from collection of taxes.

The Nara Period: Shōens, Buddhism, and Culture (710-794)

Named after the location, Nara became the permanent capital of Japan in 710. Prior to the Taika reforms, the capital of Japan was moved after the death of an emperor because of the fear of "pollution" resulting from death. During this period, interactions with China increased dramatically and Japan was greatly influenced by the Tang Dynasty. This resulted in elaborate bureaucratic structures, more buildings, and larger staff and made moving the administration extremely difficult.

The first Japanese history, *Kojiki,* [Records of Ancient Matters] written in 712 followed by *Nihon-shoki* [Chronicles of Japan] in 720 were the major source of Shinto mythology. The *Man Yo Shu* [Collection of Ten Thousand Leaves], an anthology of poems, was compiled during this era (Hooker, 1996).

Shōens. Shōens were landholdings that developed from the Chinese "equal field" system for distributing land to peasants who work the land. Taxes were assessed on all land but those held by the imperial and certain aristocratic families and the Buddhist temples and Shinto shrines. Not only were these lands passed on to succeeding generations, additional land was removed from the tax base when peasants turned their land over to the aristocracy or religious organizations. This practice emerged because the rent charged for using the land was less than the taxes assessed on the land if the peasant owned it. As a result, local administrations grew self-sufficient at the same time as land-owning peasants saw heavy increases in taxes to compensate for the diminishing amount of land still available to be taxed. This led to a system of peasants working for large landholders who were not taxed, high taxes on small landholdings, and ultimately greatly reduced income for the state.

Emperors were supposed to be Shinto chiefs. However, in reality, as in the case of Crown Prince Shotoku and others, emperors converted to Buddhism and even became Buddhist priests (Kasahara, 2001). They adopted Buddhism because they believed that its teaching would result in a peaceful society. Monasteries begin to gain political power after Buddhism was embraced by the state, and since their landholdings were exempt from taxes, their wealth also increased. Buddhism spread during this period gaining in power and assuming more influence over the government. The *Sutra of Golden Light* identified Buddha as the source of all laws of the universe and established the principle that all humans have the ability to know right from wrong. Under the *Sutra,* the Japanese emperors were provided with a moral basis not only justifying their rule, but also their decisions to adapt rules and laws to reflect new circumstances.

However, the influence of one Buddhist priest on Empress Koken ultimately resulted in limiting the power of all Buddhist priests. The

Empress had bestowed the honor title of retired emperor, *on Dōkyō,* on a favorite Buddhist priest before she abdicated her throne. Her cousin Fujiwara Nakamaro had advised the abdication but his advice was based on close ties with *on Dōkyō* who wanted to ascend the throne himself. Empress Koken learned of this and had the young emperor removed, and she regained the throne as Empress Shōtoku in 764 (Schirokauer, 1993). This resulted in three important repercussions. First, there was the commissioning of one million prayer charms, among the earliest printed works. Second, women were excluded from sitting on the throne from 764 to 1629 because the Empress's actions had distressed the Nara society.[5] Third was the removal of Buddhist priests from positions of political authority.

The Heian Period: The Rise of Military Shoguns (794-1185)

Emperor Kammu moved the court to Nagaoka in 784 in order to avoid the domination of the Buddhist's in Nara and because of an epidemic in Kyoto (Kasahara, 2001). Ten years later, the court was moved to Heian-kyō in Kyoto where it remained until 1868 (Schirokauer, 1993). As in the Nara period, regional chiefs were replaced with court-appointed governors of the provinces. In 792, universal conscription was replaced by private militia forces under local rule, which invested more power in the hands of local provincial leaders whose power would continue to expand over the centuries.

Changing power structures. A goal during this period was to unify all of Japan under Emperor Kammu's control. Military offensives were launched in order to bring the inhabitants in the northeastern "barbarian" areas of Japan under the Emperor's control. In 794 Kammu appointed Ootomo no Otomaro under the title Tai Shogun [Chief Military Commander] and in 797 appointed Sakanoue no Tamuramaro under the title *Seii Tai shogun* [barbarian-subduing generalissimo]. At this time shogun was a military title given to the commander in chief of the imperial army for a particular operation to conquer the northeastern barbarians called *emishi*. The title only lasted for the duration of a specific military campaign.[6] These actions defined the beginning of the rise in power of provincial military leaders (the *bushi* or samurai) and the decline of the court's (aristocratic) power (Library of Congress Country Studies, 1994; Schirokauer, 1993).

At the beginning of this period, the highest official ranks under the Japanese system were held by the aristocracy, who also occupied the most important offices in the bureaucracy. The power of the Fujiwara nobility continued throughout the ninth and tenth centuries. The aristocracy and religious organizations (temples and shrines) were able to obtain great power and wealth as the central control of Japan continued to decline. This resulted in a return to pre–land reforms and the expansion of the *shōen* system of powerful landowners and the peasants who worked the land.

Official contacts with China stopped in 838 and Japan's goal was continuing stability and peace while developing the Japanese infrastructure, culture, and court behavior. Roads were built, coins minted, and *Kana,* a system for writing the Japanese language, was developed. Women of the imperial court produced considerable classical literature during this era such as the famous *The Story of Genji* by Murasaki Shikibu. It was also during this period that a system of "honorifics" developed. These were rules of grammar for conversation that showed respect based on the relative rank and the gender (women spoke in tentative tense) of the participants.

Decentralization increased and the Chinese-styled land reforms declined as the aristocrats and religious institutions continued to increase their land holding. As their power increased, they became administrators not only of the family (private matters) but also of the public institutions. The nobility were given homes, household servants, and agricultural workers. Provincial officials kept the tax monies, and an increasing number of land holdings were removed from the public tax registers further reducing the official income. The *shōens* became the major source of revenue for the aristocrats and Buddhist temples. The *shōens* continue to gain in power and wealth and eventually became the primary source of military strength. The provincial *bushi* class no longer supported the imperial court (Imatani, 1993). The provincial upper class was being transformed into a military elite based on the concept of *samurai* (one who serves).

The Fujiwara, Taira, and Minamoto were the most prominent of these families. The Fujiwara family exercised considerable control in the selection of emperors thus reducing the emperors' actual power. The historian, George B. Sansom has referred to this practice as "hereditary dictators" (Library of Congress Country Studies, 1994).

The Fujiwara family lost control in 1068 when emperor Go-Sanjo took control of the throne and held control until he abdicated in 1086. However, he continued to be the power behind the throne, via the Insei emperors, until 1156 (Japan-Guide, 2005). There were clashes between rival Buddhist monasteries as well as between the Minamoto and Taira clans, who had been descendents of different emperors but had emerged as powerful military (samurai) families (Imatani, 1993).

The conflict between these families, known as the Gempei War (1180-1185), ended when the Minamoto family emerged as supreme. The Kamakura *bakufu* was established by Minamoto no Yoritomo in 1192, when he received the title of Seii Tai-Shogun from the emperor and also was granted the authority to govern the nation on behalf of the emperor. This new form of government called a *bakufu* [shogun-ate in English] was ruled through a network of personal vassals (*gokenin*) who pledged total loyalty to him in return for land and pro-tection—Japanese feudalism. It was not unusual for the vassals, who often held various bureaucratic offices, to have more power than that of the provincial governors who had been appointed by the imperial court. Thus, aristocracy-based power had been replaced by military-based power.

During the Insei period (1088-1221 AD), former emperors retired early, appointed their teenage sons as emperor, and ruled from behind the scene. This enabled them to regain control of the central functions of the imperial government from the influence of powerful court no-bles such as the Fujiwara and the Taira clans (Imatani, 1993).

The Kamakura Shogunate: Emerging Feudalism and Defeat of the Mongols (1185-1333)

The Kamakura period was named after the seat of the military-based samurai government under Yoritomo Minamoto. Minamoto shogun gained power, but his reign ended six years later when he fell from a horse and never regained consciousness. After Yoritomo died, his eighteen-year-old son, Yoriie, attempted to assume power but lacked the political backing. To fill the void, the political power was assumed by members of the Hojo family (Yoritomo's wife's family), who served as regents (E-Museum, 2005; Japan-Guide, 2005). Yoriie was assassinated in 1203 and Yoriie's younger brother, eleven-year-old Sanetomo, and not his own son Kugyo, received the title of shogun and continued to receive promotions in the court. Kugyo, in an act of jealousy, assassinated Sanetomo with his sword. Kuygo was immediately assassinated by the Hojo family in an act of retaliation, thus eliminating the Yoritomo bloodline (Schirokauer, 1993).

During the Kamakura shogunate, a fifty-one-article legal code (*Jōei* code), based on local customs, defined the rights of the warrior class and replaced the Chinese-modeled code adopted by the emperor in the eighth century. Japanese high culture, which emerged during the Nara period, continued to flourish with the addition of court poetry, *Tanka* (the thirty-one syllable poems), architecture, and elaborate ceremonial clothes for court. For example, the kimono of the well-dressed noble women would have twelve layers of coordinated colors with each layer visible on the sleeves, which extended considerably below her wrists (Schirokauer, 1993).

Feudalism. Unlike western Europe in which the feudal period began in the ninth century and had ended by the middle to late 1400s, the feudal period in Japan began in the late twelfth century and continued until about 1600 (the Kamakura and Muromachi periods). Characteristic of both western European and Japanese feudalism, is a ruler (the emperor in Japan) who shares military and political power with feudal leaders (aristocrats in the early period, followed by military elite in the later period) who controlled vast territories. There were two differences: Japan's evolution of feudalism was considerably slower, and unlike European feudalism, which was derived from Roman concepts of legal rights and obligations, Japanese feudalism was based on ethics and unquestioned loyalty (Reischauer, 1970).

The *shōens,* which grew out of the "equal field" land redistribution based on Confucian philosophy, had already begun to break down during the Nara period. The *shōens* were required to provide military forces, which was difficult for nobles with smaller land holdings. By the time of the Kamakura shogunate, not only had the small landholders relinquished their land to those who were exempt from taxes, many less powerful tax-exempt aristocrats had turned over their property to more powerful families in order to gain their protection (Schirokauer, 1993). This resulted in a greater amount of land being placed under the control of a smaller number of more powerful local samurai warlords. Most of these local samurai warlords, or *daimyō,* were originally constables or civil servants who formerly served under other samurai officers sent from the shogunate. However, they now often had more power than the governor appointed by the emperor. The power held by these provincial samurai warlords continued to expand.[7]

The samurai and *bushi* depended on the income produced by their landholdings. Because the Japanese did not practice primogeniture, in which the eldest son inherits the entire estate, ancestral estates were divided among all children and the land holding became smaller with each generation. In an attempt to preserve the landholdings, women could not inherit land after the Kamakura period. During this time wealthy men had more than one wife, which was also a way of increasing one's wealth and power base (E-Museum, 2005).

The Mongol invasions. The final blow to the power of the Kamakura shogunate was the invasion of Kublai Khan's Mongol army: first in 1274, and again in 1281. "Devine" winds, known as *Kamikaze,* produced a severe storm during the first invasion and a typhoon during the second invasion, repelling the Mongols. However, these conflicts seriously weakened the military government. The *gokenin,* the members of the shogunate's army who fought for the shogunate, suffered considerably after the Mongol invasions. Not only was the Kamakura shogunate unable to reward the *gokenin* with land or other rewards for their help in repelling the Mongols, new taxes had to be levied to cover the cost of the war efforts.

The dissatisfaction continued and confidence in the shogunate declined. In 1333, Emperor Go-Daigo attempted to seize power and restore the government to that existing in the tenth century, an event known as the Kemmu Restoration (1333-1336). After nearly a century and half, the Hojo family lost their power and the Kamakura shogunate ended.

Muromachi Period: The Daimyō, Two Courts, and European Contact (1333-1573)

The Muromachi period is named after the Muromachi district in Kyoto, which became the seat of power under the Ashikaga family's shogunate for nearly 200 years. Although the emperor Go-Daigo was able to seize power from the Kamakura shogunate, he was not able to restore the authority of the imperial throne. In 1336, Ashikaga Takauji, the warrior leader of the rebellion that defeated the Hojo clan, turned against the emperor, captured Kyoto, and two years later was able to exert political pressure on the imperial court to be appointed as the shogun.[8] One reason that the imperial family of Japan has survived numerous political and military revolutions is that the samurai warlords (e.g., *daimyōs* and shogun) needed to rely on the traditional and spiritual authorities of the emperor and the imperial court to become the "appointed rulers" of Japan (Takeuchi, October 3, 2005, personal communication).[9]

The emperor unsuccessfully attempted to reduce the power of the *daimyō* by combining the various military factions under the control of the imperial-appointed civil governors. This action resulted in the loss of the support of the *daimyōs* who had been instrumental in the emperor regaining the throne. Unable to retain control without the support of the *daimyō*, Go-Daigo fled to Yoshino in the south of Kyoto and established the Southern court (Japan-Guide, 2005). The two imperial courts, the Northern (Kyoto) and Southern court (Yoshino) existed for over fifty years until 1392 when the Northern Ashikaga court became the dominant single court.

The Ashikaga clan held power for 200 years, but during the fifteenth and sixteenth centuries, the Ashikaga shogunate and the government at Kyoto declined considerably. At the same time, the *daimyō*, who were not loyal to the central authority but to the local warrior followers, gained in power. Their power was further increased during the ten-year *Ōnin* War (1467-1477) followed by a century of warfare (*Sengoku Jidai*).[10] The Ashikaga shogunate (and vassals they controlled), the *daimyō* (and lower-level samurai warriors and peasants loyal to them), and court-appointed civil governors competed for financial and political power.

The influence of the Ashikaga *bakufu* [shogunate] in Kyoto drastically declined and the *shōen* system was severely damaged. The centralized Confucian-based government was replaced by the *daimyō* who expanded their landholdings, which varied in size from small castle towns to areas the size of former provinces. They assembled feudal armies consisting of peasants and levied taxes directly on the peasantry. However, they were able to maintain the loyalty and support of the peasants, because they also instituted improvements by promoting local economic development, building roads, reclaiming lands, and developing irrigation systems and other public works (Schir-okauer, 1993). Although the imperial court and shoguns had experienced a decline in power, their energy was redirected toward developing art and refined culture. Contact with China had resumed during the Kamakura period, and with this renewed contact came the influence of Zen Buddhism, which was adopted by the Shogun families. Zen Buddhism emphasized aesthetics and produced a renewed interest in the decorative arts, tea ceremonies, dance, drama, calligraphy and increasing the splendor of the shogunal court. Zen also emphasized rigorous discipline and practice. Thus it was well-suited for those who had endured rigorous military training. An emerging middle class developed which consisted of the offspring of the aristocracy who had become bureaucrats and the merchants who were gaining wealth, education, and power as a result of extensive national and international trade (Schirokauer, 1993).

Western contact. The first contact with Europeans occurred in 1543 when a Chinese cargo ship with three gun-owning Portuguese men arrived in the Tangashima harbor. The guns were purchased by the lords of Tanegashima and were used as models by the sword smiths to build and improve the making of guns. Within a short period of time, the *daimyō* were successfully using guns in battles as well as selling arms to other Asian countries (E-Museum, 2005).

A few years later, in 1549, Francis Xavier established a Christian mission in Kagoshima, Japan. The Buddhists opposed the establishing of Christian missions, but the *daimyō* supported them, not for religious salvation but as a mechanism for increasing European contacts for trading. The Jesuits were successful in converting some powerful *daimyō* in Kyushu who then ordered their people to adopt Christianity. For seven years, the Jesuits developed and controlled the Nagasaki port, which was granted to them by a Christian *daimyō*. Steering trade to Christian-friendly *daimyōs* resulted in them obtaining considerable wealth and power, thus the Jesuits were often caught in the middle of violent conflicts between the favored and less favored *daimyōs*. As Schirokauer (1993, p. 134) noted "The Jesuits became minor players in a deadly secular game."

Growth of trade. Throughout the Kamakura and Muromachi periods, there were technological improvements in agriculture and manufacturing along with increased trade. Japan imported cotton from

Korea, but their greatest amount of imports, consisting of medicine, art, copper coins and books, was from China. A major Japanese export was swords, but they also exported copper, sulfur, decorative screens, and, their own invention, the folding fan. Anything "Western" was popular including fashions that displayed Christian objects, which were worn as a fashion not religious statement. The Portuguese also introduced tobacco, bread, playing cards, and the method of deep frying batter-covered vegetables, which is the contemporary Japanese dish known as tempura (E-Museum, 2005; Schirokaeur, 1993). Guilds, organized by merchants and artisans who controlled the manufacturing and trading, provided a source of revenue for the *daimyō.*

New employment opportunities in agriculture, manufacturing, and trade, along with positions within the *daimyō*-controlled provincial governments provided additional revenues for the peasants to gain wealth and power. At the same time, reports of lower ranking samurai selling their prized swords and emperors reduced to selling calligraphy and lacking the funds for proper weddings, burials, and investitures were reported (Reischauer, 1970).

THE END OF CIVIL STRIFE AND REUNIFICATION

Azuchi-Momoyama Period: Reunification and Invasion of Korea (1573-1603)

From 1573 to 1603, Japan was without a shogun. A Japanese feudal warlord, Oda Nobunaga (1534-1582), the ruling *daimyō* of Gifu province, was credited with starting the unification of the country that had been torn apart by two centuries of local wars. However, before the country could be united under the control of a powerful shogunate, he first needed to destroy all other competing sources of power. In 1568, he seized Kyoto and removed the Ashikaga shogunate. He obtained muskets, both imported and locally made, and by 1578 he was able to arm 3,000 men.[11] After seizing Kyoto, he destroyed the monasteries and temples and slaughtered the monks and other insurgents who had resisted Nobunaga's power. He broke up the guilds and reorganized the administration of the land and the tax systems. He also began to disarm the peasants thus indirectly reducing the power of the local *daimyō*.

After Oda's death, one of his generals, Hashiba Hideyoshi (later given a surname of Toyotomi by the emperor), assumed control and continued the pattern of defeating all competing sources of power by subduing the *daimyō*. Hideyoshi was born a peasant but demonstrated considerable political acumen. When he became aware that he would not be able to subdue Tokugawa Ieyasu, the strongest *daimyō* warlord of eastern Japan, he gave his sister in marriage to Ieyasu. To further remove Ieyasu from the seat of power, Hideyoshi provided him with considerable holdings in Kantō in exchange for lesser holdings in central Japan (Schirokauer, 1993). In 1585, Hideyoshi was "adopted" into the Konoe family, descendents of the Fujiwara clan and appointed regent to the emperor, giving him legitimacy in his role within the feudal system as well as the Confucius-based court system (Okano, 2003).

Reunification. In 1590, after defeating the Hojo family in Odawara, Hideyoshi consolidated his power and required all *daimyō* to pledge their allegiance to him. To lessen the likelihood of peasant uprisings, he disarmed them by requesting that they turn in their swords, which would be used to build a large statue of Buddha. He forbade the samurai to be active as farmers and forced them to move into the castle towns creating a large divide between the farmer and the samurai. He carried out a nationwide land survey in order to solidify the tax base and listed the owners' names, which reinforced his decree forbidding peasants to change status and leave the fields. Although he was born a peasant and had achieved the highest court position as a samurai, he ordered citizens to remain in their hereditary social status. Hideyoshi became the prime minister as well as the regent of the emperor and received a rank from the imperial court higher than any previous shogun. He was now able to control other *daimyō* warlords, such as Tokugawa Ieyasu, by using the rational-legal authority given by the traditional court system.

This was also a period of enhanced trading with Europe which resulted in the introduction of Western culture to Japan. In addition to the Portuguese, Spaniards who had colonized the Philippines, the Franciscans from Manila, and the Protestant Dutch and English had arrived by early 1600. This increased contact with foreigners was met with suspicion (Schirokauer, 1993). Unlike the Jesuits who worked among the elite and respected Japanese society and values, the Franciscans worked among the poorest citizens and openly flaunted their beliefs. Jesuit and Franciscan missionaries had been successful in converting Japanese to Christianity with an estimated 300,000 converts by 1614. However, because Christianity was seen as an obstacle in establishing absolute control over the citizens (they pledged their loyalty to the Pope), twenty-six Franciscans were executed, and in 1587, missionaries were expelled from the country (Japan-Guide, 2005).

In 1592, Hideyoshi attempted two invasions of Korea believing that the Japanese samurai could conquer all of East Asia (or at least keep them busy so as not to challenge his authority). When he died in 1598, the invasion was abandoned and peace was made with Japan's neighbors. Reischauer (1970, p. 77) notes the impact of feudalism:

> Japan had entered into feudalism in the twelfth century as a small, weak, and economically backward land on the fringes of the civilized world. It emerged in the sixteenth century from a prolonged period of feudal anarchy an economically advanced nation, able in many ways to compete on terms of equality with the newly encountered peoples of Europe and even with the Chinese.

The Edo Period: Tokugawa Control, Trade, and the Money Economy (1600-1868)

After Hideyoshi's death, Tokugawa Ieyasu, one of the most powerful *daimyō* and a member of the ruling council, defeated the other *daimyō* at the Battle of Sekigahara in 1600. In 1603, the emperor named him shogun as a reward. Ieyasu established his shogunate in Edo (which was renamed Tokyo in 1868) while the emperor and his court remained in Kyoto. After reigning for two years, he turned the position over to his son, in order to ensure a smooth transition, but remained in actual control until his death. The Tokugawa shogunate remained in power for 265 years. The shogun was not only the emperor's primary military deputy, who had police authority, he was also the chief feudal warlord of all the *daimyō*. Several actions were taken to reduce the power of the *daimyō* including limiting them to only one castle, forbidding the repair of their castle without permission, requiring them to obtain the shogunate's permission to marry, transferring *daimyō* to other fiefs, and confiscating and/or redistributing their land.

Just as Max Weber (1904) demonstrated the importance of Protestant doctrine in facilitating modern capitalism in the United States, the importance of Confucian principles during this era facilitated actions that resulted in a society characterized (at least on the surface) as enjoying order and peace. Neo-Confucianism emphasized solidarity and peace based on a rigid, class-based bureaucratic system in which all ranks (*daimyō,* lower-ranking samurai, farmers, and merchants) followed prescribed traditions that ranged from payment of taxes to duties at court—a place for everyone and everyone in his or her place. Entrenched in a feudal, agricultural-based economy, this system became dysfunctional as a money economy controlled by the merchant class emerged.

Maintaining control. The goal of the Tokugawa shogunate was maintaining the peace and the stability of the government, as well as the entire nation (Yokota, 2002). The *daimyō* who had their own governments with local warrior armies and courts, and the ability to levy taxes controlled about 75 percent of the land; the Tokugawa family had direct control over about 25 percent of the land. Thus the shogun, as a national ruler, had the difficult task of obtaining and maintaining control. One such mechanism, noted above, was moving samurai off their land and into castle towns. They were no longer a landed class but urban citizens who served as officials in the shogunal or *daimyō* bureaucracies. Their income was now based on stipends paid by the local *daimyō,* not the rents collected from the peasant farmers. Furthermore, although they were not required to pay direct taxes to the shogunate, they were expected to contribute to the building and repair of various shogunate projects, such as castles and shrines.

Perhaps the greatest control was exercised through *sankin-kohai,* the system of alternate attendance, which required the *daimyō* lord of each han to reside in Edo for a period of time (typically every six months or alternate years). Certain high-ranking *daimyō,* including the heads of the three main Tokugawa families (the Owari, the Kii, and the Mito), had to reside in Edo permanently (Cunnigham, 2004). The legitimate heirs, all sons and the first wives, were required to permanently reside in Edo as political hostages. Not only did this require heavy expenditures for the lords and their family, the elaborate court rules extended to the various subjects who attended the *daimyō* (Jansen, 1971). Most *daimyō* lords built permanent residents in Edo to reduce the massive travel expenses and left the governing of their own territories to their local regents or ministers back home (called *Jodai-garo*). Thus, by the mid- to late-Edo period, the original purpose of the *sankin-kohtai* system was no longer valid (Yawata, 2004).

The Christian problem. Western religion, particularly its connection to Western countries, and the risk of invasion was considered to be a problem that needed to be controlled. Because Christian doctrine demanded obedience and loyalty to God (and the Pope), this was seen as weakening the loyalty and obedience to the family and shogunate. Therefore, it was important to control the *daimyō* who had been converted to Christianity and limit further contact with Christians by controlling the trade with the Europeans. Consequently, a number of drastic actions were taken. In 1606, the practice of Christianity was prohibited; in 1616, foreign trade was limited to Nagasaki and Hirado; in 1622, 120 missionaries and converts were executed; two years later, in 1624, the Spanish were expelled from Japan; and in 1629, thousands of Christians were executed (Library of Congress Country Studies, 1994; Schirokauer, 1993).

After 1635, traveling outside Japan was prohibited, and if one did leave Japan he or she was prohibited from returning. Once again Japan became virtually isolated. The Shimabara Rebellion of 1637-1638, in which the Christian *daimyō* and peasants rebelled against the shogunate, forced Edo to request the assistance of Dutch ships to bombard the rebel stronghold in order to gain control. This marked the demise of Christianity in Japan, and various strategies to rid Japan of direct Western influence were implemented.

The Portuguese were permanently expelled and members of the Portuguese diplomatic mission were executed. Dutch and Chinese trade was restricted to Deshima, a man-made island in Nagasaki harbor, thus not considered to be Japanese soil. Western trade and contact was limited to the non-Catholic Dutch. Citizens were ordered to register at a Buddhist temple or Shinto shrine.

In 1641, the shogun banned Western books except those dealing with pharmacology, surgery, and navigation. Scholars were commissioned to study the Dutch language and collect Dutch books

(Howland, 2002; Jansen, 1971; Library of Congress Country Studies, 1994). Although recent rebellions revolving around Christianity and the potential for occupation by Europeans had occurred, there was little concern about improving military technology. In fact, the reaction was to reemphasize the traditional military skills dominated by the art of swordsmanship.

The growth of commerce. Commerce grew rapidly throughout Japan. Each feudal clan (han) during this period was fairly self-sufficient. The peaceful climate throughout Japan enabled the development of commerce. Products were identified with specific areas such as sake produced in Ikeda, Itami, and Nada, rapeseed oil produced in the central part of Japan, bleached textiles produced in Nara, cotton cloths produced in Kawachi, candles of Aizu bears' gall produced in Kaga and Etchu, and seaweed from Matsumae, were sent to Edo, Osaka, and Kyoto for distribution nationally (Hoxlo, 1931; Takemitsu, 1999). The silk trade flourished throughout the country.

Honorifics, the class and gender-based forms of language that required speakers to identify their own and the other speaker's ranks, became most elaborate during the Edo Tokugawa period. It is interesting to note that during the period in which the aristocracy and military leaders experienced greatly diminished wealth, power, and privilege, the language conventions gave them the greatest amount of deference and respect. Even in contemporary Japan, one's social rank still exists in aspects of the syntax and grammar (Hooker, 1996; Takemitsu, 1999).

Learning and foreign books. The Chu Hsi school of Confucianism, popular at an earlier time, was appealing because it encouraged everyone, from emperor to peasant, to study in order to improve oneself and improve job performance. In 1313, this philosophy was officially sanctioned and became part of the civil service examinations.[12]

The samurai class, no longer engaging in military pursuits, had become well-trained, highly ethical scholars who served in various administrative positions within the government. The merchants had become literate, as had the wealthier peasants, because this was necessary in order to conduct business. In 1720, the ban on the importation of Western books was lifted, and books on military science, shipbuilding, astronomy, pharmacology, and medicine were imported. During the early Edo period, only spoken Dutch had been permitted.

However, by late Edo "Dutch learning" had resulted in the preparation of a Dutch-Japanese dictionary and the translation of texts. New nationalist schools that combined Shintoism and Confucianism, for example, the *Lu-Wang school* of Confucianism became popular. Printing and publication of books increased and education became available to the urban population.

Controlling resources. A variety of restrictions were continued or instituted to control resources. In 1635, a policy of isolation *(sakoku)*, which limited trade to the Chinese and Dutch, was one form of restriction. Suppression of Christianity, which began under Hideyoshi, was continued, and a number of restrictions based on rank or social class were established. Neo-Confucianism, which stressed the importance of social ranking, morals, and education, was strictly followed. Those of the highest rank were samurai, followed by farmers, whose labor was to produce rice and support the samurai. Artisans, merchants, and finally those who held "impure" jobs constituted the remaining ranks. Many samurai (but not all) were forced to live in the cities (where they could be watched) and be supported by stipends provided by the *daimyō* under the samurai's control. Although samurai held the highest rank, by the early 1700s, the merchant class (the fourth lowest of the five classes of occupations) was growing prosperous as a result of the growth of cities and increased commerce (Jansen, 1971).

By the middle Tokugawa period, the *chonin* or craftsmen and merchant class, although of lower rank in the Japanese system of social class, often had considerably more money than that of the samurai (privileged class of warriors and government officials). The merchant class often loaned money to the samurai whose diminishing stipends were inadequate to cover the expenses of an increasingly larger extended family that had a claim to this stipend. As a result, the merchant class increasingly gained power, became educated, and participated in cultural activities that had previously been the privilege of the upper class.

Attempts were made to control the wealth of the merchants by establishing guilds and price controls, but these were largely unsuccessful. The Confucian-based tax structure disproportionately taxed farmers whose duty was to cultivate the land in order to support the samurai and *daimyō* class by paying taxes in rice. Unlike the warrior classes who defended the land or were heirs of those who did so, or the farmers who worked the land, the *chonin* [merchants] were seen as "useless" (Honjo, 1941). Toward the end of Edo period, many lower-ranking samurai had no means of earning an income, unless they gave up their hereditary title and toiled on the land or worked in the city.

The money economy. Beasley (1972) notes that in 1800 Japan still had many elements of a feudal state despite the money economy which was gaining in dominance and weakening the bonds of feudal loyalty. Nobility still had their titles but performed low-level civil and ceremonial functions and depended on the samurai for compensation. The samurai still dominated in political terms, but their situation was problematic because of the considerable growth in the size of the samurai class. *Daimyō* lords continued to sell off part of their land-holdings to finance their required attendance in Edo. When additional monies were needed, taxes were raised, and this heavier tax burden resulted in the farmers engaging in riots. An 1842 examination of the tax revenues revealed that the samurai bore 12 percent, the merchant class bore only 4 percent, but the agricultural class bore 84 percent of the total tax burden (Honjo, 1941). Jansen (1971, p. 122) notes

> The majority of the samurai lived in honorable but austere cir-cumstance, and the literature of Tokugawa days has numerous examples of samurai who pawn their swords, run up debts, are unable to pay for desperately wanted books, and, in some areas resort to infanticide to reduce encumbrances on a limited family budget.

Thus, Japan had the emperor whose rule was strictly symbolic and without power and wealth; the samurai and older court nobility who had become scholars and government administrators and depended on the generosity of the patrons for stipends; and farmers who had to pay increasingly higher taxes to *daimyō* for use of the land. Each of these entities was growing less economically able to cover their debt and responsibilities. Only the lowly merchant class and certain *daimyō* who had engaged in trade were profiting under this new money-based economy. The merchant class was viewed as greedy, only concerned with making profit, and living a luxurious life. Furthermore, they were viewed as causing harm by creating a desire for costly items that the citizenry could not afford. There were even attempts to prohibit the purchasing of luxury items, which did not work. In describing the relative financial situation of the citizenry, Beasley (1972, p. 3) states

> The wealthiest Court nobles had a rice income smaller than that of many of the Shogun's household officers, while most, though outranking the majority of feudal lords, were forced by poverty to live at a standard much like that of a minor lord's retainer.

European warships. In 1846, Commodore James Biddle appeared in Edo Bay with two warships and the goal of establishing diplomatic relations with Japan. Japan rejected the United States' demands. However, when Commodore Matthew Perry and his four-ship squadron appeared in Edo Bay in 1853, the Japanese feared being invaded. Thus, they met the demands of the United States, who wanted to use Japanese ports as supply bases for its commercial fleet. Japan opened its door for the first time in two centuries (Jansen, 1971; Library of Congress Country Studies, 1994). This decision resulted in considerable conflict between the emperor who wanted to keep the foreigners out, the senior officials who wanted to compromise with the foreigners, and the *daimyō* who wanted to go to war but, like the merchants, wanted to increase trade. In addition to reading about Western societies, the arrival of Perry's ships forced the Japanese to address their lack of military preparedness (Jansen, 1971; Reischauer, 1970).

Increased commerce resulted in a continuing redistribution of wealth and power. The samurai and *daimyō*, who were dependent on agricultural taxes or small provincial stipends, were displaced in power and influence by a class of wealthy merchants. The peasants, burdened by increasingly heavier taxes, engaged in more frequent riots. The power and wealth once associated with the aristocracy and samurai under the government based on Confucian philosophy was now dysfunctional. The samurai warrior/scholars and other intellectuals supported a return to an earlier system.

The Meiji Period: Revolution or Restoration (1868-1912)

Emperor Mutsuhito, who ruled until 1912, adopted the name Meiji for the new era, which means "enlightened rule" (Howland, 2002). Based on the range of changes made, one could certainly conclude that they were quite modern and substantially contributed to Japan's rapid development as a major power (it was one of five nations to have permanent status along with the United States, Great Britain, France, and Germany in the League of Nations). Within a few years of the start of the Meiji Restoration *Westernization* became a national goal. Ishida (1971, p. 11) notes

> Not only Western military technology and a Western type of legal system, but all kinds of things Western from clothes to the custom of eating beef and pork, which was prohibited in the Buddhist tradition, were considered to be symbols of "civilization and enlightenment," a fashionable term in the early 1870s.

Revolution or restoration. This controversy revolved around whether the change was initiated "top down"or "bottom up." Was the change in the government structure a revolution in the Marxist sense in which the change resulted from actions taken by those without power—bottom-up change or *revolution*? Or, was the change directed by those at the head of the government—a top-down change or *restoration* of power (Nishio, 1999).

A Marxist interpretation views this as a bourgeois revolution: the peasants and intellectuals (well-educated samurai) attempted to wrest the power from those in control (rich merchant capitalists) thus producing a revolution. On the surface this appears to support a Marxist perspective, which was the view of Japanese sociologists in the 1920s and 1930s, but upon closer examination, this is only part of the paradigm shift (Ishida, 1971; Kawamura, 1994). It was the samurai and aristocrats, who had experienced diminishing power and wealth, who supported reform hoping that wealth and power congruent with their high status birth right might be restored. They assumed that restoring the emperor and transferring the power from Edo to Kyoto would return to them the glory, power, and resources characteristic of the Tokugawa shogunate. Thus, this can be viewed as the restoration of the emperor (Ishida, 1971).

In discussing the fallacy of the Marxist argument, Nishio (1990) notes that a revolution does not need a large-scale redistribution of land or violent clashes. Furthermore, the outcomes of the French and English revolutions did not really differ from the top-down revolution in Japan. Comparing the violence and inefficiency of the French Revolution, Nishio (1999) proposed that a top-down revolution, such as that experienced by Japan (orchestrated by those at the highest levels of government, the emperor), may be considerably more effective in facilitating the development of modern capitalism.

Whether it is considered a revolution or restoration, clearly momentous changes occurred, though not those that the samurai and *daimyō* lords had anticipated. Howland (2002, p. 10) notes

> The Meiji Restoration was in fact a revolution carried out in the name of the Meiji emperor . . . . Within the first decade of "restored" imperial rule, the lords were divested of their domains and the samurai of their hereditary stipends and exclusive military function; the peasants were freed from the land and the townspeople from their guild associations.

In addition to the changes noted previously, the emperor abolished Confucian-based social classes, redistributed land, and instituted a new tax system. Furthermore, compulsory education, the great social leveler, was adopted. Finally, the wearing of swords was prohibited. This was a particularly important symbolic change for the samurai as they had been permitted to wear two long swords, while the *chonin* (commoner class, craftsmen, and merchants) were only permitted to wear one, much shorter sword (Reischauer, 1970; Takeuchi, 2003). The samurai had not only lost their positions as aristocratic warrior-administrators, they were no longer permitted to wear this traditional badge of social superiority.

These actions by the newly empowered emperor resulted in a series of local samurai rebellions, culminating in the unsuccessful Satsuma (or Kagoshima) rebellion led by Saigō Takamori in 1877. This rebellion was dramatized in the movie *The Last Samurai* (Kroopf, Engelman, Zwick, Herkivitz, Cruise, & Wagner, 2003). However, the government's new conscript army, trained in modern military techniques, successfully crushed the uprisings (Reischauer, 1970; Schirokauer, 1993). Recognizing that their former traditional role was no longer viable, samurai sought power and influence by demanding a national legislature. This was strongly supported by the Meiji leaders who believed that this was modeling Western (modern) forms of government and would unify Japan. Since these samurai were highly educated and had gained considerable experience from serving in the bureaucracies of the Tokugawa, they continued to make contributions in government, business, science, and culture.

In a move to increase unity for this *new* government, the emperor moved the capital from Kyoto to Edo (now called Tokyo). The Charter Oath (1868), the first reform, provided a general statement of the goals of the Meiji leaders. It contained five provisions: (1) establish deliberative assemblies, (2) involve all classes (not just the aristocracy) in state affairs, (3) establish freedom of social and occupational mobility, (4) establish just laws of nation, and (5) open the doors to Europe in a search for knowledge to bring Japan into the modern era. An eleven-article constitution further elaborated on the form of the government, which included a Council of State, legislative bodies with a tenure limited to four years, a system of ranks for nobles and officials, and new local administrative rules (Library of Congress Country Studies, 1994).

In the following year, 1869, the *daimyō* of Chōshū, Satsuma, Tosa, and Hizen surrendered their lands and census records to the imperial government and asked that their domains' laws, institutions, and regulations be placed under the control of the new government. The *daimyō* who had not surrendered their lands had their lands placed under the government's control in 1871. The Office of Shinto Worship and government support for Shinto teachers was established and the shrines and other Shinto property returned to the Shinto. Christianity was also legalized, and there was an increased identification with Western ideology and scientific methods.

The new government financed a number of infrastructure improvements such as road, railroad, and telegraph networks, harbor improvement, schools, and modernization of the armed services. Major machinery for silk and cotton mills were imported as were factory equipment for other industries. Foreign workers, technicians, and engineers were hired to start factories, build the modern infrastructure, and train Japanese workers. Japanese were sent to the United States and Europe to study science, engineering, technology, and medicine. A modern banking system was established in the 1880s (Library of Congress Country Studies, 1994).

Colonialism. By the mid-1890s the Meiji leaders had succeeded in convincing the western powers to renegotiate the unequal treaties and returning full diplomatic equality to Japan. Extra-territoriality ended in 1899, and treaty tariffs in 1910. The Meiji leaders sought to buttress their new international position by building a colonial empire. Their motives were mixed. First, in the competitive climate of global imperialism, they wanted to improve Japan's national security by building a defensive buffer of colonial territories. Second, only "civilized" countries, such as Britain and France, possessed colonial empires, so the acquisition of colonies was a marker of international prestige. Finally, having built up their own national wealth and strength, many Japanese felt that they had a mission to spread modernization among their Asian neighbors.

By the 1890s the beginnings of industrialization were well underway. A railroad network linking the major cities of Honshū had expanded into Kyūshū and Hokkaidō; coal mines were producing fuel needed for new steam-driven factories; the cotton-spinning industry had reduced the country's dependence on foreign imports; and a domestic shipbuilding industry was developing. Except for the railroad system, however, the government no longer played a direct role either in financing or managing these enterprises. It had sold off its imported factories to private entrepreneurs and had adopted a policy of encouraging private enterprise.

The dramatic changes during the three decades after the Meiji government took power were driven by government initiatives from above, but other classes of society were not simply passive recipients of change. Although the former samurai no longer had their traditional privileges, their high level of education and public service gave them an important role in government, business, science, education, and culture in the new society. Similar adaptations to the new Japan were made by farmers, *daimyō*, and merchants. The professional army enabled the poorest peasant to learn new skills, ideas, and habits that were useful when they returned to their villages. Finally, by the 1890s, compulsory education became a formidable vehicle to promote change.

FAMILY

When discussing *society, social systems*, or *modernization* as they are applied to Japan, you cannot do so without discussing the clan and the family. To understand the historical evolution of Japanese society, you must really understand the systems of *uji* [the clan] and *ie* [the family] (see Okano, 2003). *Uji* is a kinship group organized around the same "bloodline," while *ie* is a social institution based on members' affiliation through blood, but more strongly through marriage and adoptions. Throughout Japanese history, the imperial "family" had been based on the clan system (united through a single "bloodline"), until the Meiji restoration and the official end of the clan-based system. However, the samurai class that virtually ruled Japan had been based on the family system, organized not only through a "bloodline" but more through marriage and adoptions, to operate and maintain their institutions. In this sense, it was the Kamakura shogunate after Minamoto (clan) Yoritomo's death that introduced the family based system of organizing and maintaining major social institutions. The Tokugawa shogunate of the Edo period affirmed and established the family based system to completely take over the old clan-based system. Therefore, the *ie,* the family based social system, eventually became more important than the *uji,* the clan-based social system, in Japan. Not only was the clan the organizing structure in the earliest recorded eras, the family continued to be a major component of organization throughout Japan's history. The clan was a critical factor in identifying who was in line to be emperor or aristocrat, and the family line was a critical factor in identifying who was in line to be a *daimyō* or high ranking samurai. And, in the early twentieth century, the family lineage became the basis for large manufacturing enterprises.

The Japanese term *ie* could mean both family and home. As an example, consider a family with two sons and a daughter. In Japan, the land was divided among all children until after the Kamakura period when the shrinking size of the landholding resulted in daughters no longer being permitted to inherit land. The adoption of the practice of primogeniture limited the inheritance of land to the eldest son. This son inherits the father's line of the family, the family title, and the family land. The second son starts his own branch of the family. When the eldest and second sons have children, they will follow the same pattern; their eldest sons will carry on their family line while their other sons will establish their own branches of the family. Thus all members of the family are related either through a direct line or through a branch. Ishida (1971, pp. 49-50) reports that

When the abolition of the emperor system, both as power structure and ideology, was ordered by the occupation authorities (after WWII), the family-state idea broke down.

Thus the collapse of this system was *not* the result of Westernization, but instead a change from the traditional family/clan ideology to a modern, individualistic ideology. The change was mandated by the occupation forces in the middle 1940s. They recognized that power and loyalty (and potential to rebel) was possible if the family/clan system was not eliminated.[13]

CONCLUSION

The various factors that influenced the evolution of Japanese society, especially over the last 1,500 years—the history, language and periods of exploration and isolation—were the experiences that shaped Tongo Takebe's vision of social development and the role of the family in this development. Takeshi Ishida (1971, p. 12) notes

> After Japan's victories in the wars with China in 1894-1895 and with Russia in 1904 and 1905, the Japanese people had gained enough confidence to believe that their nation was already one of the great powers of the world . . . . At this point a new slogan emerged: "Fusion between the East and the West."

This is the Japan (and world) that Tongo Takebe had experienced when he began his illustrious career as a sociologist and wrote his most important works analyzing family and society.

In 1936, Howard Becker published an article on Japanese sociology in the *American Sociological Review,* and Jesse Frederick Steiner published a similar article in *The American Journal of Sociology.* Both scholars, who obtained their information by interviewing Japanese sociologists, noted how the language barrier had limited our knowledge of Japanese sociology. Although Becker (p. 458) found fault with Takebe's Comtean-based organismic theory in which society had a *'consciousness'* and *'personality,'* he acknowledged Takebe as "perhaps the most influential single sociologist in Japan" for a quarter-century (1898-1922). He specifically identified *General Sociology* (4 vols.), "for discussing all important sociological theories in the West." Steiner (p. 709) called Takebe "an unusually gifted leader" who "combined Comte's positivism with Confucian philosophy." Both authors remarked on Takebe's desire to use or apply sociology to political and social problems.

Noting that Japanese sociologists are developing their "own distinctive systems" (p. 471), Becker implores us to recognize the research potential, "unparalleled anywhere else in the world," and hopes that we can overcome the almost insurmountable language barriers. Steiner (p. 722) states that an awareness of Japanese sociology would make our studies less provincial in outlook if we had access to these materials, and hopes that "translations of those books that make a real contribution to knowledge" will become available. Over 100 years since Takebe wrote the first volume of *General Sociology,* and seventy-one years after Steiner and Becker wrote their articles, an English translation of this work is now available.

In the following chapter, the social thinkers who influenced Japanese sociology and a biography on Tongo Takebe are presented.

The Founding Fathers of Japanese Sociology

Teruhito Sako

Every discipline has a lineage. It begins with those who first introduced the subject matter and the tradition is continued when those who have learned from them expand the knowledge base. Sociology, when compared to disciplines such as mathematics, chemistry, philosophy, history, or astronomy, is a relatively new field. Auguste Comte (1798-1857) is credited with being the founding father of sociology although one can clearly trace sociology's roots to St. Simon, Hegel, Rousseau, Hobbes, Locke, and countless others. The sociologists discussed below provide some background on the scholars who first brought sociological thought to Japan.

After briefly identifying the earliest scholars to bring sociological thought to Japan, we provide information on the life of Tongo Takebe, the first Japanese scholar to publish an original work, not translations or summaries of Western works.

EARLY JAPANESE SOCIOLOGISTS

Amane Nishi (1829-1897)

Amane Nishi was the first scholar to introduce Auguste Comte's sociology to Japan. He was also one of the key persons who introduced

Japanese Family and Society
© 2007 by The Haworth Press, Inc. All rights reserved.
doi:10.1300/5840_02

the Western liberal arts and social thought and translated basic terms such as *philosophy, subject, object, induction, deduction, reason,* and *phenomenon* into Japanese.

Nishi's background included Zhu Xi's (also known as Chu Hsi) Confucian metaphysics and Sorai Ogyu's (1666-1728) theory of state administration. He went to the Netherlands on a *Bakufu's* special mission where he learned modern theories of law, government, and society from Simon Vissering (1818-1888). After he returned to Tokyo, he entered governmental service with the Ministry of Defense and the Imperial Household Agency. Later he was designated as a member of the Senate and a member of the House of Peers. In 1870, Nishi gave his first lecture on Comte's positive philosophy in Japanese. Nishi's lectures, titled *Encyclopedia,* were given at Ikueisha (the English School that Nishi established). In these lectures Nishi outlined Comte's three-stage progressive theory of human spirit and society. He later introduced Comte's theory of system of sciences, social statics, and dynamics.

Hiroyuki Kato (1836-1916)

Hiroyuki Kato was a major intellect and politician who led Japan into becoming a modern industrial society. He began as an assistant with the Bakufu's Research Center of Western Literature (later University of Tokyo) in 1860, and received a promotion based on his scholarship. He held various important posts in the Meiji government including the undersecretary of the Ministry of Education, Ministry of Diplomacy, president of the University of Tokyo, a member of the House of Peers, and Privy Counselor. He wrote over twenty books including the following: *An Outline of Constitutionalism* (1868), *A Summary of Just Governance* (1870), *The New Theory of the State Constitution* (1875), *The New Theory of Human Rights* (1882), *The Struggle for Rights of the Powerful* (1893), and *The Harmful Influence of Christianity* (1911). In his youth Kato was a progressive democrat, an ardent admirer of the inborn universal equality of human rights who supported *people's sovereignty* or power in the hands of the people. However, later in his life, he became a conservative elitist who supported social Darwinism to justify the vested interests of the Meiji elites and *emperor's sovereignty* or power in the hands of the emperor.

Ernest Francisco Fenollosa (1853-1908)

Ernest F. Fenollosa was the first lecturer of sociology at the University of Tokyo (1878-1886). He studied Hegel's philosophy at Harvard University, before coming to Tokyo. Although his duty was to teach politics and economics, Fenollosa actually taught the modern history of philosophy, utilitarian political philosophy, and Spencer's sociology as preparation for these subjects. In addition to his teaching, Fenollosa was deeply interested in Japanese art. He collected various art objects and shipped them to Boston. His collection can now be seen at the Museum of Fine Arts, Boston.

Masakazu Toyama (1848-1900)

Masakazu Toyama was the first chair of sociology at the University of Tokyo (1893-1897). Similar to Kato, Toyama also started his academic career at the Bakufu's Research Center of Western Literature. After learning English, Toyama was admitted to the University College School in London (1866-1868) and the University of Michigan (1873-1879). When he returned to Tokyo, he was appointed as Professor of the Kaisei School (later University of Tokyo).[1] He held various posts at the University of Tokyo, as a professor, dean of the Literature Department, and president of the university. In 1898, he was appointed as the minister of education in the Meiji government. Toyama was known as an advocate of the people's rights movements. His major work, *The Arguments for People's Rights* (1880), criticized Kato's political conversion and resulted in a major disagreement among scholars in the Meiji academic community. In this debate, both Toyama and Kato used the writings of Herbert Spencer to justify their own positions. Toyama understood Spencer's social evolutionism as a theoretical foundation for the further Meiji reformations. Conversely, Kato understood Spencer as a supporter of the status quo. Toyama was also deeply interested in the reformation of art and public education. At a time when most people thought that women did not need higher education, he strongly supported those who tried to establish women's colleges. His works include *A Plan of Reformation of Theaters* (1886), *The Future of Japanese Paintings* (1890), *The History of Japanese Intellect and Morals* (1895), and *The Collection of New Style Poems* (1895). Takebe took his first sociology course from Professor Toyama.

Nagao Aruga (also spelled Ariga) (1860-1921)

Nagao Aruga was a Meiji jurist, international law theorist, teacher, and sociologist. He was one of the first generation of scholars who grew up under the Meiji national education system. Aruga was the earliest scholar whose work was not limited to translation of other scholars' works in sociology. His three volumes of *Sociology* were titled *Of Social Evolution* (1883), *Of Religious Evolution* (1883), and *Of Familial Evolution* (1884). His book *A Summary of the History of Sociology* (1888-1890) was the first history of sociology written in Japanese. His theory of evolution had a strongly teleological formation. He did not distinguish evolution from progress. As a political scientist, he wrote many books including the following: *Theory of State* (1889), *Responsibility of the Ministers* (1890), *The International Law of War* (1894), *Current Diplomacy* (1898), and *Lectures on the Constitution of the Japanese Empire* (1898). His contributions to pedagogy included *Psychology of Education* (1885) and *The Correspondence Course in Education* (1888), a book that taught pedagogy via a correspondence course.

Shotaro Yoneda (1873-1945)

Shotaro Yoneda is one of the earliest sociologists and philosophers of history in the Kyoto area. He not only expanded the teaching of sociology beyond the boundaries of Tokyo, but also introduced French social psychology (Gabriel Tarde), German formal sociology (Georg Simmel), and phenomenology (Edmund Husserl) to Japan. At that time, sociology was still heavily influenced by Spencer's and Comte's social evolution theories, which attempted to clarify the macro-level historical trend of social change. It was Yoneda who found a theoretical system of sociology that was different from those grounded in social evolution. Together with Tongo Takebe, Yoneda made an effort to establish the first national association of Japanese sociologists. Yoneda's works include *The Study of Current Social Thoughts* (3 vol., 1919-1920), *Sociological Inquiry on Modern Social Problems* (2 vol., 1920-1921), *The Issues of Philosophy of History* (1924), and *A Critical Observation on the Sociological Concepts—To Establish Sociology* (1927).

THE LIFE OF TONGO TAKEBE

Tongo Takebe (1871-1945) was a Japanese sociologist who published more than sixty books and contributed considerably to the development of Japanese sociology. However, his works have been neglected during the past sixty years. In many ways, his life parallels that of the German sociologist, Max Weber. Not only were both working at roughly the same time, both actively applied their knowledge of government and society by serving in their respective governments and working to change their respective societies.

Education and Academic Life

Takebe was born on March 21, 1871—the same year as the establishment of the German empire and the Paris Commune. His birthplace, Yokogoshi village, Niigata prefecture, is located in the northeastern part of Honshu Island, Japan. Niigata has been a major rice-producing region in the country. Also, at the time, Niigata was in the limelight as a promising petroliferous land.[2]

Takebe's family would be considered middle- or upper middle-class by contemporary standards. Takebe's father, Sadao Takebe (1835-1904),[3] was a farmer who served the local government of Tokugawa as a village head and tax collector. As a member of the landowner class during the Edo Tokugawa period (1600-1868), Sadao received an excellent education from private teachers that included academic, artistic, and military areas. However, as noted in the history chapter, the Meiji Restoration, which began in 1868, redistributed the land, changed the tax structure, and removed many privileges formerly enjoyed by this class. This placed Takebe's family in severe financial straits. After Tongo graduated from the junior high school at fifteen years of age he was forced to seek work as a substitute teacher at national elementary schools around Yokogoshi.

Three years later, in 1888, he received a private scholarship. Sota Yamakawa, the principal of Yokogoshi Elementary School where Takebe was employed, asked Sadataro Tamai, a rich landowner in a neighboring village, to give Tongo a scholarship (Kawasaki, 1982, pp. 17-18). Tamai agreed to do so. This funding enabled Takebe to go to Tokyo where he immediately took classes in a variety of subjects.

From 1888 to 1889, he learned English at Tokyo Vocational College (later Waseda University), natural sciences at Tokyo University of Physics (later Tokyo University of Science), German at Tokyo School of Foreign Languages, and Taisei Gakkan Preparatory School (later Taisei High School).

In 1889, after completing these studies, he was admitted to Tokyo Imperial High School. At this time, completing studies at the governmental high schools was virtually the only way one could enter the University of Tokyo. As such it represented the gateway to becoming a scholar.[4] In 1893, at twenty-two years of age, Takebe graduated from high school and gained admission to the University of Tokyo, the School of Liberal Arts. His major was philosophy. As a young scholar, Takebe seemed to be deeply influenced by his academic advisor, Tetsujiro Inoue (1855-1944), a recognized authority on Confucian study, and the earliest scholar to introduce modern German philosophy to Japan. It is obvious that Takebe was greatly influenced in both areas of Inoue's expertise. Before he graduated in 1896, he had published six articles concerning *Yi Jing* [Chinese Divination] in *Rikugo Zasshi,* a major scholarly journal. Takebe's first published book, *Riku Shozan* (1897) dealt with neo-Confucianism. His second book, *Tetsugaku Taikan* [Overview of Philosophy] (1898) was based on modern West European philosophy. Both books included a foreword by Inoue.

However, in 1896, when he graduated from his undergraduate studies and began his doctoral study, he did not choose philosophy but instead selected sociology. Takebe never provided an explanation for this change. In the autumn of 1896, Takebe visited the Chair and Professor of Sociology, Masakazu Toyama (1848-1900), to ask permission to enroll in the graduate sociology course. Toyama assumed that Takebe was not familiar with sociology, so he advised him to choose some small theme that could be accomplished within two or three years of study. Takebe replied that not only was he already proficient in major philosophical thought, he found that in sociology there were scarcely fundamental studies and general inquiry on society, the field's major subject. Apparently, Takebe was attracted to sociology. However his fascination was not in its accomplishments but in its questionable quality and lack of substance.

In the Meiji Japanese intellectual world, sociology was highly regarded. There were three major reasons for this. First of all, the early Meiji intellectuals believed Comte's hierarchical system of science was quite useful as a platform on which to systematically absorb Western knowledge. They treated Comte's work as a comprehensive guidebook for all the Western sciences.[5]

Second, from Meiji 10s (1877-1886) onward, Spencer's theory of social evolution came into vogue because it justified the positions of both the newly established ruling class and the nonconformists. The Meiji elites asserted that their established rule was a natural consequence of "the survival of the fittest," so it was just and fair. The non-conformists argued that such a "struggle for survival" could not be just without securing equal conditions for all competitors. In short, this period in sociology was an arena of the major ideological conflict. This was the philosophical atmosphere during Takebe's youth.

Third, at that time, many Japanese intellectuals gave credit to Spencer's theory because it was based on science not Christian theology. Although there was some interest in Christianity in Meiji Japan, the majority wanted to exclude religious thought and concentrate on science and technology.

These facts also provided insights into the reason why the Meiji intelligentsia who called themselves "sociologists" tended to rise to higher levels within the Meiji bureaucracy. The earliest scholar to introduce Spencer, Hiroyuki Kato (1836-1916), became the first president of the University of Tokyo, a delegate to the House of Peers, the Imperial Court Counselor, and the Privy Counsel Advisor. Toyama also became president of the University of Tokyo, and later the Minister of Education (Kawai & Takemura, 1998).

So, the previous anecdote about Takebe suggests not just overconfidence associated with youth but also the situation that surrounded sociology at that time. As Takebe pointed out, people read Spencer, without knowing his biggest subject—society. To argue on some system of thought without clarifying its core concepts is a tendency peculiar to the changing vogue in the academic world. Takebe was aware of the need to rediscover sociology as something more reliable, exact, and systematic. For this reason, he strategically kept Spencer at a distance and attempted to reread Comte with the full use of his philosophical and theoretical ability. His book, *General Sociology*, vol. 1, *Prolegomenon of Sociology* (1904), which has been translated into English, was the finest fruit of this project.

Takebe received a scholarship from the Japanese government for study. From August 1898 to October 1901, he went to Germany and France to study, and to Russia and the United States to observe their societies (Takebe, 1902). But frankly speaking, we can hardly say that he had thrown himself into study. He seemed to spend most of his time on sightseeing. In the first twelve months, he toured numerous cities in Germany and Austria-Hungary on an unbelievably tight schedule. In October 1899, he finally arrived at Saint Cloud, on the outskirts of Paris. His travel notes were suspended between October 1890 and January 1901. It appeared that he was absorbed in writing and polishing his doctoral dissertation, *General Sociology,* from October 1899 to March 1901 at a quiet residence in Saint Cloud (Takebe, 1902).

At the end of March 1901, Takebe awoke from the long hibernation. He left Paris for southern France, crossed the border into Italy, and energetically wandered all around the Italian peninsula. On April 18, Takebe visited Enrico Ferri in Rome, and exchanged views on sociology, criminology, religion, socialism, and international relations. He then crossed the Alps, went to Bern and Geneva, and then back to Paris. In early May after a few days rest, he went across the English Channel to Dover and observed London for about one and a half months (Takebe, 1902).

Takebe returned to the Continent and visited Brussels on July 4th to meet Guillaume De Greef. Continuing his travels, he visited Germany, Poland, and Russia, and then arrived in Moscow at the end of July. For Takebe, fatigue is a word only to be found in the dictionary of fools. A few days later, he made a two-week round trip around the Scandinavian countries.

In the middle of August 1901, Takebe started on his homeward journey. Stopping in the United States from August 20th to September 12th, he visited New York City, Philadelphia, Washington, DC, Buffalo, Niagara, Chicago, and San Francisco. On September 4th, he made a courtesy visit to Albion Small in the Sociology Department at the University of Chicago. On October 1, 1901, he returned to Tokyo. A few days later he started to give lectures as a professor of sociology to the students of the University of Tokyo.

Contributions of General Sociology

General Sociology was an epoch-making work on sociology in at least two respects. First, *General Sociology* was a groundbreaking work in Japanese sociology. Before Takebe, Japanese sociology was limited to a summary of, or commentary on, Herbert Spencer. In the worst case it was a poor adaptation of social evolution theory. Takebe made substantial contributions to the development of the Japanese understanding of sociology by his comparative examinations of the major tracks of modern sociological thoughts. Thus, *General Sociology* was the first Japanese effort that mapped various sociological theories and ideas—the seventeenth-century natural law theories, the eighteenth-century enlightenment theories, and the nineteenth century positivism, social evolution, and philosophy of history, etc.— onto a single comprehensive schema.

Second, Takebe's four-volume *General Sociology* (1904, 1905, 1909, 1918) was, as far as I know, the only and sole sociologist's work that was projected to connect the West European social thoughts with East Asian thought. That is why I chose to translate the introductory volume of *General Sociology* (1904) into English as the most important early Japanese work of sociology to be acknowledged. Written about a century ago, our knowledge base has expanded and our views on society have likewise changed. An examination of the writings of all early social theorists reveals limitation, thus reading Takebe's work through contemporary lens will reveal aspects that we do not agree with or materials that we see as inaccurate. However, what is unique in Takebe's work, and does provide considerable insights for examining contemporary society, is that he had an understanding of both Western and Eastern views of society, and he knew the appropriate perspective from which to see the relationship between the West and the East.[6]

Unfortunately, from Max Weber's *Economic Ethics in World Religions* (1915-1920) onward, sociologists seem to take the approach of characterizing every non-European system of thought as "religious." It is not difficult to see Confucianism as a subject of sociology of religion. But we must recognize that in the case of the Japanese assimilation of Western science, Confucianism played a powerful role as a major interpreter of Western sciences. At that time, in the Japanese context, sociology was a subject to be deciphered and interpreted by the Confucian system of thought. For the Japanese, Confucianism was not just a belief system, but also a system of science. Takebe was a firsthand witness who was directly involved in the encountering, questioning, and interweaving of the west European and the east Asian systems of thought. In addition, in my view, his work contains many clues to reconsidering the relationships between the indigenous and universal, in the age of globalization today.

Family and Political Life

Takebe's first marriage, in 1902, was to Yoshiko Tani (Viscount Takeki Tani's oldest daughter). But five years later they divorced. According to a piece of gossip in a newspaper, "Yoshiko has been getting along with Takebe. Their home was warm enough. But recently they decided to divorce and nobody knows the reason" (*Yomiuri Shimbun,* February 3, 1907). Just two months later Takebe married Ikuko Murayama, a teacher at Niigata Normal School (*Yomiuri Shimbun,* April 7, 1907). We do not have further details concerning Takebe's marriages and divorces. According to his descendant, Takebe was a patriarch of his home. He was extremely strict and known to severely scold his children.

Throughout his life Takebe was a well-known, staunch patriot. In May 1903, when Japan-Russia relations were shaky, Takebe independently petitioned the Prime Minister Taro Katsura (1847-1913) to immediately declare war against Russia. In August 1905, when the peace conference was held at Portsmouth, New Hampshire, Takebe along with six other colleagues petitioned *Tenno* (what Japanese emperors were called) not to seal any agreement. Also, when Japan was involved in the war against the Allied Forces (1941-1945), Takebe advocated the need for aggressive expansion of Japanese imperial rule around east Asia and southeast Asia. Given Takebe's position regarding the war, it is understandable why the post–World War II generation is quite negative toward Takebe. Takebe did not recognize the dehumanizing characteristic of the twentieth century total war. Perhaps he naively equated World War II with a premodern duel. Just like Don Quixote, Takebe was totally blind in recognizing that chivalry or samurai used in face-to-face battle are irrelevant in a mechanized war. According to Takebe's theory of the evolution of war, the more society evolves and its moral, political, and economic condition improves, the less people want to be militant. Even when war is unavoidable, people want to conduct war in a more humane and orderly manner with less damage (*Asahi Shimbun,* September 19, 1928). This theory was not Takebe's creation. In the 1920s, during the short interlude between two world wars, many of the intelligentsia posed similar optimistic views on the future of warfare.

The alumni of University of Tokyo call the twenty-one-year period from 1901 to 1922 when he was chair of sociology, "Takebe's Era" (Imai & Hayashi, 1954, p. 28). In general, the alumni evaluated Takebe as demanding, arrogant, and coercive. Several legends about Takebe remain. Every morning he came to the gate of the campus on horseback. At that time, most others used rickshaws. In the lecture room he always wore a formal frock coat, even in the middle of summer, and spoke in solemn tones. He seemed to think very highly of himself, saying, "Kant, Comte, and Tongo are the best scholars of the modern age," or "Sociology was commenced by Comte, and shall be completed by Tongo" (Imai & Hayashi, 1954, p. 29). But on the other hand, he was a true academician who often attended other young professors' lectures and took copious notes (Imai & Hayashi, 1954, p. 29).

In addition to his extensive publications of academic works, Takebe also made an effort to organize Japanese sociologists. In 1913, with Shotaro Yoneda (1873-1945), professor of sociology at Kyoto Imperial University, Takebe instituted the first nationwide sociological association, *Nippon Shakai Gakuin* [Japan Academy of Sociology] (1913-1927). From 1913 to 1922, Takebe worked as the chief editor of its *Annals* and contributed many articles, book reviews, and memoranda to the journal. From 1920 to 1927, he projected, supervised, and published the twenty-five volumes of *Studies of Contemporary Social Problems.*[7]

In September 1922, when he was fifty-two years old, Takebe suddenly resigned his post as professor. According to his career record that was written by his own hand, it was because of "the decline of his health and strength." However, Teizo Toda, his pupil (1898-1995), Masamichi Shin-mei (1898-1984), a major sociologist of the Showa Era who knew Takebe well, and Kenta Fujita, an ex-deputy mayor of

Yokogoshi Village, have stated that he took this action in order to provide the position of assistant professor to Teizo Toda (Kawasaki, 1982, pp. 31-32). Toda was a flag bearer of the new generation of sociologists, who had acquired a background in the empirical methods of social survey at the University of Chicago (1920-1921) (Kawai & Takemura, 1998). Toda also considered Takebe to be authoritarian and believed that his sociology was already outdated. Takebe must have noticed Toda's feeling. Nevertheless he presented his post to Toda. Takebe might be arrogant and authoritarian, but hc was also generous and fair, and indifferent to money and fame (Kawasaki, 1982, p. 32).

One year after the resignation, a special national election was held to fill the vacancy created when the delegate Jin-ichiro Sakaguchi (Niigata electoral district no. 6) died. Takebe ran for the House of Representatives as a member of the *Kenseikai* [Constitutionalist Party], and in December 1923, he won. Although the House of Representatives was dissolved in January 1924, he won the election held in June 1924. As a delegate, he wrestled with the population policy, reformation of the election system, and reformation of the public education system.[8] In September 1927, Takebe attended the 24th Conference of the Inter-Parliamentary Union held in Paris. As the Japanese representative, he made a speech to support publicly financed elections.[9] From 1928 to 1938, Takebe was not active in either the political or academic worlds. But he was still hale and hearty. During those ten years, he wrote and published several books and articles and taught sociology as a part-time lecturer at several colleges around Tokyo. Takebe again returned to the stage of politics when he was sixty-eight years of age. He was nominated as a delegate to the House of Peers and accepted the nomination. Until his death, Takebe energetically supported the legitimacy of the Japanese imperial ideal of the Great Commonwealth of East Asia, to emancipate the East Asian nations from the Western powers, and establish Japanese rule.

Takebe died on February 18, 1945. A few days later, his residence was destroyed by the Allied bombs. This occurred about six months before the collapse of the Great Japanese Empire. As mentioned previously, Takebe has an unsavory reputation among the postwar generations, because of his positive support of Japan's role in World War II. However, this was only one aspect of his life. He also left an important sociological legacy for us. Now, in the early twenty-first century, an era characterized as having a high level of conflict on a global level, it is time for us to open his treasure box.

Following Generations

From the Taisho period (1912-1926) onward, Japanese sociology was characterized by several methods and themes. Yasuma Takata (1883-1972) developed the sociology of economy by integrating Marx's historical materialism and Simmel's formal sociology. His major works include *Introduction to Sociology* (1922), *Class System and the Third View of History* (1925), and *A Theory of Powers* (1940). Teizo Toda (1887-1955) introduced social survey methods learned at the University of Chicago and developed sociology of the family as an empirical and practical science. His major works include *Study of Family* (1926), *Marriage and Family* (1934), and *Social Survey* (1933). Ikutaro Shimizu (1907-1988) wrote a comprehensive historical survey of modern Western social thoughts from the seventeenth century, and tried to clarify the twentieth-century mass (crowd and mob) phenomenon. His works include *Society and Individual: The Formative History of Sociology* (1935), *Rumors* (1937), and *Notes on Ethics* (1972).

Throughout the postwar era (from 1945), Japanese sociology has been struggling with contemporary social problems as they have occurred, problems such as economic growth, family-related problems, urban-rural problems, education, welfare, crime, pollution, and the like. Currently, Japanese sociologists are again seeking general theoretical schemas in an attempt to understand society as a whole.

The following chapters have been translated from Tongo Takebe's four volumes of *General Sociology*. Parts II and III in this book are from volume 1, *Shakaigaku Josetsu* [Prolegomenon of Sociology] (1904). Part IV is from volume 3, *Shakai Seigaku* [Social Statistics] (1909).

PART II:
THEORETICAL INTRODUCTION

II.1

Society

Tongo Takebe

INTRODUCTION

To begin, we need to first establish the foundation of our study as without it we cannot accurately obtain knowledge. The foundation should contain the subject, the quality, the sphere, and the method used to obtain this knowledge.

There are two modes for establishing this foundation. The first mode, theoretical, uses *deduction* to discover the foundation of inquiry through logical reasoning. The second mode, historical, uses *induction* to discover the foundation through integration of earlier studies.

Part II is from Tongo Takebe, *General Sociology* (1904). *Prolegomenon of Sociology.* Part 1, Chapters 1-4. Tokyo: Kinkodo Press.

Japanese Family and Society
© 2007 by The Haworth Press, Inc. All rights reserved.
doi:10.1300/5840_03

Four methods can be used for the study.

1. The *ideal method* contains both theoretical and historical modes of inquiry.
2. The *theoretical method* addresses theoretical issues but ignores the historical methods.
3. The *historical method* addresses historical issues but ignores the theoretical methods.
4. The *false method* imitates previous work but ignores both the theoretical and historical methods, thus reproduces inaccurate information.

The ideal method is the most desirable method for all scholarly activity because we can exclude errors when we use this approach. The theoretical method often leads us to unproductive results when it is not accompanied by the historical method. The historical method cannot avoid errors when it is not guided by the theoretical method. The false method is not worth considering here as it does not provide a sufficient foundation for scientific inquiries.

The new sciences, especially sociology, need to be guided by the ideal method. There are three reasons for this:

1. There is no consensus between scholars on the major objective of sociology, since the meaning of the word *society* is so complex and broad.
2. Under the present condition, sociologists are using various methods, working independently, so they cannot effectively communicate with each other.
3. For the reasons stated above, sociologists disagree with each other on what are the essential features of sociology. The disputes often make sociologist's own academic status unstable. This volume, *The Prolegomenon of Sociology,* contains the theoretical part (Part II) and the historical part (Part III).

Almost all the contemporary scholars believe that sociology needs its own prolegomenon (an overview or outline of topics that will appear in the book) that clarifies the relationship between human knowledge and human life in general. Auguste Comte's first volume of *Cours de Philosophie Positive* (1830-1842) contained his general remarks on the sciences. Likewise, Herbert Spencer's *First Principles* (1862)[1] was used to establish and describe his system of thought. The first half of Guillaume de Greef's book (1886 & 1889) was an overview of the subject.[2]

There are some scholars, such as Arthur Fairbanks (1896), who still ignore the need for establishing a clear foundation of study. They are satisfied with interpreting only parts of Spencer's theoretical system (see Fairbanks, 1896; Bascom, 1895; Spencer, 1876-1896). Jean Gabriel Tarde (1895), John Mackenzie (1890), and Gustav Adolph Lindner (1871) also recognize the need for establishing a foundation for their study, but they have concentrated on particular themes like psychological interpretation of sociability, or developing process of civilizations. Therefore, scholars who study sociology should place great importance on clearly identifying the foundation of their study.

WHAT IS SOCIETY?

The theoretical part should be described according to the contents of the foundation—subject, quality, sphere, and method.

Society is the subject of sociology. Therefore we should articulate the sense of the word *society,* from its ordinary uses to its academic use. It is proper to proceed with our inquiry according to the following three steps. First, we need to describe the ordinary uses of the word society. Second, we need to classify the various meanings of the word society. Third, we need to achieve a clear-cut conception of society. I'd like to call this kind of definition syllogistic.

The cooperative body[3] consisting of more than two humans can commonly be considered to be a society. The gathering consisting of more than two animals is sometimes called an animal society (Espinas, 1877), but it is just a figurative use of the word. A single individual cannot be considered to be a society. If two or more humans live a great distance from each other and were not able to cooperate, there exists no causal relation between them, they cannot be said to be a society. Each sociological researcher still conceptualizes society in his or her own way. More than that, some of them abandon conceptualizing society and, unfortunately, use society in its ordinary sense.

We should take John Stuart Mill's points seriously. Mill (1843) frequently referred to methodological issues, and stressed in his book, *System of Logic,* that science should be concluded with definitions. We should clarify the conception of society step by step, instead of rash and sometimes obscure conceptions.

SOCIETY IS A FACT

Now we are entering into the second step by which we sort out the meaning of the word *society.* Society is used in intimate relations with relatively clearer conceptions of *fact, body,* and *organism.* Scholars who claim to be social organicists such as Small and Vincent (1894), who call their theory "organic theory of society," as well as Schäffle, (1875-1878), Lilienfeld (1975, 1977, 1979), and Worms try to define society by comparing it with an organism.

Although it is not improper to define society in such a way because organism in fact often parallels society in many respects, I will try to define society by comparing it with some basic categories such as fact, body, and organism.

First, society is a fact. The word *fact* means a basic concept or idea that every human can recognize. One may recognize the statement, "Society is a fact," in two ways.

1. *Recognition by common sense.* No one can ignore that there exists some facts that qualify as *social.* We need to understand society not as an ideal to be reached, but as a *fact* before we begin any systematic inquiry.
2. *Recognition by metaphysical contemplation.* The cooperative body consisting of more than two humans is called society. The concept of *human* includes the *self.* The existence of self can be said to be a metaphysical fact, since we can find it only through self-reflection. We cannot achieve any truth without it. Every truth is derived from the awareness of self. We recognize the existence of humans who have a self, by being able to be self-reflective. In an objective world they become conscious of the social body which each human is a part of. In sum, we recognize society as a necessary consequence of the awareness of self. Therefore society is a fact.

SOCIETY IS A BODY

Second, society is an integrated body. What I call *integrated body,* unity, *einheit* [oneness], is a body that is composed of some internal parts that are functionally differentiated. It maintains itself independent of other bodies that surround it. Objects change in their appearance according to changes in our viewpoints. Thus, the goals of the inquiry and the way used to obtain the information, will influence the appearance. Since a human constantly changes his nature, the same objects appear to be different. That is why we are so slow and awkward in constructing our knowledge into an integrated body, in spite of the fact that things and matters are integrated bodies in themselves. It is an irony that academicians who think in a highly abstract way often cannot avoid this difficulty.[4]

Society is an integrated body in which the parts are closely interrelated with each other and the existence of the parts is preceded by the existence of the whole social body. Society has autonomous features which are independent of other bodies that surround it. If we underestimate the importance of knowing that society is an integrated body, it can hinder the development of our inquiry in the following four ways:

1. We could not recognize the authenticity of sociology because we are not aware that society is an integrated body. Likewise, we are also unaware of the systematic study of the rise and fall of a certain society and its autonomous activities.
2. As a consequence of the diversity and changeability[5] of human subjects, we tend to overestimate the conflict and inconsistency between the parts, and fail to recognize the social whole. This is often the problem of those dichotomists who overestimate the conflicts between science and religion, arts and morality, individual and the state.
3. We could mistake a certain part for the whole, a certain aspect of the society for the essential feature of the same society. If we theorize about society without consciousness of our own subjective biases, we shall be torn between a sociological model of society and actual society. It is absurd that some theorists criticize actual society because it is not similar to the theoretical

model they constructed. It is like putting the cart before the horse. It is also ridiculous that the narrow-minded activists look down their nose at theory construction.

4. We could hastily conclude that the whole is unknowable. The researchers who are accustomed to investigating partial phenomena tend to assume that the whole is unknowable. The quality of our knowledge depends upon our own subjective biases. We need to recognize that the accumulation of pieces of data does not automatically give us knowledge of the whole. I'm afraid that some of the current arguments and opinions on social ideals, posed by jurists, economists, moral philosophers, specialists on education, and so on, seem to lapse into this type of error. Utopists and Romanists are typical examples of this.

More than that, most of what social theories posed, until now, have fallen into this type of error. But we don't need to be pessimistic. According to Comte, sociology represents the highest phase in the history of human knowledge. It has just started. Needless to say, we sociologists have to continue to refine our methodology.

I know that the above two sections are too verbose for sensible readers. But we need to specify and share certain axiom to make our argument productive, just like a geometrical argument does. Herbert Spencer did not talk about *fact* nor *integrated body,* but I think he would agree with my view, since he treated society as an entity. It is unquestionable that Auguste Comte and his disciples, Littré, Carey, and Fiske, share my view. They emphasize that we should recognize the universe as an integrated body. Accordingly, our knowledge must also be an integrated body. In this respect, Comte should be praised as a pioneer of sociology.[6]

SOCIETY IS AN ORGANISM

Next, we should specify what kind of integrated body society is. We can categorize the integrated bodies into two kinds: simple and complex. A human is a simple integrated body. Society is a complex integrated body since it includes two or more humans. The complex integrated bodies can be classified into four types:

1. *Gathering.* There is no intimate relationship between the components except the fact that they share time and space.
2. *Compound.* The components are perfectly fused. Each component loses its original quality and acquires new quality.
3. *Mechanism.* The activity of the body is dominated by some external cause.
4. *Organism.* Every component is in itself an integrated body that develops from within.

Society is an organic type of the integrated complex body.[7] There are many differences between existing societies, but the following four characteristics are shared.

1. *Organization.*[8] Two or more humans, as the components of a society, help each other to acquire the necessities of life, that is, they live a cooperative life. If they collaborate to achieve one such need, I call this type of cooperation *simple.* If they split up the work to achieve two or more needs, I call this type *complex.* The complex type of cooperation can also be called *division of labor.* It seems that the development of division of labor causes the growth of inner-social groups. These groups are the organs of the social body. Every society has such organs, and the growth of a society is identical with the increase in number and complexity of the organs in the social body. The system of these organs can be called *organization.*[9]

2. *Growth.* Basically there is no internal cause limiting the growth of a society. The stagnation and decline are brought about from external conditions.[10] In my next book *Shakai Rigaku* [General Sociology, vol. 2, Social Logic], I will discuss some of the external conditions that can be the components of the social body (see Takebe, 1905). Two more characteristics accompany the above two.

3. *Metabolism.* Increase and decrease in the population of a society can be derived from two causes: natural and assimilative. What I call natural metabolism is the increase and decrease in the population caused by birth and death. The assimilative metabolism is caused by immigration to and emigration from that society.

4. *Reproduction.* A society grows when increases in the population are greater than decreases. If the population increases beyond the upper limit of the environment, society is compelled to reproduce itself by splitting apart. It is like cell division in lower organisms.

Every organism has these four characteristics, and society, since it is an organism, is not the exception. Later I will examine the characteristics of society again by comparing it with other organisms and integrated bodies.

The proposition that "Society is an organism" is the most abstract principle asserted by scholars who take a social organicists position. Social organicism became famous in the history of sociology. We will briefly investigate the origin of this idea.

In Japanese and Chinese philosophy, viewing society and humans analogically was quite customary. Their pantheistic schema of thought directly brought about the analogy between the universe, the state society, and the human (Takebe, 1905).[11] The Indian philosophy dealt little with social matters, but as already seen in *Manu-smriti* [The Laws of Manu] there had been many signs of the social organicism.[12]

In western Europe, Plato is commonly seen as the founder of the social organism. Plato, in his *Republic,* compared the functions of state organs such as congress and shops with human abilities such as reasoning and desire. Thomas Hobbes's *Leviathan* made progress by identifying state organs with human organs.[13]

These analogies help us to grasp the fact that society is an integrated body, but it cannot be said that this gives us scientific knowledge. These are just comparisons of some existing societies with some existing creatures, nothing more. What we need is to construct a logical cluster of the clear-cut definitions and a reliable methodology.

Comte made a great effort to establish sociology as a science, but he did not clarify the relations between organism and society. Herbert Spencer's *The Principles of Sociology* (1876-1896) heralded this idea by arguing that the political body and biological body have no teleological similarity but do have functional similarity.[14] I think highly of his effort to clarify the conceptual relationships between the political body and biological body, but there are three points that need to be improved. First, his arguments on the social ideal are not well connected to his functional analysis. Second, he tended to underestimate the functional differences between the political body and the biological body. We should clarify the characteristics of the political body more closely by investigating the functional differences of both. Third, this thought sometimes lapsed into an unrefined analogy between a particular society and a particular creature.

Spencer understood that there were problems in his analogy between society and organism. He was conscious of the difference between society and organism. So he saw society as something beyond the organism and tried to conceptualize it as a *super organism*. But currently, as his French successor De Greef (1886, 1889) suggested, we might as well continue to use the analogy of society with organism.[15] Initially Fouillée (1880) tried to defend Spencer's analogy against his critics. He intensely criticized their lack of theoretical completeness, their historical immaturity, and their ideological perspectives. But today he seems to have changed his position. Although he stresses the difference between an organism and society as well as their similarity, Worms is still defending the Spencerian analogy. Emile Vandervelde, Jean Demoor, and Jean Massart (1897) also just compare society with organism. Jacques Novicow (1897) is an outstanding scholar who tries to understand society in comparison not only with organism but also with the individual human. He distinguishes two types of conceptions of society. One is organic, the other is contractual. He uses the organic approach, but he obviously approves of other possible perspectives.

The German sociologist Albert Eberhard Schäffle argues that it might be harmful to society if we ignore the difference between society and organism (1875-1878, pp. 54-67). According to Schäffle (1875-1878), society is in one's imagination and artificial; the organism is real and natural. Lilienfeld (1896) believes that society is a real organic body (see Bordier, 1887). However, Worms notes that Lilienfeld's system of sociology is outdated unless you can resolve the gap between the natural and the artificial.

Similar to Lilienfeld, Arthur Bordier (1887) argues that sociology should be reduced to a branch of biology since society is one of the living things (see Small & Vincent, 1894). However, even those radical conservatives like Lilienfeld and Bordier approve of the important roles that human power has to control society.[16] Social organicism has its roots in the ancient poetic or common imaginations. The modern advancement of the natural sciences, especially biology, has stimulated development of the social organicism. The impact of biology upon sociology was quite big at one time, thus, many believed that sociology might be a branch of biology (see Lilienfeld, 1896; Small & Vincent, 1894).

Today, many scholars have become aware that biological laws are not equal to those of the social world. Spencer's decision to conceive of society as a *super organism* in order to distinguish society from an organism was correct. But its contents are still not clear. I think the most important role of psychological sociology will be to clarify what distinguishes society from organism.

SOCIETY IS A BODY THAT HAS CONSCIOUSNESS

Next, we will investigate the psychological aspects of the concept *organism.* We will prove that society has its own consciousness. When two or more humans cooperate with each other, they integrate and harmonize their consciousness in some way. Social consciousness is the integrated, harmonized consciousness of society's members.

Current social psychologists study how individuals harmoniously develop their consciousness and build social consciousness. I will show that social consciousness is possible in two ways. First, the consciousness of one or few members directs the rest. Second, certain social organization binds the consciousness of all members into order. Needless to say, society is not a mechanism, nor does it behave randomly. It is obvious that the social body behaves consciously to some degree.

We should note that *social consciousness* and *individual consciousness* are two representations of the same thing. I can observe my own individual consciousness by introspective or self-reflexive methods. The individual consciousness conceptualizes the functions of the individual mind. In the same way, social consciousness conceptualizes the functions of the social mind. It is just the degree of complexity that makes social consciousness and individual consciousness different in appearance.

The relationship between psychology and social psychology has been controversial. There have been various solutions offered. For example, Gustave Le Bon stressed that a crowd has a particular mind that is different from a collection of each individual's mind that composes the crowd. Gabriel Tarde criticized Le Bon and argued that the crowds' mind can be analyzed by studying the individuals' mind. There is, however, a third solution. One can conceptualize the essence of the mind as *unconsciousness.* The *social mind* (social consciousness) is the complex representation of unconsciousness. The *individual mind* (individual consciousness) is the simple representation of unconsciousness.

The notion of consciousness suggests some active factor observed in the movement of things. In our ordinary language, passive movement is not described as conscious. Society has strongly autonomous features, so we should say that society has its own consciousness.

It is said that the major difficulty in the study of social consciousness lies in whether it has physical evidence or not. No one ever made this point clear. But I think it is useless to look around for social brain, and its absence in no way threatens the value of the study of social consciousness. It is sufficient to say that the physical evidence of the social consciousness should be observed in the physical elements of humans who are the components of the society (see Takebe, 1905).

SOCIAL BODY HAS ITS OWN PERSONALITY

Next, we should articulate the degree to which society has its own consciousness. Does it only have automatic and passive abilities to respond to the change in its surroundings, just like the lower animals? Or does it have autonomous and active abilities like intellect, which can act to achieve certain goals?

Social consciousness is derived from humans who are the components of the society. When the members share the same consciousness, that is, share the value system, society appears as if it has its own consciousness independent from each member. The collective consciousness will depend on the degree to which the members share the same beliefs or have the same social consciousness. In the same way, society's conscious behavior is derived from the members' conscious behavior.

Generally speaking, the word *person* indicates the subject of human action. A human has *personality* when he or she has the ability to act as an autonomous subject. This is a formal definition of personality. The substantial definition of personality can vary according to the viewpoint we take, that is, ethical, legal, social, and so on. In an ethical sense, personality is the moral subject of voluntary action. In a legal sense, personality is another name for the qualification that is granted to the subject who has certain rights and obligations.

Society has its own personality. This statement should never be interpreted to suggest that some particular society is judged as having a higher or lower personality than another society. The point is whether society in general has a personality. For instance, in our ordinary language, we always label some people as *savage,* and other people as *civilized.* But whatever these labels may mean, we do not need to grade a certain society's personality as savage or civilized when we investigate a particular society.[17]

In this chapter we summed up major five major issues to define society. Although our definition still has limitation, we can state that society is a fact, not an illusion or fancy. Society is an organic body that has consciousness and a personality.

Currently social psychologists are trying to articulate the nature of the social personality. In 1860, a German journal *Völkerpshychologie* [Ethnic Psychology] was first published by Moriz Lazarus and Heymann Steinthal. The journal encouraged many historians, linguists, jurists, and anthropologists to submit essays (see Lazarus, 1855-1896; Steinthal, 1864, 1871,1885). After that Wilhelm Maximilian Wundt (1896, 1900-1911) and Gustav Adolf Lindner (1871) made advances in social psychology. Charles Bouglé (1896, p. 20) stated "social science provides insights into human history in general just like psychology provides insights into the path of individual life, and it is the very thing that sociology should study."

Ludwig Gumplowicz, (1885, chapter 4), Gustav Ratzenhofer (1893a,b, 1898, chapter 2) and many other sociologists tried to construct sociological systems that were based on psychological observation. Gabriel Tarde (1890a, 1895a) focused on the imitation-innovation process. Gustave Le Bon (1894, 1895, 1898) studied the psychological characteristics of crowds.

Franklin Henry Giddings (1897) proposed the concept of *consciousness of kind* and tried to illustrate the process of socialization. Jacque Novicow (1897) examined the relation between social consciousnesses with individual consciousness, and concluded that the relationship is beyond a simple analogy.

Alfred Fouillée pointed out that every individual's consciousness is actually the collective consciousness from the experimental, physiological, and psychological perspective.[18] Fouillée's perspective was supported by Haeckel, von Hartmann, Espinas, and Schäffle, and

I also share this view. But I have to question some of Fouillée's points (see Fouillée, 1880, p. 227). He stressed that social consciousness is nothing more than the sum total of individual consciousness. But we cannot say that society is an autonomous body in psychological terms. He is not willing to say that society has its own consciousness. He also maintained that individual consciousness and social consciousness can be unified only in the contractual organism (Fouillée, 1880, pp. 390-400). We can ignore this argument because when we say that society is a conscious body, we do not necessarily mean every social consciousness is the sum total of the individual consciousness. Fouillée has reworked and expanded on these ideas in his more recent work. René Worms (1895b, chapter 10 "Fonction de Relation"), Albert Eberhard Schäffle (1875-1878, vol. 1), Ward (1893), and James Sully (1877) also considered this problem. Paul von Lilienfeld (1873-1881) paid attention to the nervous system of society.

Many scholars understand the psychological viewpoint as one of the fundamental apparatus useful for sociological inquiry. They see society as an integrated body and use this as a basis for clarifying various social laws. But there were errors in their work. For example, Albion Small and George Vincent (1894) did no more than explain social consciousness by providing an analogy. Of course analogies are useful for stimulating our thinking, but they do not provide a reliable basis for constructing knowledge.[19] Social psychology is not yet mature.

The psychological inquiry of society had developed from the study of ethnicity. Today it diverges into two directions and we should not confuse one with another. One is *Völkerspsychologie,* which examines the psychological characteristics of each ethnic body. Another is social psychology, which examines the collective psychological phenomena in order to discover their general laws.

THE STATUS OF SOCIETY IN THE UNIVERSE

We have clarified some ideas regarding the concept of society in the previous sections. In this section we will clarify the meaning of society by observing the status of society in the universe. There are two ways to view the universe: philosophical and scientific. The philosophical perspective abstracts and summarizes the universe as a whole and treats the universe as an abstract system of categories. The scientific perspective empirically observes the parts of the universe, and treats the universe as a system of entities.[20]

Many systems for studying society have been proposed. Currently the evolutionary system is the most developed and refined system. One could subdivide the entities in the universe into inorganic objects and organic objects. Inorganic matter is constant and exists at all times. Organic matter lives and dies over time. There are three stages through which organic bodies evolve. First, there is the organic body that is made of a single organ, that is, a cell. Second, there is the organic body that consists of many organs that are functionally correlated, or living creatures in general. Third, there is the organic body that is made of living creatures that are functionally correlated, known as society. Among living creatures, human beings alone form society. Therefore, society is the highest, most developed, and the most recent to emerge among all the entities in the universe.

Currently new sciences are disproving commonly held dualisms such as inorganic and organic, human and other animals, individual and society, as being simplistic. Chemistry is trying to clarify the process through which inorganic matter gives birth to organic matter.[21] Evolutionary biology provides an explanation for understanding the continuities between various creatures (see Haeckel, 1868; Darwin, 1859, 1871; Lamarck, 1809). Sociology is trying to understand the way individual behaviors form the social order and conversely how social order regulates individual behaviors. Sociology is a science that can address the latest stage of the evolving process of entities in the universe.[22] Four ages can be distinguished in the continual process of evolution in the universe. The first age is the physical universe. It is a fundamental condition of evolution that matter and energy exist. The second age is the astronomical universe. Heavenly bodies were created as a consequence of the evolution of matter and energy. The third age is the biological universe. Organic bodies arose. The fourth age is the sociological universe. The human race was born. The age of human and social evolution began.

Ratzenhofer (1898, p. 11) disagreed with the view that society is the highest entity in the universe. He emphasized that the individual body is the very thing that characterizes the fourth age, since society is a passive body actuated by the individuals. He also stressed that sociability and individuality conflict with each other, and the winner is always individuality. In fact, individual behaviors shape social institutions, but I think it is also true that social institutions shape individual behaviors into a mold. So which is the active and which is the passive is a false question. Herbert Spencer and Auguste Comte have already stated my view that society is the highest entity in the universe. But Spencer's theory of super-organism is obscure and not well defined. That is why I had to elaborate on this point.

THE CONCEPTION OF SOCIETY

In the previous sections, we have fully sorted out the meanings of the word *society*. Now we can go ahead to the next step in order to achieve a clear-cut conception of society. To review—*Society is the organic, personal unity of the association of humans*. From this proposition we can deduce the following three corollaries.

1. For individuals, society is the closest and most familiar entity in the universe. The individual lives a life as an organic part of the society just like a cell in certain creatures. When we talk about human life, society is necessarily derived; when we talk about society, human life is necessarily derived.
2. Human life has, in its profound meaning, society. Humans live not only as an organic component of society, but also as the source of social consciousness and its personality. Humans give society higher characteristics and act as its higher element. It is obvious that a human loses the higher meaning of life when he or she leaves society.
3. The entities in the universe are subordinated to society, especially from the teleological point of view. Society occupies the highest position in the system of the entities. Its essence is in the law of evolution. The law of evolution does not vary based on material, spiritual, natural, or artificial things. The above three corollaries are deduced from the observations we made through this chapter.

We have now succeeded in describing the first step of social inquiry. The object of sociology is the study of society, so in this chapter I wanted to discuss sociologists' definitions. However, I found that most of them are useless. Some definitions are too simple and brief, others spend full chapters of a book on it.[23] Therefore, I defined society by the three steps above.

The word *society* has been overused. We should be especially aware of the following three misuses. The first error is to use the word *society* to indicate every social phenomenon except political, economic, and so on. Its meanings are diverse and will vary case-by-case. The second error is to use the word *society* to indicate non-governmental aspects of human life in general. The third error is to use *society* to indicate non-individual aspects of human life. Socialists often use the word society in the second and third way. Ordinary people use the word society in the first way.[24]

Sociology

Tongo Takebe

STUDY

Before asking the question *What is sociology?* we need to consider the more general category, *Gakumon* [learning, science, knowledge, or study].[1] All human enterprise has certain aims. Learning constitutes one of the important human activities. Then what is the goal of learning?

We may say that the goal of learning is to facilitate human progress. The notion of progress needs to be clarified after acquiring a whole system of knowledge, but for now, I will briefly try to illustrate the relation between knowledge and progress. Human life is a continuous chain of goal attainments. Goal attainment is a *doing* phenomenon, not a *being* phenomenon. Doing phenomena have two elements, the representation of goal and the action to achieve it.[2] The ultimate principle that permits humans to realize the ideal is the dependability of the order of nature, or *reason*.[3] Analytically, reason appears as laws. Everything operates by the universal existence of reason. So the goal of learning is to understand the laws that occur in the universe. By behaving in harmony with these laws, society can be improved. These laws that are discovered through science are called scientific imperatives.[4] Advances in science make our ideals appropriate. When we have appropriate ideals in mind and try to realize them, we shall progress.

Knowing the goal attainment constitutes the pivotal aspects of human life, so its improvement makes our life better. This is the goal of learning. This was especially true in ancient Chinese philosophy.[5] For example, ancient Chinese philosophers expressed the advancement of learning in the following order: learning, questioning, contemplation, discussion, and practice. Later, knowledge was subdivided into various genres and concentrated on each specific aspect of human life, and called science. It was the fate of human evolution, since differentiation is a major sign of evolution. But we should not forget that modern science is still connected with human goal attainment. We should try hard to discover the path between scientific knowledge and its practical uses.

Above, we briefly clarified the meaning of progress and the goal of learning. Learning is a human activity that tries to achieve certain human goals by certain methods.[6] There are three ways to obtain knowledge: the dogmatic method (which includes the theological), the skeptical method (which includes the metaphysical), and the critical method (which includes positivism).[7] The reader might think that this view appears as if it is derived from Hegel. But, I confess, it is actually derived from Comte.

1. The dogmatic method focuses on acquiring knowledge but pays little attention to understanding the foundation and the validity of the method. There are two forms of dogmatism. One is traditional dogmatism (or imitation) that relies on legendary tales, religious teachings, or foreign folks and rumors without critical investigation.[8] The other is intolerant dogmatism that erroneously equates one's narrow experiences and beliefs as ultimate truth without critical investigation.[9]

2. The skeptical method has an awareness of the need to explore the foundation and confirm the validity of certain knowledge, but still does not know the exact method to achieve it. The skeptical method gives us some exercises in logical thinking, but its consequence gives us no clue as to how to achieve human goals. There are two modes in the skeptical method. One is negative skepticism that negates the validity of our knowledge in general, and therefore negates the existence of beings in general. The other is positive skepticism that probes deeply into the questions and discovers the ultimate question that one can not answer.[10] Skeptical philosophy is the other name given to negative skepticism. Metaphysics is the other name of positive skepticism.

Some of the positive skeptics try to explain the way in which we acquire true knowledge. Those explanations are called epistemology. There is no substantial achievement in metaphysics except epistemology.

3. The critical method tries to find positive laws that control things in the universe, by criticizing our own knowledge of these things, and further investigating into things to correct the knowledge (Comte called this phase "positive"). The critical method is the only way to achieve knowledge.

The above provides a general view of the different methods of study. Of course there can be further classifications according to the subdivisions of science. But that is not necessary to provide a detailed explanation on those subdivisions at this point. Here we clarified *What is knowledge?* Knowledge is what provides the positive imperative for the progress of human life. Laymen often misunderstand knowledge in two ways: they see knowledge as sacrosanct or they discard knowledge as useless.

First, there are those who treat scientific knowledge as if it is the knowledge itself that is the ultimate value. They scoff at the question, *Knowledge for what?* They note, *Knowledge itself is the goal.* I think dogmatic and pedantic people are well matched with ultra-nationalists and art maniacs. But it is also true that this view is often posed as refuting the view that study is useless because it makes no money. Recently Gustav Ratzenhofer explained the matter in detail.[11] Traditionally, German philosophy understood the aim of study as satisfying their thirst for knowledge, so Germans placed the classics at the center of the curriculum of their public education. But, as a result, students are not familiar with contemporary issues.[12]

Second, in contrast, there are people who find no value in knowledge and say that human progress cannot be achieved by study since scientific law is not the same thing as practical law that is based on common sense and experience. Methodologically, this is a kind of dogmatism. Experience results in limiting our knowledge to a particular law that is valid in a particular situation. Common sense law is the accumulation of those experiences without clear-cut methodology. Thus, the power and applicability of these laws is very limited.

Johann Gottlieb Fichte (1794) and Auguste Comte provided the clearest examples of the positive method that contains critical investigation into the goal and the meaning of study. As contrasted with the Western scholars who have often neglected this issue, the Eastern thinkers always begin with a clarification of the phenomena that they are studying. *Six Arts* is the best example[13] (see also the opening pages and three learning principles in Concucius' *Daxue* [Great Learning]). Even Ssuma Ch'ien in *Shin Chi* [Record of History] (1961, preface) gave the outline of the positive method. Those ancient examples represent the major characteristics of the Eastern academic traditions.[14] Although there are almost no successors of Fichte's teachings, in the current Western tradition, we may find many disciples of Comte.[15] Today, the Eastern and Western traditions are getting closer and sharing the view that science and human life should be tightly connected.

Ancient Eastern thinkers had expressed the universal consistency of the laws in a general way as did ancient Western thinkers. But in the medieval period, the emphasis on religion corrupted the study of laws. The laws were subordinated to the arbitrary will of God. As people's minds awoke in the early modern age, new logic arose, and various sciences arose. As a result, the idea of the universal consistency of the laws was revived. A scholar in France at the end of the eighteenth century, explained the laws of nature, united them to the laws of society, and promoted the sociological thought.[16] Comte established sociology. And Spencer, Carey, and Fiske all followed in this tradition.[17] Eugéne Fournière (1898) rightly said that human evolution occurs when humans come to know the laws that drive things and give birth to various phenomena. By acquiring this understanding, sociology developed a firm positivist basis.

HIERARCHY OF SCIENCES

Science offers us empirical instruction for understanding human advances. Human advances are a part of the advances of the universe. So scholars who use empirical research for human advancement should start from a general inquiry of the universe. Since humans and the universe work together, it is not too difficult to consider humans to be a thing in the universe [18] and to consider the universe to be a thing that only humans can understand.[19] It comes from the difference in the viewpoint. These two viewpoints help us understand the interaction between humans and the universe.[20]

At first glance, sciences appear to be quite different, but essentially sciences constitute a single body since in the universe only one law exists. If it appears that there are two different laws, one is false or both are false. All science shares as a goal the discovery of the law that drives all things in the universe. The objective of all sciences is the improvement of human life. The subject matter and the objective of all sciences should be integrated into a single system. This is the ultimate aim of study.

To understand the system of all things in the universe, we need to view it as an evolutionary system.[21] Evolutionary thought tells us that all things in the universe are formed into a system in two ways, which can be integrated into single system. One way is by a taxonomical system that classifies the things into kinds and species. The other is a causal system that articulates the lawful interactions between the things. The evolutionary system is essentially a hierarchical one.[22]

The lower species are included in the more general kind, though the things in each level of the hierarchy are different in appearance. The highest and most general level of the classification includes all the previous characteristics and attributes of all those things in the lower levels of classification in the universe. Thus, an, evolutionary system of things is not parallel but hierarchical—the relationship between inferiority and superiority.[23] In this taxonomy, the highest-ranked things include all other things in the universe; therefore those things in the highest rank include an integrated conception of humans and the universe.

The whole body of sciences can also be understood as an evolutionary system, that is, a hierarchical system. The study of logic constitutes the lowest rank in the hierarchy. Logic inquires into pure forms of true knowledge and existence.[24] Physics constitutes the second rank of the hierarchy because physics examines the primitive existence of the universe. The third rank in the hierarchy is occupied by astronomy, and the next rank biology, according to the evolutionary stages of the universe. Sociology constitutes the highest rank because it studies the highest, most evolved thing, society in the universe. We describe each stage of the hierarchy as follows.

Logic. Logic assumes the pure form of knowledge to be its subject, and proves the first principle that enables real existence and its knowledge. Logic just proves the real existence of beings, so it does not have direct relation to humans and the universe. In itself, logic is worthless. Logic becomes valuable when it relates to the things in the following ranks.

Physics. Physics studies the beginning stages of the evolution of the universe, that is, the primitive state of the universe. In other words, physics studies the conditions of evolution. Physics observes the objective real existence; however, the objective real existence that physics understood was not the real existence for a long time. Just recently physics began to investigate into the real existence. Physics should become more worthy when it relates to the things in the following ranks.

Astronomy. Astronomy examines the first stage of evolution of the universe. The evolution actually becomes possible when the conditions of evolution that physics clarifies are sufficient. The evolution at this stage is inorganic. Science in this stage researches the objective things. As contrasted with physics, astronomy, which researches inorganic evolution, has value in itself, but its value is lower than the sciences in the fourth and fifth stages.[25]

Biology. Biology examines the second stage of evolution of the universe. Biology uses not only logic and physics but also astronomy as the material.

Sociology. Sociology examines the third stage of evolution of the universe. Sociology researches conscious evolution while biology researches organic evolution. Sociology uses the sciences from the first four stages as its material. Sociology researches the evolution of all knowledge in the universe. Therefore, its value is extremely high. The oneness of the things in the universe can be proven for the first time by sociology. The hierarchy of the sciences is completed by sociology.

It was Comte's great achievement to have described the hierarchy of sciences.[26] His hierarchical theory was superior not only because it was highly rational but also because it considered the latest developments of the sciences at that time. A reason why we might be dissatisfied with his schema is because sciences had advanced considerably after he had developed it. One example of this is that there are still a lot of uncertainties and defects on the periodic table of the elements. Scholars who succeeded him, for example, Fouillée, De Greef, and Adolphe Coste, did not forget the importance of this problem.[27]

However, there are careless scholars who rushed to adopt Comte's hierarchy theory.

Spencer's classification of sciences[28] seems to be precise, and he considers recent scientific progress in detail. It is regrettable that Spencer did not connect it closely to his general system of philosophy. Ward (1883) completely agreed with Comte. Albert Piche (1892) recently wrote a summary of Comte's classification of sciences.

Scholars who rush to investigate particular themes of biology, psychology, and sociology fail to use a systematic theory of sciences. They try to decide the range of the research appropriate for sociology without comparing it with other sciences.[29] Each sociologist has his or her own strengths and weaknesses, however, this approach ultimately weakens sociology. This section was intended to provide insights into understanding sociology's position in the system of sciences.

PHILOSOPHY AND SCIENCE

In the ordinary world it is often the case that people employ vague concepts for convenience. Similarly, in the academic world, scholars often employ vague concepts such as *philosophy* or *science*. Of course we should not be content with such vague concepts. For the purpose of articulating the qualities and attributes of sociology, we should examine the meanings of the concepts philosophy and science.

There are so many variations of philosophy that it is exhausting and futile to enumerate them.[30] We will classify the concepts of philosophy into three types, and describe the points and the characteristics of each type, below.

1. *Philosophy that is identical to metaphysics (epistemology).* As contrasted with physics, which investigates real phenomenon, philosophy as metaphysics clarifies the human cognitive forms toward objective beings.
2. *Philosophy that is identical to ethics.* As contrasted with mere description of phenomenon, this kind of philosophy includes normative statement.
3. *Philosophy that explores the universal principle.* This is compared to the study of particular principles.

Though these distinctions do not appear in each philosopher's definitions of philosophy, we can point out the meanings of the notion of philosophy as above. Among those, traditional West European philosophy normally tends to adopt the first type. It is a necessary consequence of the spirit of inquiry in general. The Indian philosophy also tends to adopt it, and recently the Chinese philosophy has finally begun to recognize the importance of it. The school of positive philosophy rejects it as second stage of metaphysical thought.

The second definition is the primary one adopted by Chinese philosophy, religious teachings, and various kinds of popular precepts of these days.

The third definition appeared in the process of modern development in West European thought. It dichotomizes the partial study and the whole study, and calls the latter philosophy.[31] Compared to philosophy, it is more difficult to understand the idea of study we call science, because thinkers have been using the notion in an undisciplined manner. We can roughly identify the ideas that describe science.

Science is the result of a logical investigation of things. To construct a theory, science in this sense should be totally based on logic to prevent false logic. In this sense, science has no positive function other than to avoid false logic. Science from this perspective developed as a rejection of theory based on superstitions and fanatical theology. Modern science began during the Renaissance when Francis Bacon proposed a new logic that provided a foundation for this new method of science.

Science is the result of systematic investigation of things. Science in this sense is opposed to fragmentary knowledge. Fragmentary knowledge that enables us to forget the original nature or generality of things of the universe, often results in contradictions and inconsistencies. While it seems to increase knowledge concerning each part, fragmentary knowledge hardly brings valid knowledge concerning the whole. Responding to the upsurge of a philosophical trend at the dawn of the modern age, thinkers such as Comte, Hegel, and Spencer tried to investigate the details of the world after constructing a general view of the universe. In ancient times, Aristotle already had this approach. Eduard von Hartmann's philosophy of unconsciousness (1873, chapter 1) provides the name *science* in this sense as science for the first time. The above-mentioned two kinds of science distinguish scholastic knowledge and popular knowledge, and label scholastic knowledge as scientific.

Science is a result of the division of academic work. The research on a part of human life or the universe is called a science, while the research on the whole of the life or the universe is called a philosophy. This kind of science has the merit of the division of labor and a weak point as well in the nineteenth-century social enterprises.

We defined both philosophy and science in three ways. Among those, the first and second definitions of philosophy (metaphysics and ethics) and science (logic and systematic observation of things) are almost identical. And, today the distinction between metaphysics and physics is increasingly insignificant. The reader needs to recognize that in the past, people had mistaken metaphysical ideas as a pedantic game of *ideas,*[32] as *objective real existence,*[33] or *absolute real existence.*[34] However, all of these misguided ideas vanish when we take a positivistic approach. Needless to say, there is no fundamental distinction between philosophy and science in the second definitions. There can be descriptive philosophy and normative science and it is usual in this world. The major difference between philosophy and science is in the third definition, that is, the difference between the total study and partial study.

There are advantages and disadvantages in the division of scientific study. The division of scientific work causes conflicts with philosophy. Of course science developed as a result of the division of labor, but it is also true that philosophy is needed at the critical point of the progress of science. Now we will explain this issue from the following three aspects.

No matter how science develops, there are limits that cannot be exceeded as long as it is science. Three kinds of limits exist. First, no matter how science investigates the parts and phenomenon, all sciences are partial investigations of things, so they cannot be the total study of the universe. Also, sciences cannot clarify the relations between one branch of science and the other. Second, all sciences provide just partial knowledge, so we cannot derive any general principle of human life. The general principle of human life can be derived only from the result of the total approach. Third, every scientific law is valid under certain assumptions called *axioms.*[35] In a word, morality or ethics cannot be a research subject in sciences. Science has those three limits so it needs the assistance of philosophy.

Two questions arise. Does philosophy provide the proper principles of human life? Can philosophy remain independent from science? First, because philosophy is the general study of humans and the universe, it is able to clarify the relation between the branches of science. Moreover, philosophy is able to analyze the assumptions and axioms of sciences. The disadvantages of sciences should be controlled by philosophy if philosophy remains on a general level. Second, as many philosophers' failures have proved, it is easy to state the importance of the general study but it is very difficult to do this type of study. However, it is not possible to advance philosophy when it cannot interact with sciences, and vice versa.[36]

Philosophy and the sciences advance by interaction. Therefore, even if philosophy is not yet complete, and even if we do understand certain principles of human life, we should not stop studying science. At this stage of progress, sociology, which exists in the highest rank in the hierarchy of sciences, should use both the philosophical and scientific methods.[37]

It is not shameful eclecticism that sociology uses both the philosophical and scientific methods together. Sociology stands in the highest rank of the hierarchy; therefore, true philosophical knowledge must be a part of sociology. And sociology can freely use the finding of sciences for the same reason.

Many scholars in western Europe have ignored the relationship between philosophy and science. The reason for this might be that philosophy and science have not been effectively interrelated. Following the old convention of the academic circles, those who call themselves scientists look upon philosophers as the enemy, and vice versa, although there are a few important exceptions like Spencer, Jevons (1874b), Comte, and Hegel.

SYSTEM OF SCIENCES

The hierarchy of sciences discussed above was purely a taxonomy. It is obvious that sciences in a hierarchical taxonomy and the present state of sciences are different. Knowledge in our present sciences is not crystallized but rather cluttered fragments of knowledge. Under these limitations, we have tried to construct a new science named *sociology*. It is necessary to clarify the position of sociology in relation with existing sciences. It is convenient to classify various sciences from two points of view. One is a classification by the objects of sciences, that is, material or non-material. Another is a classification by the functions of sciences, either theory or application. We can systematically classify the present sciences as follows.

I. Theoretical Sciences.
   A. Material and theoretical sciences.
      1. Physics in a broader sense.
         a) *Physics in a narrow sense.* The study of the relations of molecules.
         b) *Chemistry.* The study of the inner structure of a molecule.
         c) *Kinetics or dynamics.* The study of the relations between bodies.
      2. Astronomy in a broader sense.
         a) *Astronomy in a narrow sense.* The study of the relations between heavenly bodies.
         b) *Astrophysics and geology.* The study of the history of heavenly bodies.
         c) *Mineralogy.* The study of the constituents of heavenly bodies.
      3. Biology in a broader sense.
         a) Physiology.
         b) Biology in narrow sense.
      4. Sociology in a broader sense.
         a) *Geography.* The study of the external conditions of society.
         b) *Ethnology and archeology.* The study of the internal situations of society.
   B. Non-material and theoretical sciences.
      1. *Logic in a broader sense.* The study of metaphysical entities.
         a) *Ontology.* The study of the existence of metaphysical entities.
         b) *Epistemology.* The study of the existence of metaphysical knowledge.
         c) *Mathematics.* The study of the formal laws of entities.

        d) *Logic in narrow sense.* The study of the formal laws of knowledge.
     2. *Psychology in a broader sense.* The study of consciousness.
        a) *Psychology in a narrow sense.* The study of the subject of consciousness.
        b) *Esthetics.* The study of the subject of free choices.
        c) *Ethics.* The study of the human actions.
     3. Sociology in a broader sense.
        a) *History.* The study of the history of society.
        b) *Sociology in a narrow sense.* The study of the laws of society.
II. Applied sciences.
  A. Material and applied sciences.
     1. *Industrial art and technologies.* Contribution to the need of humans in a positive way.
     2. *Medical science and pharmacy.* Contribution to the need of humans in a negative way.
  B. Immaterial and applied sciences.
     1. *Economics, politics, and pedagogy.* Contribution to the development of humans in a positive way.
     2. *Theology, jurisprudence, and international law.* Contribution to the development of humans in negative way.

This classification has organized the most recent knowledge in the sciences in the most systematic way possible. There are various sciences that are not noted in this classification which can be classified into two kinds because they are part of two or more categories. For instance, statistics applies the method of mathematics and logic in both sociology and economics. Statistics is one of the methods of sociology and economics. Furthermore, there are various sciences that constitute subdivisions in a single category. For example, condensed matter physics, acoustics, optics, thermodynamics, and the study of electricity constitute subdivisions of physics. The subdivisions also have further subdivisions.

When we clarify the position of sociology in this classification, it is necessary to note the following three points. First, sociology extends over both the material theoretical science and the non-material theoretical science. This shows that sociology stands in the position that integrates the material and the formless. Second, sociology is at the highest position in the hierarchy. Third, there is both a narrower and a broader perspective in sociology. This book is intended to clarify sociology in the narrower sense.

We must not put too much emphasis on the hierarchical classification of knowledge. However, by using it, the scientists confirm their own position and learn its relationship to other sciences. Also, the philosophers confirm how their own knowledge is correlated to the knowledge from other disciplines. Until now, the scientists have not cited the hierarchical theory of knowledge sufficiently, and the philosophers have likewise made this error. This is the biggest defect in the western European academic system of knowledge. Comte was an outstanding exception. Today Comte's disciples are paying attention to the hierarchical theory of studies. Among them, Carey's tree of knowledge is remarkable (Carey, 1874, vol. 1). As having already seen, the modern scholars often neglect non-scientific divisions of knowledge such as philosophy. By citing the classification table above, scholars might avoid a number of problems found in the classification of sciences.

DEFINITION OF SOCIOLOGY

From the previous text, we can derive the following definitions of sociology.

1. Sociology in its broader sense is a study of society.
2. Sociology in its narrower sense is a science of the laws of society.
3. Sociology is to unify society and study in general.

Based on material from the previous chapter as well as that in this chapter, we can define sociology in the following three ways. First, sociology studies the correlations between humans and society.[38] Second, sociology seeks the general principle for human life. And third, sociology stands in the highest rank in the hierarchy of studies.

All scientific knowledge flows toward sociology because sociology is the highest form of scholarship that articulates the general principle for human life. In other words, advances in sociology will influence the development of research in other branches of science that will contribute to the improvement of human life. The existence of sociology should not depend on the existence of society. Some self-centered people say that the study of sociology is simply an activity to gratify one's desire to learn about society. This is a mistake.

It is useless to name the sociologists whose goals are just to fulfill their own desire for knowledge. The goal of sociological knowledge is to activate the human conscience, to move the human will, and to achieve practical good. A desire to learn might activate the human conscience, but this does not mean that the person will use the knowledge to improve society. Sociology sets forth the human ideal and seeks the way to achieve it.

Sociology takes a general view and examines the meaning that the study originally had, and explores the meanings of human life. Sociology tries to make the person understand himself and the universe. As a result, sociology tries to prove the oneness of humans and the universe.

In the primitive state, we leave individuals on their own to survive in nature. Now we have ethics and education. However, we leave society on its own to survive in nature. This is strange. Recent advances put the survival of society under our control. Society is a collective body of individuals and it should have a system that corresponds to ethics and education for individuals. We need the normative system to set and achieve the ideals of society. Sociology has taken on the study of the normative system.

Individualistic social theory obstructs the development of sociology. It is not true that the normative force of society has harmful effects toward individuality. Laissez-faire theory also obstructs the development of sociology. It totally negates the artificial control over the natural course of things.[39]

Until now, scholars saw sociology in a variety of different ways, so it is not easy to put those views in order. We may classify these views in two ways. The first is a classification by the difference in ontological perspectives. The second is a classification by the motives and aims. The classification, described below, is nominal and abstract, but there are exemplary cases that correspond to each category.

I. ONTOLOGICAL CLASSIFICATION
OF THE TYPES OF SOCIOLOGICAL STUDY

1. *Materialist sociology.* This type of sociology sees society as a material entity. Biological sociology and organist sociology belongs to this type. Spencer and Lilienfeld are excellent examples of theorists using a materialist sociology approach. The human society is nothing but a material entity, just the same as all other natural organics. Lilienfeld (1873) says, "the human society is in the foundation of the knowledge of all natural organics, and it is the most advanced real existence in the universe" (see Chapter 1, pp. 15-19). He also believes that the ultimate aim of science is to identify the single, absolute law that rules the universe. Society is a phenomenon that resulted from the same absolute law. But in the present stage, it is very difficult to articulate the laws. So we should not ignore any kind of knowledge that includes sociology, even though the findings may still be questionable.

Arthur Bordier (1887) considered society to be a living body, and put sociology in the genre of natural history. Fouillée (1880) says it is necessary to study society in comparison with organics. De Greef, and Fouillée believe that society develops from human conventions and contracts.[40]

2. *Idealistic sociology.* This type of sociology sees society as an ideal entity, and psychological sociology and ethnic psychology belong to this type. Idealistic sociology is developed in social psychology by Lazarus, Steinthal, Lindner, Simmel, Giddings, and Ludwig Stein. According to Simmel (1895, vol. 6, No. 3, pp. 52-63), the themes in sociology as a branch of science are the development of society, cooperation, and symbiotic life of the individuals. Simmel and Giddings's conception of sociability focuses on the changes in the social crowd and in the symbiotic life of the individuals. Giddings (1897, pp. 1-2) defines sociology as a special science that studies sociability. Socialization has an effect of changing forms of the social crowd and symbiosis of the individuals. Stein also emphasizes the study of the psychological aspects of society (Stein, 1897). Recently Tarde, Le Bon, Abramowski (1897), and Brinton (1902) are trying to develop a new phase of the idealist sociology.

3. *Dualistic sociology.* This type of sociology views society as a unity between the material and ideal. Dualistic sociology has no strict distinction between the materialist and the idealist. Schäffle, Stein (1897), Gumplowicz, Ratzenhofer, Combes de Lestrade (1889), and Novicow (1893, 1894a,b, 1895) are the representatives of the dualist sociology. Schäffle was formerly inclined towards organist theory, but in his revised edition of the masterpiece, he confesses that he could not evaluate the psychological aspect of society in the first edition (see Schäffle, 1875-1878, vol.1; Ratzenhofer, 1893, 1898). Ratzenhofer (1893, 1898) and Novicow (1895, 1897) are the most complete examples of dualist sociology. They discuss the conflicts between the psychological aspect and the material aspect of society.

4. *General sociology.* This type of sociology sees society as a unified body. When dualist sociology develops fully, it becomes general sociology. General sociology will correspond to the complete development of a systematic study. This is what I am trying to establish in this book. For the time being, John Stuart Mackenzie's sociology best represents general sociology. Mackenzie (1890, pp. 11-13) says that there are three kinds of social researches. First, just as Aristotle constructed his philosophy by the collection of *endoxa* [the opinion that is accepted by the ordinary people as true. Eds.], we can formulate a study of society. Second, we can name the experimental science of society as sociology. Third, we can find the laws of society by the deduction from philosophically analyzed principles. Mackenzie uses the third type of study.

Mackenzie also cites Aristotle's four methods of explanation: (1) the explanation of a thing by analyzing the various elements, (2) the explanation of a thing by finding the laws that determines the quality of thing, (3) the explanation of a thing by finding the origin of it, and (4) the explanation of a thing by clarifying the purposes. According to Mackenzie, natural history and taxonomy use the first method, exact and empirical science use the second, metaphysics and social philosophy use the third, and ethics uses the fourth. Mackenzie (1890, pp. 14-16) states that he uses all four methods of explanation that Aristotle posed.

Usually sociologists understand sociology in the second sense [the experimental science of society. Eds.], but according to Mackenzie, it is not enough. It should accompany the first and third method [collection of endoxa and logical deduction. Eds.]. However, under the present conditions we sociologists have to be content with borrowing those from other branches of study.

Adolphe Coste (1899, p. 1) strongly recommends the need to have a general sociology from a viewpoint that is different from Mackenzie's. In the preface of his book, Coste criticizes recent psychological sociology. He says psychological sociology is confused with the study of morals and politics. Sociology should be a study concerning facts; therefore, the basis of sociology should not be subjective and psychological, it should be objective and experimental. He also says it is necessary for sociology to become independent from biology, since organisms vary and even biologists do not have reliable methods to compare various organisms and their relationships (Coste, 1899, p. 48). To our regret, Coste's alternative proposal is hackneyed.

II. CLASSIFICATION OF SOCIOLOGIES BY THE AIMS AND MOTIVES

1. *Descriptive sociology.* The goal is the description of social phenomenon. Coste's sociology might become descriptive sociology or social statistics. Coste defines sociology as the clarification of the phenomena that constitutes human society based on evolutionary theory. In his definition, the difference between the descriptive sociology and social statics is the same thing as the difference between qualitative study and quantitative study.

Letourneau is a representative of descriptive sociology. He states that today sociology is nothing but pieces of information from various studies (1892, preface). Sociologists always say that they will find the laws of society. However, nobody has actually discovered the laws yet. So under the present circumstances, sociologists should concentrate on collecting and recording the facts. Spencer is also inclined toward descriptive sociology. Social statistics takes one step forward from such descriptive sociology, aiming at the discovery of the laws of society. Le Play and Mayo-Smith (1895) are representatives of social statistics.

2. *Positive sociology.* The goal is to investigate the development of society (Le Play, 1864; Mayo-Smith, 1895). The founder of positive sociology is Comte. Carey, Courcelle-Seneuil (1862), and Funck-

Brentano (1897) wrote summaries of Comte's sociology. Ward agrees to the practical purpose that Comte advocates, and recently Fouillée and Victor Considérant also agree with Comte. Carey (1858-1867, vol. 1, pp. 9-40) says that current knowledge has advanced from the theoretical to the positive, and it provides a foundation for sociology. However, sociology has not been established because it still has not progressed beyond the metaphysical stage in the research of humans. According to Carey (1858-1867, vol. 1, p. 64), sociology should unite physical laws with social laws. Carey notes that: "Sociology investigates the laws that enable humans to live together in the most excellent way."

Courcelle-Seneuil (1862, pp. 26-29) suggests that sociology studies humans in a general way and investigates the conscious activities of humans. Sociology investigates society as if it was an animate creature that has emotions. According to Ward (1883, vol. 1, preface), in the United States, the true aim of study is to enrich human life. He stated that knowledge is no longer valuable when it no longer enriches human life. Although sociology started as a true study to enrich human potential to the utmost, it is becoming a toy of dilettantes. Ward tries to restore the original sociology as a true study. Recently Ward (1903) published an excellent book, *Pure Sociology*. Like Ward, my goal is positive sociology. There may be dogmatic sociology as a counterpart to the positive sociology. The majority of dogmatic sociology is so-called Christian sociology. Wilbur F. Crafts (1895), Carl Bonhoff (1900), and Jean Gaume (1863) are the representatives. Helion (1894) is not religious but he is a dogmatic sociologist. As mentioned, the dogmatic method is not worth the name of knowledge.[41]

II.3

Problems and System

Tongo Takebe

SUBJECTS AND PROBLEMS

In each branch of science, there is a clearly defined subject matter that researchers address. However, the limitations of each branch of science, the inner properties, and obvious characteristics of the problems, have not been successfully clarified. In order for each branch of science to distinguish itself from the other branches, it is necessary to clearly identify its objects. However, the characteristics of a certain branch are not fully determined until its problems are clearly identified.[1]

Such problems could be identified in various ways according to the nature of the objects and the interest of each researcher, but here we will articulate the characteristics of sociology by going beyond just clarifying "the object to be noticed." Here we will draw a rough sketch of the problems that sociologists identify. The object that sociology investigates is *society*—sociologists in every school agree with this. But they do not share the same methodology, they do not agree in their evaluation of the result, and in the last resort, sociologists appear as if they do not share any problems and themes. We can determine the problems of sociology only after we successfully articulate the themes of sociology.

In various scientific activities, we observe an unfortunate practice in which sociologists neglect the analysis of their own themes and problems. We know of dozens of studies that have fallen into obscurity because of useless and inaccurate knowledge. I think German

Japanese Family and Society
© 2007 by The Haworth Press, Inc. All rights reserved.
doi:10.1300/5840_05

scholars, in this respect, are superior to French. Sometimes German scholars are criticized for excessive formalism. However, the formalization of the method and discourse is the most valuable part of establishing and creating science. As a good example, I recommend that you read the first part of Adolf Wagner's (1892-1893) *Grundlegung der politischen Oekonomie* [Foundations of Political Economics].

THE PROBLEMS OF SOCIOLOGY

Sociology has a number of problems that should be noted. These are theoretically categorized and summarized in the following seven groups.

1. *What is the essential significance of knowledge? What is the ultimate nature of knowledge?* When we start studying something with a serious and earnest mind, and with sufficient consciousness, we first have to identify the essential significance, the ultimate nature of knowledge.

2. *What are the characteristics of and grounds for sociology?* As the general characteristics of knowledge have been identified, it is now necessary to begin with an investigation into the characteristics of sociology. Sociology has already become established as a serious field of study. However, sociologists have only begun to identify and apply appropriate methods of study in their own area.

The two items noted above are basic and urgent problems that need to be solved. In the second chapter we developed some philosophical arguments to indicate the existence of these problems. We may call them *fundamental problems of sociology.* Once we solve those problems we can establish the foundation of sociology, as well as develop a detailed discussion in each specialized division of sociology.

3. *How does society exist?* The first riddles that a sociologist must face are the conditions and ways in which society exists. We should clarify this problem by articulating the laws of the relationships between society and other beings in the universe, and understand the inner laws of society's birth, its maintenance, and metamorphosis.

4. *What kind of phenomena occur in present societies?* This is technically the easiest question to answer. We can answer this by describing the real phenomena and situations of existing societies, and

putting them into certain theoretical and methodological order. In answering this question we can enhance our understanding of existing societies.

5. *What is the fate of societies? What are the problems that societies should overcome?*[2] Following are the facts mentioned above, the question that next comes into our sight is the fate of societies. That is, how will societies be, versus how should societies be, in the future? Through these two lines of questioning we can establish the framework describing the current state of society and how it could be changed.[3] We will include these two as the problems of sociology because sociology should ultimately be the study of human life in general.

The third, fourth, and fifth problems are concerned with the identification of existing societies, the articulation of social phenomena, and the prediction of the future of societies.[4] These are important issues which sociologists should not neglect. The fourth problem, the study of phenomena in societies, may be highly scientific. We can call this the *second problem of sociology.* Once we have answered these questions, we will have improved our knowledge of societies, and we can apply that knowledge to further improve society.

6. *What is the historical context that has shaped existing societies?* This is a question concerning how the existing societies developed. Before trying to apply our knowledge to practical and current issues, we first need to reflect on societies' past. Practical applications are applied to existing societies that have a historical context. In order to understand current societies we need to examine the past history of societies and apply this knowledge. In studying society, we need to use the ideal method as previously discussed in the beginning of Chapter 1 and put those two ideas (history and application) together [see Part II, Chapter 1, Introduction in this book. Eds.].

7. *How can we put the outcomes of sociological study into practice? What are the reliable laws for the practical application of sociological knowledge?* When we try to take the information from our study and apply it, it is necessary to summarize and explain the practical meanings of study (problems 1-6). To summarize and explain the practical meaning of sociological studies, we should answer the questions concerning members of society and their interrelations,

their obligations toward ensuring the future of the society, and the regulatory frameworks for social relationships.

The above two problems are those of the practical application of sociology. Needless to say, it requires considerable support from related disciplines. By synthesizing the body of knowledge of these disciplines, and using it to formulate the ultimate foundation of sociology, we can establish a social ideal between society's theoretical model and actual society. We may call it the *third problem of sociology*.

Many shortsighted sociologists neglect the matters categorized in *the fundamental problems of sociology*. Even the leaders in the field often pay little or no attention to them. Comte's intent was to answer these fundamental problems. Mediocre scholars, who have relied on common sense without critical examination, overwhelmingly ignore these fundamental problems. The second problem of sociology involves the central issues of theoretical sociology, so scholars have never neglected them. However, there are different evaluations toward the importance of the second problem.

Descriptive sociologists see the fourth problem as the sole problem to be resolved. Sociologists whose training was in philosophy of history, see problem five as the only question that should be solved in sociology.

Materialists and spiritualists see problem three as the only problem in sociology. Most of the materialists and spiritualists are amateurs who did not receive academic training. So we do not need to be concerned with them. But it is true that the diversity among the existing sociological theories comes primarily from the different approaches towards the third problem, *How does society exist?*

Scholars who call themselves *historians of civilization* or *sociologists of the history of civilizations* understand the problem in sociology only from the sixth problem. They take the same position as that of philosophers of history and their sociological sympathizers, but the latter are superior to the former because they address the core arguments of sociology. Those who equate sociological study with superficial investigations of social problems and socialism tend to understand sociology as the study of the sixth and seventh problems. But they do nothing more than pose poorly developed quasi-theories on the actual social situation and social ideals. Of course these two problems, six and seven, are very important, and they need to be resolved.

But unless we clarify problems one through five, we can hardly find proper answers to the sixth and seventh problems. Those who do not recognize this tend to pose his or her personal views on history and social ideal as if they are the objective truth. The western European scholars, especially German pseudo-philosophers and scholars under the government's thumb, tend to fall into this type of error.[5]

The most neglected issue of all is the relationship between sociology and other social sciences like history, history of civilizations, and philosophy of history. Gumprlowicz,[6] for example, comes to a deadlock on this issue. This results from insufficient analysis and clarification of the problems. If we are willing to understand sociology, understand its inner structure, and its position in the system of knowledge as a whole, we need to clarify its shortcomings. French sociology is far above all in this respect, but even it has many omissions.

PROBLEMS AND SYSTEM

To clarify the characteristics of the contents of a particular branch of science, the first thing to do is to articulate the problems that constitute the fundamental principles of research. After clarifying the problems, it may appear that we can immediately begin to discuss the substantial arguments. However, since science should be an integrated body of knowledge, the form of a particular branch should also constitute a system. In addition, systematization is necessary for developing well-ordered research. The problems provide the foundation for the systematization of a body of knowledge.

The meaning of the word *system* is not as simple as the words *object* and *problem*. I will explain the meaning of the word *system* shortly. System is a name given to the form of knowledge that is well ordered. If knowledge has sufficient reasonableness, clearness, and exactness,[7] it will become systematic to some degree. Although we usually use the term *system* to indicate the knowledge that is comparatively broad, of course there is no clear boundary line between broad knowledge and narrow knowledge. The difference between broad and narrow knowledge is based on the forms of the objects.

We may explain the status of *system* in the whole body of knowledge as follows: An idea expresses each real entity. A concept expresses the type and character of the entity. A judgment expresses the relationship of each entity. Reasoning expresses the laws. Thus, when the stages of our knowledge are distinguished in this way, there will be the broadest form of knowledge that integrates the whole process (idea-concept-judgment-reasoning), which we call *system* (see Ueberweg, 1857).

The rational idea of *system* can be deducted by the above argument. Of course, as stated, "the lawful nature of real entities in general" could be broad or narrow according to the genre of the field to be studied. In the present situation, even if we could not discover the ultimate rational system of the universe, we should be content with finding some partial systems. When actually studying sociology, the meaning of the word *system* should be understood simply as the unit that has relatively autonomous features.

The systematized body of knowledge is knowledge that is arranged in order. We have to satisfy the following three requirements in order to study systematically. In the first place, we should have the method of distinguishing certain branches of knowledge from others. We need to be especially careful that we do not mistake cross classification for linear classification, we have clarified the standards of a classification, and we have avoided duplication or gaps in knowledge. Second, we should specify the logical correlation of each portion that constitutes a certain branch of knowledge. One must identify the methodology and indicate the limitations in the study. Third, equal attention should be given to each portion of the study. If these requirements are satisfied, then the necessary and sufficient conditions for the systematization of a certain branch of knowledge will also be satisfied.

The above is a discussion of the system of knowledge in general. If it is not a relatively big branch of science, scholars are not concerned if it is not systematized.[8] This may be caused by the lack of development of the branch of science, or by the circumstances that surround it. Because of its size and circumstances, sociology needs to be systematic. The circumstances that characterize sociology are summarized in the following three points. First, the societies, which are the objects of sociology, are vast and various. Moreover, most of the problems of sociology are highly complicated ones. Second, sociology has many research methods. Good sociological research cannot be performed unless it uses those methods together.[9] Third, sociology develops through the synthesis of small, unrelated studies in order to get meaningful principles for the improvement of social life. A certain systematic guide is required for synthesizing the outcomes of the various research studies.

I have briefly explained the reason why sociology needs to be systematized. We now need to go to the next step and articulate the substantial contents of the system of sociology.

Sociologists today forget that sociology should be systematic. This tendency inevitably came from the lack of an awareness of the discipline's problems. Schäffle, Lilienfeld, and others have pointed out the importance to some degree. We have nothing to say about the sociologists of France on this point. In Germany and Austria, Ratzenhofer and Gumplowicz recognize the importance but do not show a sufficient plan. Thus, they cannot develop sociology in a systematic fashion. Recently there have been many instances in which sociology has been criticized by other branches of science for these limitations.

A SYSTEM OF SOCIOLOGY

According to its problems, the system of sociology may be as follows.

1. The system of sociology consists of three divisions according to the three categories of its problems. The first division of the system corresponds to *the fundamental problems of sociology,* and we may call it the principle of sociology.
2. The first division is subdivided into two parts. The first part could be general outline of knowledge.
3. General outline of knowledge is the foundational study clarifying the nature and the characteristics of knowledge itself. In order to begin studying sociology with full consciousness and earnestness, we have to provide the ultimate answer to the question, What is knowledge? The answer must simultaneously address the following five questions:
   What is life?
   What is study for one's life?

What are the branches of knowledge?

What is the limit of each branch?

What methodology should be used for obtaining knowledge?

4. If the nature and the characteristics of knowledge become sufficiently clear and if this knowledge is needed to understand human life, then this should provide a comprehensive view of this domain of knowledge.

5. As a proverb of Confucius states: "discover new things by studying the past," we should examine past knowledge and explore the history of its development. This approach also gives us useful data for the systematic research of existing societies. So we should attach great importance to the study of the past development of knowledge.

   Therefore, the third part of the general outline of knowledge serves as history of knowledge. The history of knowledge elucidates the relationship between the progress of knowledge and the development of world civilizations. Thus, the history of knowledge is the history of intellectual activities of humans at large, as well as the history of world civilizations as a whole.[10]

6. The general outline of knowledge consists of the three parts noted above. This is the preface to the system of sociology. After that, we will discuss the main contents of sociology. According to the general outline of knowledge, sociology is a systematic kind of learning, which generalizes all sciences, and aims to bring about the highest understanding of human life. Those who are going to succeed in the interpretation of *the second problems of sociology* should read the general theory of sociology, that is, the second part of the first division.

7. The general theory of sociology is subdivided into two parts. The first part is an outline of sociology. The outline of sociology deals with enactment, the meaning, the status, system, and the inquiring method of sociology. It connects the general outline of knowledge and each portion of sociological studies.

8. Once the outline of sociology becomes settled and the content is established, the next area to be developed would be the history of sociology. The history of sociology studies the rise and fall of sociological ideas in the past and provides references for substantial sociological research. It is convenient to distinguish

it from the general history of the development of knowledge. The history of sociology more closely resembles present-day sociology. When we inquire into the history of knowledge it is necessary that we do not overemphasize the history of sociology.

9. The main subject of sociology is the study of societies. It is the second division of the system of sociology that corresponds to the second problem of sociology.

10. The main subject of sociology consists of three parts. The first part asked how does society exist,[11] and what are the laws guiding the existence of society.

11. The first part consists of two elements. The first element, the study of general laws, examines the existence of beings in general in the universe and seeks to discover the laws of these beings' existence as a whole. It will provide the fundamental laws of the existence of society (Astronomy, Physics, Chemistry, Biology).

12. The second element is the study of special laws, the particular laws dealing with the roles of humans in society (Sociology).

13. The second part of the main subject of sociology is theory of social phenomena, or social statics.

14. The theory of social phenomena is subdivided into two elements. The first element, embryology of society, is concerned with the question of the prerequisites of the birth of society. The second element is the morphology of society, which is concerned with the forms of the existing societies.

15. The morphology of society, or the theory of social structure, investigates the structure of society and the functions of its parts. The theory of social structure is subdivided into two elements. The first examines the formation of each organ, the correlations between organs, and their functions in the whole social structure.

16. The goal of the second element of the morphology is to articulate the administration of those organs.

17. The third part of the main subjects of sociology is social dynamics, or the theory of the future of society.

18. The theory of social evolution is the first element of social dynamics. Along with social statics it deals with the future of society.

19. The second element of social dynamics is the theory of social ideals. It is concerned with the guiding principles for the improvement of society. It may be also called the ultimate theory of civilization.

20. Applied sociology is the third division of the sociological system. It corresponds to *the third problem of sociology* and is subdivided in two parts.
21. The first part of the applied sociology corresponds to the question of how contemporary societies developed and is called description of society.
22. For convenience, the description of society can be subdivided into two elements. The first element deals with the past of a particular society, and it is called the historical profile of society. It is different from the history, since it emphasizes the positivistic evaluations of historical phenomena.
23. The second element deals with the present condition of a particular society, and is called the present profile of society. It observes inter-social problems and intra-social problems. Among those inter-social problems, the race problem is central.
24. The second part of applied sociology corresponds to the question of how we try to apply the outcomes of sociological study into practice. It is called social administration.
25. Social administration consists of three elements. The first, principles of pedagogy, focuses on understanding the process of socialization of individuals.
26. The second is the principle of politics, with a goal to articulate the proper policy to lead the people.
27. Finally, to understand the laws operating between societies, the third element, the principle of international relationships, is needed. Below is an outline of the system of sociology.

System of Sociology

Division 1. Principles of Sociology

    Part 1. General Outline of Knowledge
      1. Principles of Knowledge
      2. System of Knowledge
      3. History of Knowledge
    Part 2. General Theory of Sociology
      1. Outline of Sociology
      2. History of Sociology

Division 2. Main Subject of Sociology

Part 1. Social Physics or Theory of Social Existence
1. General Laws
2. Special Laws

Part 2. Social Statics or Theory of Social Phenomena
1. Embryology of Society
2. Morphology of Society
3. Administration of Social Organs

Part 3. Social Dynamics or Theory of the Fate of Society
1. Theory of Social Evolution
2. Theory of Social Ideal

Division 3. Applied Sociology

Part 1. Description of Society
1. Historical Profile of Society
2. Present Profile of Society

Part 2. Social Administration
1. Principle of Pedagogy
2. Principle of Politics
3. Principle of International Relations

As noted earlier, past sociologists have paid little attention to the systematization of sociology. But the system I proposed above is not genuinely my creation. The basic distinction between *Social Statics* and *Social Dynamics* came from Comte, although I cannot agree with him on minor technical procedures in systematization. The current advances in social psychology made me aware of the need to distinguish *social laws* from other branches. I referred to Stuckenberg's (1898) suggestion that the system should be constructed by three divisions.[12]

The need to distinguish the historical profile of society from history may be justified by citing Raoul Rogières's (1884) *Histoire de la Société française au Moyen-age:* 987-1483 and Charles de Ribbe's (1879) *Les Familles et la Société en France avant la Révolution.* De Ribbe inquired into the past society by applying the Le Play Method.

GENERAL SOCIOLOGY

Sociology will be a broad and systematic branch of science. We should cover all branches of the system, but unfortunately, at the present sociology does not have the sufficient ability to do so. Sociology is still too young. Thus, I would like to propose *General Sociology*. General sociology allows us to draw the outline of the system of sociology, as a preparatory study or preliminary investigation. General sociology has the following four characteristics:

1. Maintaining coherence within the system, it concentrates on the most conspicuous characteristics of sociology.
2. Detailed explanations on serious and familiar matters are investigated. Things that are not serious or are unfamiliar can more or less be neglected.
3. The order of the observations will not necessarily be systematic. It can include the subjects of the different branches of the system in a single chapter or section.
4. It should be simple and clear.

Thus, general sociology neglects division 3 of the system. Applied sociology can be established only after we make clear the main subject of sociology. Also, general sociology pays minimum attention to division 1. We will just grasp the general tendency of knowledge. Especially neglected are the historical branches of knowledge. Therefore our main concern is about division 2. *General Sociology* consists of four parts below:

Volume I. Prolegomenon (Introduction)
Volume II. Social Physics
Volume III. Social Statics
Volume IV. Social Dynamics

I believe that general sociology provides an introductory guide for the successors.

In sociology, it is difficult to assess the perspective or use of a given work—a handbook or a special treatise. Without this, other branches of science cannot place confidence in sociology.

II.4

Methodology

Tongo Takebe

GENERAL METHODOLOGY

In the previous chapter, I discussed the subject, nature, characteristics, and system, and provided an outline of science. Next, I will provide a clarification of methodology. This, I believe, is the proper order in the progress of the study. Unfortunately, science has been slow in making progress. The major reason for this is our unfortunate habit of attempting to quickly achieve success by using common sense methods without critically recognizing the difference between generally shared methods and special methods. Currently, it seems that many scholars have begun to recognize that we cannot achieve any of the goals of science in such a primitive way. Today, methodology has become a major point of discussion in the various branches of science. This is especially a problem in sociology. The various theories and levels of abstraction result in the need for discussions of methodology among researchers.

Methodology consists of the procedures used for building theory. Methodology consists of a special application of epistemology and logic which focuses on how to achieve knowledge, that is, how we know what is what. The main objectives of methodology are first to clarify what kind of method we can use when we discover laws, and second to clarify the range and the limit of the validity of a particular methodology.

Japanese Family and Society
© 2007 by The Haworth Press, Inc. All rights reserved.
doi:10.1300/5840_06

There are two kinds of methods used in sociology. One is the same method shared by science in general; the other is specific to methodology in sociology. The latter needs a more detailed examination. I will explain these points in greater detail in this chapter.

Before we had any awareness of the discipline of sociology, we did not discuss the methods for observing society. It may be said that one of the biggest motivations for the separation of sociology from philosophy in the nineteenth century was an awareness of methodology. You can gain insights into this separation [of sociology from philosophy] if you remember the rise of Comte's positive philosophy.[1] Following Comte, Mill (1843, part 6) elaborated on the methods to observe society. Spencer constructed a huge system of philosophy, but he did not seem to be interested in abstract methodology. In France, Le Play proposed a novel method, but it has few followers.[2] The development of Le Play's method has been influenced by advances in statistical techniques. From the new continent (North America) Mayo-Smith (1895) advocated the use of the Le Play Method. Many other current sociologists also have a deep interest in methodological arguments.

The diversity of methods for studying society developed from a variety of definitions of society and sociology. Frequently, problems in conceptualization and in definitions result from the problems that occur during the actual observations. This is because people often neglect the difference between definitions of society and the methods for observing society. Currently there is the practice of giving strange names to different methods. Some examples of this are the *organic method* or the *psychological method* (see Lilienfeld, 1898; Stein, 1898).

COMMONLY ACCEPTED METHODS

In all scientific activities, there are two commonly accepted methods: deductive and inductive. Deduction is a method of reasoning from the relatively general to the relatively specific. It applies knowledge of general matters to particular matters. Conversely, induction is a method of reasoning from the relatively specific to the relatively general; it applies knowledge of particular matters to general matters.

When we divert laws that are found in a certain branch of science to another branch by using the deductive method, we should divert the laws from the higher branch to the lower, or else we will experience serious complications. Induction is suitable for finding laws in every branch at every level of advancement. Thus, the diversion can be made more safely using induction than when using deduction. Ideally, the laws found by both highest and lowest must be irrefutable truths, although the highest general knowledge tends to be acquired by intuition of the mind, the lowest-specific knowledge tends to be acquired by intuition of the five senses. Intuition is the basis for discovering both the most and least abstract reality, that is, both the deductive and inductive method. The distinction between the mind and senses is compatible with *subject* and *object.*

An additional explanation on the above *high-low* distinction is needed here. Suppose we examine the case of deductive from a higher-level science to a lower-level science. This is called decomposition or analysis and is useful for obtaining specific knowledge. Conversely, the inductive diversion from the lower to the higher is the process of composition or synthesis. At last we will reach true general knowledge.

Both methods should be used jointly. The distance from starting point to ending point, that is, from particular to general, from general to particular, of the two methods is too lengthy and such a lengthy process of reasoning may easily have serious errors. We can minimize the risk of such errors by starting from both the particular and the general.

Of course the two basic methods are also applicable to sociological study, although they need to be modified in a sociological manner. Next, we discuss the special methods that are particularly sociological.

Worms (1896b, p. 79) once pointed out that there are five kinds of methods in science, that is, observation, experiment, classification, induction, and deduction, although their applications are diverse according to the diversity of the objects to be studied. I think his argument has some elements that are true and others that are false. We cannot say that observation, experiment, and classification are accepted as useful methods in all branches of science. But other than these points, I agree with him.

Kant (1884), Mill (1843), and Jevons contributed much to the methodological discussion of induction and deduction. Every other logician argues all the various small points (see Hamilton, 1873; Ueberweg, 1857, 1872).

PARTICULARLY SOCIOLOGICAL METHODS

Methods of sociology need to be designed as apparatus that are useful for solving its problems. Considering the peculiarity of the problems of sociology, sociological methods needs to be two fold, that is, subjective-rational and objective-empirical.[3]

It is well-known that rationalism and empiricism are the most powerful sources of modern Western European philosophy. Each has its own characteristics. The rational method is a form of deduction that is suitable for general studies. The empirical method, that is a form of induction, is suitable for particular studies. One is a subjective, philosophical method; the other is an objective, scientific method. The flow of modern history of thought was divided between those two. Sociology arose as the criticism of subjective-philosophical faction, so it tended to neglect the rational method.

Many sociologists believe that the elimination of the subjective-rational method represents an advancement of science, but this is wrong. We should use the two methods together. However, it is also true that empiricists are sufficiently aware of the need to critically examine the method that rationalists often disregard. In this respect the methods used by the empiricist are superior to those used by the rationalist.

Auguste Comte is considered to be an example of a pure empiricist. It is true that in some paragraphs of his work, Comte rejected the validity of the subjective-rational method entirely.[4] However, he also stressed the need for the subjective-rational method. He said that human knowledge has progressed through three stages. The first stage was *theological*. During the theological stage, scholars had explained phenomena and the effects on the world from the perspective of the existence of a super natural being. The theological stage was unavoidably dogmatic and visionary. The second stage was *metaphysical*. Based on the human ability of abstraction, scholars have isolated themselves from facts and toyed with abstract notions. The third stage will be *positive*. Based both on the ability of reasoning and observation, our thoughts and our knowledge shall come to perfection. Comte is not a mere objectivist-empiricist. His positive method contains both subjective-empirical and objective-rational approaches. He warned that when we use the subjective-rational method, we should avoid supernaturalism and metaphysical games. I think that Comte employed the new term *positive* because the term *empirical* does not convey the need for the subjective-rational method.

Those who proclaim to be disciples of Comte do not understand the need for both methods, and wrongly equate the positive method with the objective-empirical method. For example, Henry Charles Carey says that advances in science are based on a move from abstractness to concreteness, from general to specific, complex to simple, metaphysical to methodical (Carey, 1858-1867, vol. 1, pp. 9-37). In short, he places too much weight on objectivism-empiricism. John Fiske, in his badly formulated book *Outlines of Cosmic Philosophy,* says that there are two types of methods in science (1874, p. 98). One is subjective, and metaphysical philosophy is its main outcome. The other is objective, and cosmic philosophy is its achievement. He completely misunderstands Comte's argument and regresses into the theological stage.

Herbert Spencer, in his *First Principles,* rigorously differentiated between the knowable and the unknowable and declared that his science treats only the knowable. His *synthetic* method is a kind of induction. It is disappointing that he told us nothing about the unknowable. If he had, the relationship between the knowable and the unknowable would be clearer. He may have achieved his personal goals, but I think sociology needs more.[5]

Currently, Durkheim, Fouillée, Harris, Menger, and especially Mackenzie are trying to rehabilitate Comte's true positivism.[6] I place my hope for accomplishing this on Mackenzie. His creativity stimulates me.

SUBJECTIVE-RATIONAL METHOD

The subjective-rational method has been employed mainly in the philosophical branch of sociology. Comte's positive method corresponds roughly to *reasoning* (inference). But Comte's account of inference is narrower than that of the subjective-rational method. Inference is just one aspect, although an important one, of human intelligence. We can acquire knowledge without both the inference and the five senses through intuition. By using intuition we can recognize the truth directly. The philosophical branch of sociology ought to employ both inference and intuition.

The subjective-rational method has three functions: defining concepts, theory construction, and ideal production. We begin using the subjective-rational study approach by defining concepts, putting them together into a single logically consistent system of theory. The preconditions of the subjective-rational method are the epistemological conditions of intuitive knowledge and the logical conditions of deductive inference. The subjective-rational method should not be used by itself. Although this method is quite effective when employed for collecting and putting facts in order, to establish a perfect positive method, we need the empirical method as well as the rational method.

OBJECTIVE-EMPIRICAL METHOD

The objective-empirical method is a special application of induction, and has mainly been employed in the scientific branch of sociology.[7] Scientific inquiry begins from the objective observation of external phenomena. In Comte's positive method, it roughly corresponds to *observation,* but it is narrower than that of Comte's account. The conditions that validate the objective-empirical method are the laws of time, space, causation, and logic, and the validity of deduction.[8]

The objective-empirical method consists of two parts:[9] qualitative-descriptive and quantitative-statistical.[10] The qualitative-descriptive method is useful when we develop a list of particular facts. The goal of the quantitative-statistical method is to find the laws of coexistence or the connection between two or more particular facts or phenomena by functional analysis.

The qualitative method operated through four stages: the existence of the facts, the recognition of facts, statements about facts, and the integration of the statements. We have to be aware that a single error occurring in a single stage could be fatal to the validity of the whole study. In the first and second stages we may fail to distinguish real existence from fancy and illusion. In the second stage we may fail to make a valid correlation between the existence and our intuitive of recognition. We could mistakenly misinterpret the facts because of biased thinking.[11] In the third stage we may be faced with the problem of naming the facts. As experience shows, it is often very difficult to avoid the contradictions between a technical term and the mundane usage of the term. In the last stage we would experience difficulty in organizing statements and constructing the whole system of sociology.[12] It has been said that descriptive sociology is full of mistakes. Those mistakes seem to come from disregarding the subjective-rational method.

The quantitative method has four stages. They are the simultaneous or successive occurrence of two or more phenomena, and the recognition, analysis, and explanation of these phenomena. Similar to the errors found in the qualitative method, we can also make serious errors when using the quantitative method. In the first and second stages, we may overanalyze a single phenomenon and misrepresent the simultaneous or successive occurrence of two or more phenomena. It may be meaningless and tautological. In the second and third stages *chance* may wrongly preconceive as *necessary*. In the last stage *hypothetical laws* may misconceive as *substantial truth*.[13]

The goal of the statistical method is to find the laws of simultaneous or successive occurrence of two or more phenomena in a quantitative manner. To achieve that goal, the statistical method has to obey the rules of mathematics. Theories of mathematical approximation no doubt represent major advances in current applied mathematics, but they have limits. Theories of mathematical approximation apply the method of difference (differential calculus) and the method of concomitant variation, to establish causation in quantitative expressions. We should not overestimate the capability of those theories, since they only calculate the degree of probability. For example, *highly probable* is not the same as the general idea of *necessary*. Likewise, *low probability* is not the same as our general concept of *chance*. In nature, they are incapable of judging such causation as necessary.[14]

In addition, when we apply those theories to actual observations, we often cannot collect a large enough sample to determine the degree of probability.[15] The smaller the samples, the less likely the outcome of the calculus will be statistically significant. Also, until now, studies based on actual observations have often ignored analysis that could identify multiple causes. So we should be cautious when we employ the statistical method to actual sociological observation.

Mayo-Smith (1895, p. 7) is a typical example of someone who understands the method of sociology as empirical, not to mention other methods. He said that sociology is a science to study the social structure and social change. To obtain this objective, he argued that sociologists should employ the qualitative-descriptive method and the quantitative-statistical method, and no other is needed. Although, he occasionally pointed out that both methods and their combination are not omnipotent; thus, we should explore this further.

In his early career, Durkheim (1893) stressed the objective-empirical method. But in his later work, *The Rules of the Sociological Methods* (1895), he demonstrated a proper and moderate argument. He says that we should study social facts as if they are crude facts. But in addition, he knows that we need certain theoretical assumptions before we can study social facts. Also he characterizes social facts as general, not particular, facts. I think he emphasized the physical treatment of social facts only because he felt the need to notify people that sociology had not yet awoken from the metaphysical period.

Adolphe Quételet (1869), Ernst Engel (1861), Gustav Rümelin (1875-1894), and others established statistics as a well-ordered branch of science. In its broader definition statistics included meteorological or chemical branches, but its narrower definition is more familiar. In its narrower definition, statistics is the same thing as demography. Georg Mayr (1877) and August Meitzen (1886) are the current major scholars in statistics.

COLLECTION OF DATA

We can achieve the perfect positive method by combining the subjective-rational method with the objective-empirical method. In collecting empirical data, we should use the objective-empirical method. To put those empirical data in order, we should use the subjective-rational method.

There are two kinds of empirical data: quantitative-statistical and qualitative-descriptive. The collection of those two kinds of data is not the same as the physical gathering of the data at the same place and same time, but rather mental gathering of data in a theoretical order. When we collect the data, we have already gone one step forward in order to synthesize the objective-empirical method and the subjective-rational method. The collection of data is the medium of exchange between the subjective-rational method and the objective-empirical method.

Ego's intuition. The ego's intuition is the stage in which all mental phenomena arise and become active. By the ego's intuition, we recognize the phenomena without distinguishing subject and object. Its essence is in the unconsciousness; but it functions in the consciousness. When viewed from its functions, the ego's intuition is the basis of our awareness—that which makes us aware that our awareness does exist.[16] Also, the ego's intuition gives us the ultimate basis for both the deductive and inductive method, although the ego's intuition itself cannot analyze the matters. Thus, it cannot develop both methods sufficiently.

Awareness. If the ego's intuition develops and is able to distinguish subject and object, we can call it *awareness.* Awareness is the first sign of ideas, or what we call knowledge. Also, awareness is the concept that generally indicates ego. In other words, awareness is knowledge acquired by ego's self-reflection. Knowledge is the facts that are to be collected, so the awareness gives us the second and strong basis to both deductive and inductive methods.[17] This is the starting point for the rational collection of facts. All of our knowledge of matters comes from ego's self-reflection.

Category (basic schema of human perception). Awareness is derived from the ego. Awareness accompanies category, which makes it possible to know the relationship between objective things. Awareness and perception, subject and object are mediated by category.[18]

Perception. Perception is the ability to understand objective facts. All facts have their own characteristics. The variation in the characteristics is in direct proportion to the sensitivity of the ego. Sensitivity is itself a category. If our sensitivity quantitatively increases or decreases, our perception, in the future, would be different from today.[19] When compared to category, perception goes one step forward to the objective world. When the objective matter stimulates us, our perception arises. The perceptive image in our mind is created from the sensitivity of the five senses (e.g., taste, smell, hearing, vision, and touch).

From a methodological viewpoint, these four components or stages of the state of mind form the rational collection of data. Objective data are influenced by the subjective viewpoint. Empirical data can be collected by observation, experiment, comparison, and historical observation.

Observation. Observation is used to collect data on ordinary phenomena. Perception helps us collect objective-empirical facts. Perception deals with internal images, whereas observation deals with facts. Observation provides the starting point for the objective-empirical method and from the logician's viewpoint, the starting point for the inductive method.

Experiment. The experimental method is used to observe the objective phenomenon, by manipulating the situation according to the observer's goal. Jevons (1874a, pp. 233-234) suggested that the observation and experimental methods differ by the degree of manipulation. Observation uses passive surveillance of the phenomena. In the experiment one observes the outcome of a manipulation of the setting. The only difference between the two methods is whether we can control the conditions in which certain phenomenon occurs. Comte stressed that observation and experiments are both necessary methods of sociology. Le Play emphasized observation as the axiomatic method of sociology.

Spencer, a descriptive sociologist, encouraged the observation method, but noted that most observational studies are still based on the unreliable records of a traveler. Le Play's plan is outstanding and magnificent. According to Le Play (1864, vol. 1, pp. 63-72), the best way for gathering information in order to propose social reforms is by the observation of social facts: (1) Researchers should study the unique social systems in their own country. (2) They should obtain accurate information from political groups and missionary associations. (3) They should have frequent visits with the families—at least 300 families, seven to thirty days—in each country, each region, and each class in order to observe their material, mental, and moral conditions. This third method is called the Le Play Method. It would be best to try to meet the necessary conditions of the Le Play Method, but in reality it is very difficult. The Le Play Method is meaningful when we understand it as an antithesis of Saint Simon's speculative method for proposing social reform.

Comparative method. Both observation and experiment, based on the collection of simple external data, help us understand the laws that regulate the relationships between phenomena, that is, it gives us perception, not category. There are two ways to acquire knowledge of laws: spatial comparisons, that is, comparing phenomena between two or more entities at the same time (comparison in ordinary sense), and temporal comparison, that is, comparing a particular phenomena at two or more different times (historical observation).

There are three kinds of comparison.

1. Comparing similar and coexistent phenomenon enables us to properly exclude accidental cases from the samples. For the sake of research, we have to accentuate major trends rather than focus on minor differences.
2. By comparing different kinds of phenomena that are coexistent, we can closely examine the similarity and the difference. But if we lack certain standards for the comparisons, it will not be fruitful. It may fail because it is overly complex.
3. By comparing different kinds of phenomena, we can discover certain similarities at given levels of abstraction, and discover the essence common in those phenomena. This is ordinarily called *comparison* in science. For instance, in anatomy, researchers may compare the circulatory organs of gorilla and chimpanzee to discover the evolutionary processes of primates. In linguistics, researchers may compare the processes of development of two or more languages, in order to understand general laws of language development. Similarly in psychology, researchers may compare the human child and lesser animals so that they can articulate the developmental process of the human mind. In employing comparison, we can make errors especially in the process of analytical, inductive integration.

Historical observation. The historical observation is a special case of the comparison method used to articulate causation. As stated above, the comparative method is capable of categorical distinctions and identifications, but not capable of articulating the causal relationships between two or more phenomena. By comparing two or more phenomena at different points in time, historical observation tries to provide causal explanations. However, historical observation can be extremely complex to conduct. The goal is not only to observe single pairs of cause and effect, but also to observe several coexistent processes of causation and their configurations. Suppose we wanted to study world history. When we try to acquire valid knowledge by historical observations, we have to meticulously observe not only the rules guiding the empirical collection of data, but also the rules guiding the *use of the ideas* regarding the data.[20]

Comte gave the closest analysis to the empirical method. He believed that sociological methodology consisted of two divisions. One, the indirect method, is used in all branches of science. The other, the direct method, is specifically used in the study of sociology. He subdivided the direct method in three parts: observation, experiment, and comparison. The comparison method has three elements:

1. Comparing human society and that of the lesser animals.
2. Comparing two or more existing human societies.
3. Comparing a single society at two different times.

Then he added that there should be a fourth kind of comparison. It is the historical method that deals with the most complex phenomena, social phenomena. I think Comte's argument is generally right, although he was not careful about the logical coherence.

Recently many articles have been published that emphasize the importance of the historical method (see Lamprecht, 1896; Rappoport, 1896; Langlois & Seignobos, 1898). Fouillée, as a representative of French sociology, published an article concerning the methodology of Worms (1895a, p. 5) in which he summarized Worms's methodology in three points:

1. Every social phenomenon correlates with each other, so when we try to understand a single phenomenon, we must take all other phenomena into account, without exception.
2. In each partial study of social phenomenon, we should use the objective method. To prevent unconscious value biases, we should devote all our attention to observation and classification of the phenomenon.
3. Only after we have done this is it appropriate to describe existing problems in society, and plan studies for improving the situation.

USE OF IDEAS

A *fact,* which can be empirical and logical, is the name given to the basic material that constitutes knowledge. Knowledge inevitably begins with ideas and categories. After facts are collected, we use ideas (or categories for perception) to convert these facts into knowledge. To use the idea accurately and with confidence, we should study logic that teaches the laws of thinking. Therefore, in this section we just enumerate the essentials of logic.

The existence of rational facts is the necessary prerequisite of the subjective-rational method. In terms of logic, a rational fact is the prerequisite of the deductive method. An empirical fact is the prerequisite of the objective-empirical method. In terms of logic, an empirical fact is the prerequisite of induction. The order of using the idea can be reversed according to whether we choose to use the deductive or inductive method. We divide the usages of the idea roughly into two kinds: internal usage and external usage. The internal usage is further divided into analysis and synthesis. The external usage is further divided into deduction and induction.

The goal of analysis is to enumerate various attributes of a certain idea and to make it clear that a complex idea is the synthesis of simple ideas. Such simple ideas are called categories. Synthesis, the opposite of analysis, clarifies how those categories create a complex idea that varies according to the kinds of material collected.

In addition, there are two subtypes of analysis and syntheses: *connotative* (the attribute of a certain notion) and *denotative* (the applicable limit of the notion). Usually, when we use the terms analysis and synthesis, we mean connotative analysis and connotative synthesis. Denotative analysis is called listings, and denotative synthesis is called summary. The first logical use of the idea is deduction. Deduction is the process of reasoning that starts from the universal and arrives at the particulars. There are two kinds of deduction: direct reasoning and indirect reasoning.

The second logical use of the idea is induction. Induction is the process of reasoning that starts from the particulars and arrives at the universal. Induction is sometimes divided further into two kinds: perfect induction and imperfect induction.

Needless to say there are also two kinds of deduction and induction respectively, according to the nature of the idea (simple or complex) that is chosen at the starting point of reasoning. In sum, we can use ideas in two ways.

1. Start from synthesis, via deduction, arrive at the listing—the deductive method.
2. Start from analysis, via induction, arrive at the summary—the inductive method.

We should entrust logicians with further details of the above argument. To conclude, we should put the arguments in this chapter in order.

 I. Methodology in General
   A. Normal methods (deductive and inductive)
   B. Special methods
     1. Subjective-Rational (intuitive, reasoning)
     2. Objective-Empirical (descriptive, statistical)
II. Elements (variables)
   A. Collection of facts
     1. Collection of rational facts (Ego's intuition, self-consciousness, category)
     2. Collection of empirical facts
       a) Simple (observation, experiment)
       b) Complex (comparison, historical observation)
   B. Usages of ideas
     1. Theoretical (analytical, synthetic)
     2. Logical (inductive, deductive)
     3. Systems (inductive, deductive)

PART III:
HISTORICAL INTRODUCTION

III.1

General Remarks on Historical Study

Tongo Takebe

HISTORICAL STUDY

In recent years, historical study has been developing in academic circles as a method of scientific inquiry. Unfortunately, there is an undesirable trend in which the name "historical study" is now being used in various ways. However, it is natural that we tend to imagine the course of our future by looking back upon the past. And, it is also natural that such studies adopt complicated methodologies, since this appears at the last and the highest stage of the development in scientific inquiries. Of course, historical study would have no value if it did not have a reliable methodology. Below, I will investigate the history of science—its nature, goals, and limits—with reliable methodology.

Part III is from Tongo Takebe, *General Sociology* (1904). *Prolegomenon of Sociology.* Part 2, Chapters 1-4. Tokyo: Kinkodo Press.

Japanese Family and Society
© 2007 by The Haworth Press, Inc. All rights reserved.
doi:10.1300/5840_07

The history of science aims to clarify the characteristics of science itself and strengthen the second meaning of science. We should understand that the history of science gives us the third meaning of science.[1] The history of science does not provide a detailed discussion on the substantial contents of each science; it only decides the general framework. The history of science estimates the course of future science by looking back upon the past.

Therefore the goal of the history of science is not only to observe past events in scientific activity, but also to clarify past contexts and general tendencies. From this point of view, we can say that the history of science is a part of the history of civilization and represents the subjective aspect of the history of civilization. So the history of particular branches of science must also be a part of the history of civilization, although each branch has its own characteristics and goals.

In order for historical description to be appealing to the readers, it is necessary to contain the second and third meanings of the description. However, it is a history of sociology that I am going to discuss here. I would like to contribute mainly to predicting the future of sociology, so I will employ the findings from the general history of civilizations when it is necessary. After all, historical study in general deals with the development of certain past events that impacted certain societies. Therefore, we should describe the general nature of society before we inquire into particular events. Since civilization is the goal of society, the history of civilization describes the process by which it is accomplished. Civilization and society cannot be separated in nature: They form a single unified body. So we need to reinforce our argument by citing the history of civilization.

In our study of the history of sociology, we should not be particular about whether the authors employed the term *sociology*. If we disregard authors who did not use the term *sociology*, our history will be full of mistakes. In the history of sociology, as in the history of civilization, the most important points are the phases in which there are complications:

1. The dawn of sociological thinking.
2. The formative phase.
3. The reformative phase.
4. The phase immediately before us.

In the first phase, sociology was quite unstructured and obscure, so we will begin our investigation of this phase by investigating the work of authors who did not call themselves sociologists.

Auguste Comte was the first man who tried to establish the history of sociology. His history of sociological thoughts was combined with the developmental history of civilization. The most noteworthy contemporary scholars in this field are Ludwig von Stein (1897), Friedrich von Baerenbach (1882), and Robert S. Hamilton (1873). They maintained that theoretical study and historical study should work together. Although their systems of sociology seem to be excessively complex, their historical descriptions are worth reading. Jean Gaspard Bluntschli and Johannes Weitzel are early scholars who studied the history of sociological thought. Other contemporary scholars like Harald Höffding, Gustav Schmoller, Robert von Mohl, and Célestin Charles Alfred Bouglé tried to describe the history of sociology.[2]

Max Landmann (1896) and Otto Friedrich Gierke (1880) described the formation of sociological thought by different authors. Friedrich Julius Stahl (1846-1847) and August Johann Geyer (1863) wrote books concerning the history of jurisprudence. In addition, Fouillée made some contributions to this subject in his new books (Fouillée, 1896a,b). Except for Fouillée, recent French scholars seem to be neglecting this subject.

DATA OF THE HISTORY OF SOCIOLOGY

Besides works that are identified as sociology, the following nine factors may be counted as data for a history of sociology. Some of these have a right to claim that they are independent, systematic branches of science. Some of them are new areas containing much confusion and omissions. But I will list the areas of study that are relevant.

Confucianism. Since the history of Confucianism is far older than that of sociology, it might appear that there is an unbridgeable abyss between the two. But the major concern shared by the truest Confucians is how to influence society. Therefore, although Confucianism and sociology each have their own methodologies, they share a similar problem to be resolved. The difference between Confucianism and sociology is not as critical as that between metaphysics and sociology in Comte's terms. In fact, in a comparison of the ancient systems of knowledge, Confucianism is the most similar to sociology. It is unreasonable to think that sociology has been, and shall continually be, exclusively Western. We who aim to make sociology a major branch of science can claim Confucianism as one of our origins.

History. History is the record of the development of a society and is an archive useful for sociological studies. It is unavoidable that historians' facts are collected according to their own opinions and ideas. Therefore, historical study cannot be neutral and objective, but that does not mean that it is meaningless and false. If it is properly developed, the historian's subjective opinion can be seen as a social ideal. Just like sociology, historical study can help to establish a suitable social ideal.[3]

Philosophy of history. As historical study proceeds, two paths of development arise. The first is the methodological crystallization of subjective ideas. Philosophy of history attempts to discover the fundamental principle of historical development. The second is objective crystallization of the subjective ideas. History of civilization compiles major historical facts according to their developmental order. Thus, we need another branch of science, one that has been named sociology, to collect the historical data that has been omitted and to establish a social ideal. Philosophy of history can be seen as the medium between historical study and sociological study. In fact some scholars in this field have made the pioneering contributions toward sociology.

The history of civilization. The history of civilization can also be seen as the intersection between historical study and sociological study. It has made contributions toward sociology, but its contributions are smaller than that of the philosophy of history, since each study of civilization depends strongly upon the scholar's scope. Furthermore, philosophy of history and history of civilization do not share the same problems, methodology, or characteristics, so they scarcely reach a consensus even on the most fundamental issues. Both philosophy of history and the history of civilization have inadequate methodology to be able to interpret the problems of sociology. But, the data from each study contain profound knowledge that can be used to construct a system of sociology.

The Western academic world failed to adequately clarify the relationship between history, philosophy of history, history of civilization, and sociology. Today, at the end of nineteenth century, I feel the need to apologize to our students for this blunder. But there are some clues for resolving this confusion. Paul Barth (1897a) and Fustel de Coulange (1916, 1934) maintain that sociology should be a history that describes the causes of social changes. Bouglé (1896) and Simmel (1892) argue that sociology should become independent of the philosophy of history and sociologists should concentrate their research on the forms of society. Funck-Brentano (1897) says that the laws of history and the laws of society are the same, and the laws of history should be articulated by sociological methods.

Fouillée (1880) proclaims that the difference between philosophy of history and sociology is in the difference between teleonomy and causation. He says philosophy discovers the fundamental principle of historical change in a theological, poetic, and mystic manner. Sociology discovers it in a positivistic manner. Both should be integrated in the present study of society. Formerly his position was unclear, but later he clarified his position. Recently Fouillée (1895) commented on Fustel de Coulange's view that sociology is nothing but another name for history since both deal with social actions (see Worms, 1895a). Fouillée commented that Coulange is a typical historian who lacks a grounding in philosophical thinking, so he is not able to clarify the nature or characteristics of the fundamental social body that constitutes history. For the time being, the debate is fruitless. The two sides remain as far apart as ever.

As I noted earlier, this kind of controversy results from the inconsistencies between the different positions and the lack of comprehensiveness (see Part II, Chapter 2, System of Sciences). Not only is philosophy of history not studied in a systematic way, sociology lacks an awareness of the accumulated knowledge in the field of philosophy of history. From Schlegel (1829) and Hegel (1837) onward, countless numbers of followers have written books copying Schlegelian or Hegelian style.

The German scholars disliked the name *sociology*. The policy of *Grossdeutschtum* [German expansionism] could not be tolerated by the social democrats. This is one of the reasons why the universities and colleges in Germany are so reluctant to create chairs of sociology. Scholars are not angels, the earth is not paradise, and as a result, this kind of narrow-mindedness seems to be unavoidable. But it is inexcusable to arrogantly exclude possible alternatives without a close examination. Recently Gumplowicz and other German sociologists are making efforts to clarify the relationship between history, philosophy of history, history of civilization, and sociology, but at present they have not reached an agreement.[4] I doubt that they will succeed in surmounting the German narrow-mindedness. However, it is too early to evaluate their works.

The heart of history is world history, which represents the author's view of the world that reflects his nationality and the status quo of his nation. In education this characteristic of world history should be emphasized. The world history by Leopold von Ranke (1881-1888) is simply a German's version of history. Likewise, Gustave Ducoudray's history of civilization (1888, 1891) is a French-Latin version of history. These examples do not indicate that the study of world history is worthless. World history is useful when the authors and the readers understand its characteristics. Hegel was a philosopher who served the Hohenzollern court. Schopenhauer denounced Hegel as being a pawn of the government, but it is unfair to criticize Hegel's philosophical understanding of history without considering his pragmatic desire to improve human life. It is said that Hegel always lectured to the students as if he knew the ultimate truth. But this is no different than when the presiding judge declares the decision in a solemn tone. The most miserable nation is the nation that has no one who can provide prophecies for the people.

Philosophy. Among all the branches of science, philosophy is most ambiguous. It includes virtually all knowledge that has customarily been called *philosophical*. From the time of the ancient Greeks, philosophy has undoubtedly contained many sociological ideas. Also, every branch of science has its roots in a particular philosophical view, and certain branches influenced the development of new philosophical principles. In some nations today, philosophy comes close to sociology; in other nations, philosophy and sociology are developing in a parallel fashion. In the most desirable situation, there should be almost no separation between the two. We should support current efforts to provide clear definitions of philosophy and sociology. The aim is to express the close interdependence between the two.

Anthropology. Anthropology is equally as ambiguous as philosophy and sociology. Until recently, anthropologists have not been able to successfully explain how they systematize their scientific activity. It seems that anthropology is now reclaiming their discipline. Among anthropologists, the study of Homo sapiens [humans] is similar in many respects to ideas in sociology.[5]

The Study of State. Kokka-gaku [the study of state] in most cases is the equivalent of the study of society, so *Kokka-gaku* must have a very close relationship with sociology. Some authorities of *Staatslehre* [study of states] are also regarded as experts in sociology. *Staatslehre* is a special product of Germany, and scholars in this field are aware that it is the specific study of German national law.[6] So there must be some general category that includes the study of national law[7] and practical politics.[8] The general study of the state must be a part of sociology.[9] The major reason why German scholars label this study *staatslehre* is their commitment to overcome their own national crisis. The present state of German academia reflects the high cost of unification under the leadership of Prussia. Japan does not want to follow Germany's path.

Economics. In the broadest sense political science is a collective term that indicates all branches of science concerning the state. So some scholars argue that economics is just a subdivision of political science. But I disagree. Although it is true that economics began as a dogmatic, deductive science, based upon weaker assumptions, the scope and methods have advanced rapidly as the civilized world grew. Now economics is a major, autonomous, highly systematic division of science that has a close interrelationship with sociology. Economic studies are also credited with accelerating current advances in sociology. The cooperation between the two sciences is especially evident in the study of human misfortune. Some scholars have suggested establishing a new subdivision of applied sociology called social economics.[10] The integration of sociology and economics will be favorable, but the field is not yet mature.

Socialism and study of social problems.[11] In general use, sociology is currently misunderstood as an equivalent to the study of social problems. But we may overlook this because social problems arise in the intersection between sociology and economics. The two branches can and should cooperate in analyzing and interpreting social problems. The study of social problems may be strategic for integrating the two branches. Below we will conduct a general examination of the history of sociology.

THE GENESIS AND DEVELOPMENT
OF SOCIOLOGY

Generally, certain ideas or thoughts develop from unconscious to conscious. This is the genesis of an idea. A conscious idea develops from simple-consciousness to awareness; this is the genesis of science. Awareness develops from simple-awareness to the ideal; this is the genesis of social science. The ideal develops from the simple ideal to the pragmatic, realizable ideal; this is the genesis of sociology. Sociology has emerged at the latest phase of the development of human ideas.

From a more analytical viewpoint, it can be said that sociology emerged when:

1. A person became conscious of the existence of the integrated social body.
2. A person became conscious of the existence of an integrated body of science.
3. Thus, a person became a sociologist when the social consciousness penetrated into one's own consciousness and made one aware of the need to reform society.
4. Finally, a person becomes a sociologist when he or she perceived the absence of a systematic division of science, or noticed the negative effects of the already-established vertical division of science.

There have been three phases in the development of sociology. The first phase was that of philosophical inquiry. There was no division of science and people were only vaguely conscious of the existence of self and society. Sciences in ancient Greece, medieval Europe, and historical China are examples of this stage. Scholars were not aware of any difference between philosophy and sociology. However, when viewed from a modern eye, we find some scholars who tended to be philosophical, and others who tended to be sociological.

The goal of the second phase was scientific inquiry. There was no sociology in the truest sense, but scholars were not content with the outcomes of the prior phase, and started to reexamine, criticize, and improve each hypothesis by empirical tests. Then science broke up into many branches according to the differences in the objects they researched. Sociology reached this phase at the dawn of the modern era, as preparation for the next phase.

The third phase was the integration of knowledge. Sociology evolved in the truest sense when knowledge from the prior phases was integrated into a single system. This is the system for the future of sociology. Above we sketched the developmental process of sociology. Now we will investigate the historical sources of sociology in various societies.

III.2

Historical Sources of Sociology

Tongo Takebe

SOCIOLOGICAL IDEAS IN JAPAN

There are four centers of civilization in the world: China, India, western Europe, and Japan. Among them, Japanese civilization can be characterized by its perfect agreement between thinking and practicing. Because Japan was a solitary island, the simple and uniform organizations of clans were blessed with peace, although sometimes they were in conflict with each other. Original Japanese thought emerged naturally under that circumstance. However, at the beginning, Japanese thought was very simple and lacked a written language. Therefore, very little regarding its development was recorded and preserved.

Chinese thought influenced the earliest Japanese thought and provided many ideas for understanding and governing a more complex society. Buddhism was introduced into Japanese society during the middle ages, where it gradually fused with existing thought. Early Japanese sociological ideas reflect this characteristic of the developmental process of Japanese society. The society, based on the family-clan organizations, developed with very little internal and external influences.

Under this situation a unique idea of collectivity developed. That was the idea of the concept of *Kokutai* [state body] which suggests a unified society in perfect harmony.[1] *Kokutai* has an active nature, unlike the idea of patriotism that arises as a reaction to the enemy's attacks. But I cannot describe the significances of *kokutai* further because its

Japanese Family and Society
© 2007 by The Haworth Press, Inc. All rights reserved.
doi:10.1300/5840_08

essence is difficult to express verbally. We can detect its existence only in people's practices. Because *kokutai,* does not correspond with science, I currently advise young students not to waste time on this concept.

The Japanese easily assimilated both Chinese and Indian thought and did not see any conflicts in doing this because they just borrowed the logical forms. The Japanese succeeded in pouring their native spirit into Chinese and Indian molds. I did not find anything concerning original Japanese sociological ideas, which need further explanation. Below we will examine Confucian and Indian thought. This chapter will conclude with a discussion of the age of internationalism and the Meiji period.[2]

SOCIOLOGICAL IDEAS IN CHINA

Chinese thought can be characterized by its writing system and systematic construction of ideas that have a high-level of consistency between thought and practice. Recently some western European scholars have begun to study Chinese thought. But it appears that the language barriers made it impossible for them to understand the ancient civilization of China. As a result, there is a tendency to interpret ancient China by using information from present day China. You should not assume that contemporary Chinese society provides a reliable picture of ancient Chinese civilization. You would not expect the present culture of Greece to be similar to that of ancient Greece.[3] I regret that the Western scholars cannot see into the essence of ancient Chinese civilization, and that the Japanese have no interest in contemporary China.[4]

In the *Yi Jing* [Book of Change], we learn that the earliest hunting period was led by the godly king Fu-xi. The godly king Shen-nong is credited with inventing farming. The emperor Huang-di was the next leader to be identified in *Yi Jing*. During this period the Chinese ideographic system of writing, kanji, accelerated the development of civilization. Huang-di developed the calendar and established dynastic dominion, universal metrology (a measuring system), costumes that identified one's social class, and ritualistic-political music. The invention and diffusion of a written language made it possible for these social institutions to develop.

The written language in early Chinese society was used in a highly pragmatic way. Unlike the ancient Greek alphabet, it did not serve other purposes. This initial characteristic of Chinese civilization was later reflected in Confucian thought. The Confucian system of thought was gradually formed during four phases.

First phase. The first phase was that of the teachings of politics and economy. In ancient China, the pioneers of social thought were also the pioneers of practicing new life styles at the same time. They not only taught the people the technique of agriculture that made it possible to increase and stabilize food production, they also taught the moral-ethical ideas, which expand the sphere of human communication. In sum, every pioneer of Chinese social thought was a leader in both the industrial and moral aspect of society.

Second phase. The second phase was that of the ethical teachings of law and governance. Thousands of years after Fu-xi, emperors Yao and Shun introduced a large-scale system of statutory regulations. They also developed the philosophical idea of *Natural Reason,* to strengthen the cohesive force of the statutes.[5]

Third phase. The third phase was that of a systematic description of the world. Yu compiled *Hong-fan* which contains a general system of categories to be used in analyzing the beings in the universe. These were

> *Five elements:* water, fire, wood, metal, earth.
> *Five deeds:* attitude, speech, observation, hearing, thinking.
> *Eight government affairs:* food supply, financial and commercial management, offer of sacrifices, administration of settlements, public security, education, diplomacy, military affairs.
> *Five measurements of time:* year, month, day, observing stars, calculating zodiac degrees.
> Supreme principles
> *Three virtues:* upright and outspoken, strong and tough, kind and amiable.
> *Removing doubts by divination:* If turtle shells are used for divination, the signs can look like one of the following: (1) rain; (2) sun shines after the rain; (3) mist; (4) cloud; (5) a battle between two armies. (If Alpine yarrow is used for divination, it will display either the inner side or the outer side.)

Omens: rain, sunny day, warmness, coldness, and wind. [Meaning: if the five omens appear and they appear in the right order and time, then plants and crops will grow luxuriantly.]

Five sources of happiness: longevity, wealth and rank, health and safety, moral conduct, and happy death at an old age.

Six sources of adversity: premature death, disease, sorrow, poverty, ugliness, and cowardice.

Hong-fan's system included not only political and economic matters, but also the cycle of natural phenomena that was of crucial importance to people's lives.

Fourth phase. The fourth phase was that of perfection. The Zhou dynasty (BCE 122-256) integrated the outcomes from those three phases and established a highly advanced system of philosophy and government. The ancient Chinese thought had developed as noted above. They limited their knowledge to what they ought to do in terms of ruling people, unlike Western thought which tends to broaden their sphere of knowledge beyond practice. In the ancient development of orthodox Chinese thought, the fusion between knowing and practicing has been the principle guiding individual activity as well as the principle guiding society. They understood that the emperor and saint were the same. Later in the era of Confucius, they distinguished between ruling and knowing, and social matter and personal matter, and enhanced the latter. Confucianism developed in this way.[6]

The Chinese civilization stagnated after Confucianism became accepted as the sole dogma, and the saint's activities came to be understood as the superhuman master's extraordinary deeds. Confucian thought has remained for over a thousand years, but unlike the ancient period, it lost its direct connection to the development of society and civilization. Apart from the practical stimuli and the debate with other strong schools of thought, the Confucian school no longer significantly contributed to the advancement of science.[7] What is sociologically important regarding Chinese thought is their early thought and their attempts to establish the perfect connection between knowing and practicing.

CONFUCIANISM

Today Confucianism is understood as the major school of Chinese philosophy. However, I think calling Confucianism a "philosophy" is not appropriate. Western European and Indian thought can be called "philosophy," as they developed the metaphysical systematization of their knowledge. Confucians were only slightly interested in such developments although they developed abstract ideas such as *human nature, natural reason, providence,* and *love.* In the Song dynasty (960-1279), Zhu Xi (1130-1200) was known for integrating Confucian ideas metaphysically. Unlike the western European and Indian philosophy, Confucianism focuses on *how to live one's life* rather than to think about *what is the world after death.* I think *sociology* is the more appropriate name for Confucianism, rather than *philosophy.* The goal of Confucianism is to provide a better form of government for society and a better life for people. Currently, Chinese intellectuals are discussing the idea of socialism and trying to use sociological terms to persuade the adoption of this form of government. I think this movement may give rebirth to the original essence of Confucianism.

The Confucian conception of society is one of wholesomeness and common sense, a fact that has both advantages and disadvantages. The Confucian conception of society has no basis in science and has no theoretical apparatus to analyze the formation of social organizations. Because Confucian scholars lack scientific thinking, they often make erroneous assumptions. According to Comte, sociology is the most complex and most systematic science and other simple sciences, such as astronomy and biology, are subordinate to sociology. Advances in those simple sciences give birth to the more complex sciences. Confucianism has astrology and medical classification of creatures, but they are not scientific. However, when we view this from a different perspective, Confucianism may have an advantage because it avoids the negative effects which occur when sciences are over-differentiated. The Confucian conception of society is based on ordinary experiences and historical records. Clearly it has an advantage in the development of the inductive sciences. So its outcome becomes similar to the outcome of scientific inquiry.[8] Thus, we should not reject Confucian thought in our future development of sociology. We should utilize it but compensate for the weaknesses in methodology.

Confucianism gives no special attention to the origin of human society. It just explains that the universe gave birth to humans and
humans have laws just like every worldly being has laws. Also it
provides no explanation on the birth of individuals or races. It concentrates on how to ease people's lives and how to cultivate their virtue. That is to say, it conceptualizes humans not as Homo sapiens
universally, nor as individuals specifically, but as people in contrast
with rulers. In terms of sociology, societies can be classified according to their degree of differentiation. The Confucians see society
mostly as a state, and so we may name it *sociology of state.* They just
say the universe gave rise to all beings: among all beings, humans are
superior beings and they have superior spirit. Among all humans, the
most superior human is called ruler or saint.[9] They understand human
relations primarily as the process of spiritual or moral cultivation of
the inferiors by the superior. They provide no explanation on how and
why such differentiation exists. They do not need any contract theories or conflict theories of the origin and the development of society.

The Confucians classified the forms of social relations into five
types:

1. the ruler and the ruled
2. the parent and the child
3. the husband and the wife
4. the elder and the younger
5. friends

The potential number of human relationships will increase in proportion to the number of people in the society. When we have just two
members, there will be only one possible relationship. But when the
population reaches one hundred, there will potentially 4,950 relationships using the following formula:

$nr = np(np - 1)/2$

when nr = number of relations, np = number of population

The Confucians successfully reduce the large number of relationships into the above simple five forms. We may understand this as the
Confucian principle of social statics. Each form has its own moral
principle. Between the ruler and the ruled there should be loyalty.
Between parents and the child there should be piety. Husband-wife

relations should be discreet; elder-younger relations should be orderly; and relationships between friends should be faithful. Among these five types of relationships, ruler-ruled, parent-child, and husband-wife are understood as the foundation of all social relations.

The Confucians are satisfied with knowing that those are empirical facts. The Confucian social dynamics do not contain progressive ideas. The historical progress of Chinese society is understood only in terms of a change in rulers as seen in *Zhou Yi* (*Zhou Dynasty's Divination,* the main body of the *Book of Change*) and *Chun Qiu* [Spring and Autumn Annals].

Zhou Yi was a major attempt to clarify the principles of the dynamics of the universe as a whole. It was understood as the genesis of later Chinese philosophical thought. *Chun Qiu* dealt with changes in the national society and the rises and falls of the dynasties. It was understood as the genesis of Chinese historical thought. *Zhou Yi* sees the universe, from the movements of heavenly bodies to human life, in a single perspective and single principle, and observes their fateful rise and fall. The principle that *Zhou Yi* employed was called *the reason of divination.* The essence of the reason of divination can be summarized in the following three articles:[10]

1. Every being in the universe—stars, states, families, persons, and so forth—grows and strengthens itself by the power of heat and light.[11]
2. Every object and matter develops according to the power of natural tendency from birth to maturation to decline.[12] It is very important to control the power of natural tendency for the improvement of life, regardless of whether the person is saintly or common. Later the *Lu* and *Wang's* school of Confucianism (twelfth century to sixteenth century) developed this idea.
3. The above two are the absolute, immutable powers that rule every corner of the universe. Of course it can never be said that *Zhou Yi* had a modern conception of evolution. But no doubt it had a unique conception of social dynamics.[13] *Zhou Yi* had an empirical methodology, although it was obscure, and the Chinese used it for practical applications, [i.e., to determine the proper time and place for marriage, to decide the timing for the rice planting, etc. Eds.]. Using the five moral principles, *Zhou Yi* and *Chun Qiu* assessed each historical state and each actor and provided

explanations on why some states were stable and other states did not last long.[14] Ssu-ma Ch'ien's *Book of History* systematized those historical descriptions, establishing history as a major genre of Chinese thought.

In its ancient period, the Confucian ideas of society had arisen from practical need, and had already been refined to a considerable degree. It can be summarized as below. Zhou Dynasty's ideal image of society was codified in *Zhou Li* [Zhou Dynasty's Rites]. This book represents the Confucian conceptions of society. After *Zhou Li,* Confucian schools experienced a long period of decline. In the period of the Han dynasty (206 BCE-220 CE), scholars lost their creativity. In the period of the Song dynasty (960-1279), the focus was on metaphysical integration of the classics. In the period of the Qing dynasty (1699-1912), scholars again lost their creativity. However rulers in each dynasty continued to study Confucian thought and applied it to practical needs.

When Confucius and his disciples were active in both the philosophical and political world, there were nine schools of thought in Chinese philosophy: Yin-Yang, Confucianism, Mohism, Legalist, Logicist, Daoist, Militarist, Political Strategist, and Agriculturist. Each had its own characteristics, but beyond those differences, they shared the same tendency that governed Chinese philosophy in general; that is, they never isolated knowledge from practical application. There are few exceptions in the Yin-Yang and Daoist schools of philosophy. Some of those schools indulged in metaphysical meditation. Sociological aspects within Confucianism are clearly observed in Confucius's *Da Xue* [The Great Learning] and *Zhong Yong* [The Moderation].[15]

Prior to Zhu Xi, philosophical integration of Confucian thought was only slightly successful. Currently the Western positivists like Henry Charles Carey and Harrison are interested in the similarities between Comte's religious teachings and Confucian thought.[16]

SOCIOLOGICAL IDEAS IN INDIAN THOUGHT

Among Oriental civilizations Chinese thought has the most sociological significance. Indian thought has almost no sociological significance. It is interesting that those geographically neighboring civilizations have extremely different natures. Indian thought flowed into Japanese culture, together with Chinese thought. We should not ignore the effect of Indian thought on the Japanese.

In sum, Indian thought had been quite religious and metaphysical. The society in ancient India was constituted of four classes of people.[17]

1. The Brahman class was comprised of wise men or poets. They controlled the relationships between the gods and humans.
2. The Kshatriya class was constituted of secular political leaders like kings, peers, and warriors.
3. Traders, merchants constituted the Vaisya class.
4. The Sudra was the class of laborers.

The Brahman, the Kshatriya, and the Vaisya classes were the Aryan conquerors. The Sudra class consisted of the conquered indigenous people.

Indian regimes had been typically theocratic. They understood the basis of their sovereignty as the divine will, so the Brahman class enjoyed great prestige. Their religion, Brahmanism, has strong effect on Indian society. The theology of Brahmanism says that there exists a single Supreme Being. There are three gods according to the Supreme Being's three virtues: strength, goodness, and malice. The Brahma is the god of creation, the Vishnu is the god of preservation, and the Siva is the god of destruction. The gods permeate into human bodies and cause feelings of pleasure and pain, ability to see oneself as different from others, and judging things as good or evil. The best state humans can realize is the state of no feeling, no separation, and no judgment. Humans reach this state called Nirvana or *Mukti* through the ascetic exercises of self restraint. The Indian religious beliefs may be understood as resulting from their climate and natural surroundings. After death, people will transmigrate as gods, humans, or animals based on their ability to eliminate negative intrusions. Before transmigrating, people go to various heavens or hells according to their degree of deliverance.

Indian thought appeared to be influenced by their extraordinary piousness as well as their geographical location. Indian thought was thoroughly nonsociological because it understood society as just a temporary residence. Human life was considered to be an illusion. Their practical teachings concentrated on how to leave social life, regardless of the fact that this kind of thought is possible only when they live a social life. As I pointed out earlier, science is possible as a result of consciousness and awareness of one's own life. But Indians attempted to exclude life from their own consciousness, so they did not formulate the science of human society. The Indian society did not have either sociology or historical studies. So it was unavoidable that their society collapsed. The Indian case provides insights into understanding the history of sociology from the reverse position.

After Brahmanism emerged there were six schools of philosophy in the dualistic religion of Jaina.[18] In the era of the Gupta dynasty, Buddha established a new religious philosophy, but its diffusion could not eliminate the influence of Brahmanism among the Indian people. The development of Buddhism as secular, practical, social knowledge was mainly achieved in China and Japan.

SOCIOLOGICAL IDEAS IN ANCIENT GREECE

As far as we can trace, the Western sciences have their origins in the Ionian and Assyrian civilizations. But we know very little about their details. We begin the investigation of the history of Western sociological ideas with ancient Greece.

In contrast to Chinese thought, which was motivated by practical interests to reform their social life, the Ionian thought seemed to be motivated by a pure desire to learn. But it was also one of the roots of later Greek philosophy. Other influences also played a vital role in the formulation of Greek philosophy.

Imagination of poets. Prior to the seventh century BCE, Homer, Hesiod, Orpheus, and Pericles described human affairs and divine activities in mythological and poetic ways (Ueberweg, 1872). Their verse and prose influenced later Greek thought both directly and indirectly. They also recorded the practical admonitions that were based on their ethnic experiences.

Legislation. As seen in Solon's legislation, the Greeks accumulated practical experiences in social and political governance and compiled them into simple codes. This legislation developed the social consciousness of the Greek people. Solon was the most distinguished legislator and social educator of the time. He was also a paragon of the Greek political spirit of democracy.

Philosophical thought. The Ionian philosophers studied the first principle of the universe as a whole. They explored their knowledge beyond the practical necessities of life. This signaled the rise of Greek philosophy as they developed the abstractions of beings and matters and arranged them into a categorical system.

Historical observation. Together with the emergence of philosophical thought, they began observing historical facts on an empirical basis. The earliest Greek historian, Herodotus, tried to place the Greeks' own social life in a historical context. These four streams of thought provided the foundation for the rise of Greek philosophy. Socrates, Plato, and Aristotle succeeded in integrating these four streams.

Socrates, who belonged to the same generation as Herodotus, reformed the methodology and defined the themes of philosophy. He integrated not only philosophical thought and historical observation, but also poetical imagination. His style of thinking was essentially based on proverb; his phrases were quoted from the colloquial speech of traditional folklores. But he seemed to miss the second stream, that is legislation. Plato overcame this weakness by combining the philosophical and historical methods to investigate society as a politically controlled entity. This can be understood as the oldest genesis of modern Western sociology.

Plato's system began from observing the relationship between human intellect and the universe, and concluded with presenting ideas on human social life. Plato's idealism is as follows. Humans acquire certain concepts by summarizing and abstracting similar things and matters. Therefore a concept is a mental representation that reflects the nature of the external world. He thought that the external world is not the material world that is tangible to human senses, but the ideal world that is tangible by human reason. The material world is an imperfect copy of the ideal world. For Plato, among those ideas, the idea of *good* is the most sublime idea that should rule the universe. As a rational being, a human in the material world has to reach beyond the current state to realize the ideal world. Agape (love, longing) is its practical principle. And the pursuit of agape should not be based on obligation or motivated by rewards. According to Plato, the world has two aspects: mundane and rational. The mundane or commonplace world is a fictitious world that is dominated by opinions and beliefs.

The rational world is the real world that is dominated by reason (see Plato, *The Republic*, chapter 6).

At this time in Greece there were class conflicts and disputes over the form of government, international struggles, and the corruption of public morals.[19] In Plato's eyes, Greek society was driven into a corner by those problems. His *Republic* may be understood as illustrating the countermeasures needed to settle these conflicts. He thought that among the fundamental norms of the time, justice was the most powerful and universal. He believed that a man of virtue should exercise justice, so the state has to organize training schools on theology, literature, medicine, and gymnastics in order to cultivate the civil virtues of intelligence, courage, temperance, and justice. He also declared that philosophers should govern the state because philosophers are the embodiment of all virtues and true knowledge. The power of the philosopher-ruler resides in his ability to discuss and persuade. According to Plato, philosophers rule the state just like Demiurge (the God) rules the universe. His ultimate good is not in sensual pleasure, nor in knowledge. It is the perfect copy of the God-universe relation. Plato developed a schema to establish the ideal state in the Italian peninsula. He visited there twice. But after the assassination of Dion (BCE 354), his close friend, Plato's plan was halted. In addition, Plato in his *Law* says that there should be the second-best principle of governance in case we cannot have a reliable philosopher-ruler. The principle of a law-governed state would be an acceptable system as a substitute for the philosopher-ruler governance.[20]

Plato's sociological ideas, as stated above, contain many insights but it is typical Greek metaphysical thought. Many years after Plato, Comte began to overcome the limits imposed by metaphysical thought and attempted to establish the philosopher-ruler governance.[21]

Aristotle succeeded Plato. Aristotle refined and revised Plato's theory of ideas. He negated Plato's transcendentalism and redefined the concept of ideas as attributes of material things and matter. He also developed the organicist theory of substances and described the phenomena of the world in an evolutionary order. The core of his methodology was logic that analyzes the relations between the universal and the particular. Aristotles's theory of human society can be seen in his two works *Ethics* and *Politics*.[22]

Aristotle maintained that it is in man's nature to be political. Only in politics can we understand the ethical questions. The original function of the state is in the protection of people's lives, but its aim is in the advancement of human virtues. The existence of the whole must be prior to the existence of the particular, and the choice of means must be preceded by the mental representation of end. Similarly he argued that the existence of the state must precede the existence of individuals. Aristotle did not mean to neglect the individual interests; he stressed the harmony of the individual interests with the state. It was Aristotle who clearly distinguished the forms of government into monarchy, aristocracy, and democracy. He methodologically developed sociological ideas, but he neglected to inquire about the social ideal.

At the declining period of Greek philosophy, Stoicism and Epicureanism emerged and their opinions clashed. Stoicism maintained that humans are social in nature and they reflected God's attributes. Epicureanism took an opposing viewpoint and believed that humans are cruel by nature, and this is reflected in their animal-like attributes. The Neo-Platonist, Plotinus, tried to establish Plato's ideal republic, but its failure signaled the end of ancient Greek philosophy.

SOCIOLOGICAL IDEAS IN MEDIEVAL EUROPE

All the current historical studies agree[23] that the later western European scholars were influenced by the ancient Greek philosophical perspective,[24] Roman legislative perspective, and Jewish religious belief. But here we will concentrate on Greek influence. Judaism gave birth to Christianity, and Christianity has been the most influential system of thought among western European people. But it is only slightly connected with the development of sociological thought. It did not develop to the degree necessary to understand and resolve the practical problems.

From the beginning to the end of the medieval era, Christianity was based on the church fathers' teachings and scholastic philosophy. Thomas Aquinas was an exception. He absorbed and developed the Aristotelian system, arguing that humans are not only political beings but also social beings.[25] But this argument was based on the belief that God's rule, and not the king's rule, is absolute. He thought that humans need God to rule society. The king's rule can be justified only when it promotes social happiness among humans. Only God and his representatives know the ultimate implication of this happiness. So kings must obey God and the Pope; the states must obey the churches. Many scholars agreed with this teaching. This was called the theory of divine right of kings.[26]

Two opponents threatened this theocratic teaching. Arabian thinkers like Averroes, also known as Ibn Rushd (ca 1179-1180), argued that from the moral point of view every religion has the same functions, and from the logical point of view all religions are false (see Ibn Khaldun, 1896; Ibn Tofayl, 1782). Averroes used a comparative method for studying religions, rejected all miracles, and tried to resist the Catholic orthodoxy and the Pope's secular power. Averroes's theory gained enthusiastic support from many kings and nobles in western Europe. Marshilius of Padova (1328) further elaborated Averroes's theory and adapted it to the practical problem of that time. Marshilius argued that the Pope's intervention, Plenitude Potestates [perfect power or perfect rule], in the kingdoms is unjustifiable. Christ prohibited it. The right to make laws [Universitas Civium or civil world] resides in each state. Subjects of each kingdom enact their own codes.

The medieval intellectual world, as described above, was in severe turmoil. It may be said that the medieval era did not have social problems but it did have political problems (Stein, 1897, p. 257). The public philosophy had been developed in ancient Greece and Rome, but it seemed that the savage people of Gaul failed to absorb it. [Gaul (Gallia) is the name of the area under the Roman Empire that is roughly France, Belgium, Luxembourg, and Germany today. Eds.] In the medieval era, only the most superior people, like kings and nobles, observed social consciousness. So they concentrated on the power relations of kings, nobles, and priests. Medieval people were not aware of the need for sociology.

SOCIOLOGICAL IDEAS IN THE MODERN ERA

The beginning of modern science occurred in the Renaissance period. The Renaissance was a multidirectional movement of thoughts, not restricted into the field of literature and art. It was a complex social movement that occurred in the human mind and civilization, and awoke the human emotions and reason from a thousand years' sleep.[27] The rise of modern civilization was based in the Renaissance movement so, we should not neglect its importance. Generally speaking the total reconstruction of society becomes necessary when the foundation of a prior era has collapsed. Lacking the foundation, people will attempt to reestablish the foundation and try to overcome the unstable condition. And nostalgia accompanies every reconstruction process.

Renaissance thought was not an exception. People became suspicious of the foundation of medieval thought because they were familiar with the rational thought of ancient Greece and realized that Roman Catholicism was strongly limiting their intellectual ability. So they tried to reestablish the earlier foundation of scholarly thought in their society. The movement developed in two ways, the reevaluation of the works of classical theorists and the advancement of new sciences. They gave new interpretations to Plato and Aristotle and developed new sciences of nature, god, and state.[28]

The rise of modern sociological thought was based on the new theories on state's constitution and government that were proposed during the Renaissance movement. The Renaissance theories tried to establish the supremacy of the secular power instead of the religious power. They replaced the foundation of natural law from divine command to human nature and prepared for the rise of the modern forms of law-based governance. Also, in the development of foreign trade, they tried to adapt the new natural law theory to international relations. These movements coincided with the Reformation in the religious world.

Dante's resistance toward the religious power was further developed in Machiavelli's theory of state government (see Dante's *De Monarchia,* ca 1310). Machiavelli (1531) argued that the ideal political goal should be the cultivation of a nation's autonomy.[29] The church prevents this, so secular powers should take over control. Francesco Guicciardini (1527) agreed with Machiavelli. Thomas More (1515) described the utopia where people have equal property and praise religious freedom. Jan Bodin (1576) disagreed with Machiavelli on many points but approved his idea of the legitimacy of monarchy and religious freedom. He constructed the political theory of natural law from his own ethnological and historical viewpoint. Albericus Gentilis (1582, 1589) formulated a jurisprudential theory of human rights from the idea of universal human nature, and asserted religious freedom and freedom of trade. Hugo Grotius (1604, 1625) integrated those theories of natural law and tried to establish the foundation of international law. He dealt with the freedom of Dutch traders on the East Indian Sea and articulated the principles of maritime law. Acknowledging human reason, Grotius negated the efficacy of the divine law (*Göttliches Recht* [God's law]) and constructed a system of human law (*Menschliches Recht* [human law]) as the foundation of human society. According to Grotius, the state is founded on the member's contract, and state government can exercise its coercive force only to maintain the society's security or *Positives Recht* [positive law].

Above is the prehistory of modern sociological thought. The full-scale development of sociological thought can be found in the English Civil War period. Thomas Hobbes (1651), John Locke (1689), John Milton, and German political thinkers sought the ground for the legitimacy and authority of state government, and began to study this. Other continental thinkers were not able to decide on the foundation of state government, but their indecisiveness gave rise to the eighteenth century philosophy of Enlightenment movements. Hobbes (1651) argued that humans are not social in nature but endeavor to destroy each other. So humans need the absolute power of sovereign authority to compel them to obey and to protect them. The moral capacity of humans to distinguish good from evil is not the precondition of society; it is the result of the existence of society, the existence of the absolute power. Locke (1689) maintained that humans in the natural state did not have leader-subjects relationships, but they knew the familial order. Therefore, the familial order should be the foundation for the state governance. According to Locke, the belief in absolute sovereign power, held by Hobbes and his followers, is useless and should not be permitted.

The power of the state government comes from the people's trust. The government is legitimate as far as it preserves people's rights. Samuel Pufendorf, a German political philosopher, appraised the modern theory of natural law and advocated liberalism and religious tolerance (see Alberti, 1678; Pufendorf, 1660, 1672; Seckendorf, 1685). He introduced Christian Thomasius's philosophy and constructed a theory of human sociability. Valentine Alberti and Veit Ludwig von Seckendorf argued that natural law is based on the Roman Catholic orthodoxy, and they tried to persuade people and rulers to obey the Church. Gottfried von Leibniz and Christian Wolff proposed some mediation plans between the new and old natural law theories. Giovanni Battista Vico (1720) investigated the spiritual and behavioral structure of society.

The enlightenment movement in the eighteenth century was a short break in the long development toward modern western Europe. In the eighteenth century, the seventeenth century rationalism fell out of favor yet the nineteenth century skepticism had not yet arisen.

In England, Anthony Cooper Ashley (3rd Earl of Shaftsbury) and Francis Hutchison blended ancient Greek thought with deistic teaching of ethics. Similar theories were held by German philosophers such as Alexander Gottlieb Baumgarten and Gotthold Ephraim Lessing. Inspired by Aristotle, they developed a theory of evolution in the field of esthetics. In France, materialists and pantheists such as Etienne Bonnot de Condillac, Charles Bonnet, Denis Diderot, Jean d'Alembert, and Claude Adrian Helvétius compiled an encyclopedia of natural history. In the late eighteenth century, the English thinkers concentrated on the study of the individual, and did not consider the study of society. German thinkers Immanuel Kant and Johann Gottlieb Fichte developed the study of society, but they said very little about government and state administration. French thinkers, just prior to the French Revolution, rushed to study state constitutions and human rights. Charles de Montesquieu (1734, 1748) argued to preserve the freedom of thought. He had a cyclical view on the state's fate and insisted on the importance of governance based on law. He described the separation of the three branches of government and a bicameral system. To negate his opponent Jacques Bénigne Bossuet's theory of the divine rule, Montesquieu (1748) formulated a political-social theory based entirely on humans' spontaneous self-control.[30] Jean-Jacques Rousseau (1754, 1755, 1762a,b) inherited it and posed a theory of radical liberal democracy. But he could not establish any practical method of social reformation. He could only say "go back to the innocent savage state." Marquis de Condorcet (1822) upheld the idea of a communist society.

Those theories were actuated in the French Revolution. In this disturbance the sociological ideas went to the next phase.

The Formation of Sociology

Tongo Takebe

THE CAUSE OF THE RISE OF SOCIOLOGY

The French Revolution was a great social and political incident generated by the developments of modern thought. At the same time, it fostered intellectual development because it stimulated social theorists. It is quite natural to think that the French Revolution was the epoch-making incident not only for political history but also for the history of social thought. In this chapter we explore the development of sociological thought in the post-revolution era.

Generally speaking, from the end of the eighteenth century until the end of the nineteenth century, the development of sociological thought experienced several twists and turns. At the end of the eighteenth century, sociological thought flourished. However, it suffered a decline in the first half of the nineteenth century. It was in the middle of the nineteenth century that sociological thought gained a foothold in the Western intellectual world and began to make steady progress.

There were five noteworthy conditions characterizing the European social and national scene.

1. *Political problems.* England had already overcome the problems of state-government both theoretically and practically through two revolutions in the seventeenth century. At the time, France, under the absolute monarch King Louis XIV, enjoyed power and luxury. As a consequence, the privileged people around the

Japanese Family and Society
© 2007 by The Haworth Press, Inc. All rights reserved.
doi:10.1300/5840_09

Versailles court became corrupted, resulting in severe conflict with the general public. The citizens' anger exploded at the end of eighteenth century. Then, at last, thinkers and patriots began to redefine the relationships between the king and the subject, and between the king and the nobility, the monks, the third class, and the general public. France, among the European countries, experienced the most intense movement in terms of general public demand for political participation. In Germany, the problems concerning the relationships between the Holy Roman Empire and states arose as the Hapsburg dynasty began to lose its authority. The rise of the Hohenzollern dynasty seemed to settle the crisis. But even for the intelligentsias whether its authority has been reliable or not is difficult to judge. From the seventeenth century until now, Russia was the only country that did not redefine political-legal relationships.

2. *Economic problems.* Problems in defining social happiness resulted from debates on political problems. Some radical reformation was needed in the distribution of economic resources. Thus, the economic aspects of social problems began to be recognized.

3. *International problems.* Since the seventeenth century onward, the relationship between major governments and the colonies they controlled resulted in various social phenomena. Gradually the colonies demanded new resolution. The War of Independence in North America (1775-1783) was the decisive blow to the old way of defining power relations between the major governments and the colonies they controlled. Equality among the sovereign states became a big problem not only theoretically but practically.

4. *Academic problems.* The development of science in western Europe began when scholars shook off primitive religious beliefs. It was accelerated by various innovations in the seventeenth and eighteenth centuries.[1] However, they still relied on old-fashioned methodologies. In the nineteenth century the intelligentsias realized the need for methodological reformation in science.

5. *Problems of civilization.* Academic innovations stimulated the development of industrial technologies.[2] The development of transportation and communication channels promoted the En-

lightenment and improved the standard of living. At this point, society underwent drastic changes, and people became aware of the need to resolve the imbalance between the levels of development in each sector. In other words, people became aware of the problem of civilization and the social ideal arose. The current sociological inquiries are stimulated by those circumstances.

There are six theoretical sources in the development of current sociology: socialism, natural sciences, philosophy, historical studies, economics, and jurisprudence (Worms, 1895b).[3] The development of those branches of science has been stimulated by the transformation of the world, and vice versa. Sociology attempts to integrate those branches and tries to find the desirable future of society.

THE RISE OF SOCIALISM

The rise of socialism is a remarkable phenomenon in the current world of thought. "Socialism" was the name given to Robert Owen's (1813) movement in England in 1835.[4] We can find many signs of socialistic ideas even at the dawn of human history. Every respectable conception of justice, humanity, and the divine includes socialistic images of the ideal. But it was in the nineteenth century that socialism became recognized as the dominant ideal of society and international relations. Political problems triggered the rise of socialism in the nineteenth century. Its major causes were economic problems and the problem of civilization; minor causes were international and academic problems.[5]

As the medieval, feudalistic social structure waned, sympathetic-reciprocal human relations disappeared. As the modern industrial social organization developed, the fourth class, or labor class, arose. The economic gap between the capitalists and the laborers had been growing larger. The poor hate the arrogant rich; the rich hate the obsequious beggar. Class antagonism became widespread. The adherents of the doctrine of laissez-faire argue that it is an unavoidable, natural way for things to develop. The socialistic reformers courageously attempted to provide relief to the poor.

At the beginning there were three types of socialist reformers: the traditionalist, who advocated restoring the feudalistic social condition that had been steadily declining; the communist, who maintained the necessity of total economic equality; and those who believed in the distributive justice theory. The latter two have been growing and joined together to provide relief for the oppressed. The name *socialist* has been used in ambiguous ways, but all share some characteristics. They maintain that democracy is the best form of government for a society. Ethically, they emphasize sympathy, benevolence, and tolerance. Socially and economically, they advocate altruistic labor. Practically, they see the relief of extreme poverty as the most vital project to be accomplished.

Of course those doctrines existed before the eighteenth century, but the teaching in earlier times was done by small groups, such as Christian religious associations.[6] Also, like Plato in Greece and Thomas More in England, those advocating these doctrines tended to be visionaries. The modern socialist no longer supports those traditions and depends on solid methodology to observe the economy, and acts internationally to solve the problems of capitalism.

Throughout the nineteenth century, socialism gained support but then relapsed. Its present situation is as follows:

1. French socialism tends to be dogmatic and radical such as exemplified by François Noël Babeuf, Etienne Cabet (Babeuf and Cabet are communists), Henri de Saint Simon (a founder of socialism, wrote numerous books), Barthélémy Enfantin, Saint Amand Bazard, Charles Fourier, Victor Considérant (a Fourier disciple), Louis Blanc (a founder of national socialism), Pierre Joseph Proudhon (an individualist-socialist), and Louis Auguste Blanqui (the leader of the destructionist organization *Blanquistes*). Petr Alexeïvich Kropotkin was a Russian anarchist. German socialism tends to be academic and systematic as Karl Johann Rodbertus-Jagetzow, Karl Marx, Ferdinand Lassalle (a founder of the social democrat party), Friedrich Engels, Adolf Heinrich Gotthilf Wagner, Gustav von Schmoller, Lujo Brentano, and Adolf Held. The latter four are leading figures of *Kathedersozialismus*.

2. There are three methodological positions in socialism. First are the private experiments conducted by Owen and Fourier. This view tends to correspond with certain ethical or religious teach-

ings. Second are nationwide reform by legislation such as carried out by Louis Blanc and Las salle. This view tends to correspond with economics and political science. Third is international co-operation. Marx is its representative and this view tends to correspond to sociology.

In addition, Christian Socialism, originated by Félicité Robert de Lamennais in France, attempts social reform in accordance with the Christian faith. Charles Kingsley, John Frederick Denison Maurice, and Thomas Hugh in England see the church as the spiritual medium to foster close ties among individual economic and religious lives. In Russia, in 1870, socialism developed out of criticism of its despotic form of government. Recently the nihilist movement developed in Russia. The socialist movement or social reform movement is also becoming more popular in the United States of America. Marx organized The International Workingmen's Association and attempted to integrate the various social movements.

In its primitive form, socialism needs the general study of society. In its advanced form, socialism needs the analytical study of the social body. So socialism hastens the growth of sociology. In the future, socialism shall be National Socialism. Its theoretical base shall be economics; its practice shall be social policy. In the future, sociology may be the study of national societies.

Most of the giants in the history of socialism are also the giants in the history of sociology. Among those, Saint Simon, as the teacher of Comte, and Marx, as the founder of historical materialism, were the most influential socialists, but I will not discuss this further here.[8]

ADVANCEMENT OF NATURAL SCIENCE: THE THEORY OF ENERGY

Current natural science advances in two directions: the theory of energy and the theory of evolution. The theory of energy provides a revolutionary principle for physics and other sciences concerning non-living beings. James Prescott Joule and Sir William Grove in England, and Julius Robert von Meyer in Germany began this revolution. Sir William [Lord Kelvin] Thomson, Peter Guthrie Tait, Hermann Ludwig von Helmholz, and James Clerk Maxwell succeeded in establishing new principles (see Stewart, 1873; Helmholtz, 1873; Tait, 1876; Thomson & Tait, 1872; Thompson, 1891-1894; Tyndall, 1863). This theory clarifies the following eight facts.

1. The theory of energy demonstrates that all the physical phenomena, light, heat, sound, and electricity, are the effect of the oscillation of molecules. Traditional physics treated those phenomena separately. But the new theory found that the different oscillation results in various phenomena. It is called the principle of energy conversion.
2. The new theory found that energy conversion is a zero-sum phenomenon. It is called the principle of the conservation of energy.[9] This knowledge was made possible by great advances in experimental methods and mathematics.
3. Energy in the universe decays as time goes by. The transmission of energy from one system to the other finally produces an absolute equilibrium in the distribution of energy. Motion is only possible when differences in the volume of energy exist between two or more points in space. So, in the state of absolute equilibrium of energy, there cannot be any motion in the universe. It is called the *principle of increase of entropy.*
4. After the establishment of the new theory of energy, it is no longer necessary to consider material as the sole ultimate prerequisite for physical science. But when we explain the transmission of energy, we need to assume that certain materials exist as a conductor between two or more points in space. Nevertheless, the results from every experiment suggest that the universe is not filled with materials. Therefore, many scholars agree with the ether hypothesis, but it seems untenable since most experiments suggest that the speed of light is a constant. [In the second half of the nineteenth century, scientists hypothesized that "ether" filled the entire space. Eds.] Today the situation of physical science has become confused.
5. Not only physical phenomena, but also chemical phenomena are under the rule of the new theory of energy. Chemical combinations can be described as the radiation of energy. Chemical decomposition can be described as the absorption of energy. Today chemical thermodynamics has become the dominant meth-

odology of chemistry and is clarifying chemical phenomena in a quantitative way.[10]

6. This new theory of energy has also influenced physiology. Traditionally, life is understood as a unique phenomenon different from other physical or chemical phenomena. But as anatomy advanced, we recognized that life is not the exception to the order that governs inanimate things. Life, although it is very complex, is a phenomenon that is under the principles of energy. In this way the new theory of energy has made inroads into biology.

7. Traditional psychology consisted of mystical and primitive attempts to describe all mental phenomena by only three categories: intelligence, emotion, and intention. But the influence of the theory of pluralistic integration or monistic theory of polyaspects is currently increasing. These modern psychological theories emphasize the close correlation between mind and body. Some psychologists focus on how the image in one's mind stimulates bodily movement and attempt to understand it from the viewpoint of the energy theory.

8. The theory of energy has broader influences as noted above. It also attempts to clarify astronomical questions. The gross quantity of energy in the universe does not change. However, beings in the universe and the forms of their interactions have been changing and shall continue to change, although the universe is on a trajectory towards absolute extinction. Today the invention of spectrum analysis makes physical astronomy, such as the work by Joseph von Fraunhofer and Gustav Robert Kirchhoff, more precise. The advancement of geometry and the improvement of observation devices make theoretical astronomy and spherical astronomy more profound. Those facts suggest that we can establish a study of the universe or worldview that is based on the methodology of exact science. I think that the theory of evolution clarifies the normative aspects of this view.

ADVANCEMENT OF NATURAL SCIENCE: THE THEORY OF EVOLUTION

It seems that some modern thinkers want to find ethical implications in past thought. It is true that we can find the awakening of the idea of evolution even in the ancient Greek philosophers. Also in the medieval era, scholars continuously attempted to inquire about the developmental laws of the universe.[11] But each of them faced obstacles because their arguments were deduced from dogmatic first principles or religious belief. From the eighteenth century onward the development of both natural sciences and the inductive method flourished.[12] As a consequence, the theory of evolution as an empirical science arose.[13] Charles Darwin (1859, 1871) and Alfred Russel Wallace (1864, 1870) established this theory.[14] We can summarize the current scientific view of the world, which is closely interrelated with the theory of evolution, in the following six points.

1. Concerning the origin of the planetary system, Laplace in France and Kant in Germany developed the nebular hypothesis. Lagrange built on Laplace's ideas. William Herschel discovered Uranus. Johann Gottfried Galle discovered Neptune on the point predicted by Urbain Jean Joseph Le Virrier. Those discoveries were made possible by the nebular hypothesis and the development of spherical geometry. Today the nebular hypothesis is regarded as the most reliable ground for scientific cosmology[15] and is consistent with the laws found by modern physics.

2. Since Joseph Louis Lagrange succeeded and completed the Newtonian system of gravitation, the tidal evolution theory has expanded its applications from geology to astronomy. Thomson and Tait (1891-1894) provided geometrical expressions on tidal evolution in their appendix. Today tidal evolution theory is regarded as the most promising theory to unify the planetary evolution and the microscopic physical phenomena.

3. Geology is a very young science. The sixteenth-century German scholar Johannes Agricola laid the foundation for the development of geology. In the seventeenth century, Nicolaus Steno in Denmark named the discipline and the eighteenth-century Professor Abraham Gottlob Werner of Freiburg and his pupil Buch systematized it. Alexander von Humbolt (1845-1858) made remarkable progress in geology along with Jean-Baptiste Élie de Beaumont in France and Sir Charles Lyell (1841) in England. Charles Darwin's work in paleontology (1859, 1871) contributed to geology and attempted to build a bridge between

planetary evolution and organic evolution. Physical law governs not only life but also the formation of geological features.

4. To articulate the relation between inanimate and animate beings, we have to resolve the question of the origin of organisms. Traditionally, organic matter was thought to be completely different from inorganic matter, so there was a wide gulf between organic and inorganic chemistry. Even the major adherents of the idea of evolution, from ancient Greek philosophers to modern scholars like Darwin and Lamark, believed that animals and plants made of organic matters have *pneuma* or *vital force*. They did not try to further inquire into the origin of life. But Denis Diderot and Charles Bonnet, pioneers of the theory of protoplasm, clarified that organic matter is synthesized from inorganic matter.

   This theory is supported by both astronomical and chemical facts. Occasionally, meteorites contain hydrocarbons. Some kinds of comets contain carbon, hydrogen, and their organic compounds. In 1828, Friedrich Wöhler synthesized urea. Shortly after, Pierre Eugene Marcellin Berthelot synthesized formic acid. Currently, various techniques for the production of organic compounds developed, and now many chemists hope that we can produce every organic compound by artificial synthesis. There is no longer a gulf between organic and inorganic matter. Organic protoplasm forms cytodes. When a nucleus is created in a cytode, it is called a cell. The cell is the minimum unit of living matter. So there is no essential difference between inorganic matter and life. In the process of the evolution of the universe, inorganic, organic, beings and living beings have formed a continuous chain.

5. Before Charles Darwin's (1859) *Origin of Species* every species was thought to be unchangeable. Even scholars supposed that there was no interrelation between different species. But Darwin and Wallace argued that the variety of species is made possible by evolution from very simple creatures. Today their disciples are collecting evidences to reinforce the Darwinian theory of evolution. The Darwinian system is constructed on two fundamental laws: mutation and heredity. Mutation is the species' transformation as it adapts to the environment when the environ-

ment changes. Heredity is the name given to the process through which parental characteristics are passed on to the child. Most biologists support the validity of heredity hypothesis, but its physical and chemical process remains unclear. Today theorists studying evolution are attempting to uncover the process.[16] However, it is already clear that life has evolved according to the laws of heredity and mutation, from single species to various species.

6. Herbert Spencer was the first to describe the evolution of human society. The human race is not an exception to the laws mentioned above. Although he notes the uniqueness of the human race, he hastily adapted the outcomes of the theory of evolution to human society. Although in the study of psychology he referred to the comparative study of human and other species, this is not sufficient. I think Spencer's achievement was to attempt to apply the theory of evolution to human society. It is our role to clarify the evolution of human society more completely.

To summarize, the theory of energy arose and attempts were made to resolve some scientific problems found in the nineteenth century. When the theory of energy expanded its field of application to cosmology, it produced the theory of evolution. At this point, the theory of evolution made a great stride forward. The theory of evolution saw all beings in the universe as a single continuous body. Osborne (1894) provides a good history of the theory of evolution, which was expanded to the study of human society.

THE ADVANCEMENT OF PHILOSOPHY

Today's philosophy is based on the theoretical foundation constructed by Hume's and Kant's *rationalism,* the prevailing philosophy on the continent, and *empiricism,* characteristic of English philosophy, which flourished and created a new phase in western European thought. However, both decayed and changed their nature into the philosophy of the Enlightenment. True philosophical spirit was revived in Hume's skeptical philosophy and developed in Kant's critical philosophy. Kant's philosophy is not adequate for analyzing his own subjects. Also, his system left many gaps. Until now, most of the philosophical thinking has been nothing more than the rehash of Kant. Germany is now the center for scholarship on philosophy.

For Kant, the fundamental problem of philosophy is found in the essence and character of reason. To resolve the problem, Kant drew a plan to integrate various expressions of reason, pure reason, practical reason, moral reason, and natural reason. But his plan was not completed. In an attempt to remedy Kant's problem, the philosophy of integration was introduced.

The problems in the post-Kantian age can be summarized in the following three points: (1) theoretical integration of various functions into a single principle; (2) theoretical integration of pure reason and practical reason; and (3) theoretical integration of being and its perception, natural order, and human liberty. In a word, our goal is to establish a general monolithic theory to provide a rational explanation of beings in the universe and their relationships.

Karl Leonhard Reinhold (1790) attempted to supplement the Kantian system of philosophy by clarifying the first problem noted above. He argued that there is no reliable ground in Kant's philosophy, since it lacks a general explanation on how we acquire knowledge. Reinhold raised the theory of cognitive representation.

Johann Gottlieb Fichte (1794) provides an answer to the second problem in his philosophy of subjective idealism. Fichte argued that ego is the sole existence. People incorrectly believe that external conditions restrict the ego's activity, but actually the ego's activity can only be restricted by the ego itself. It is the image of alter-ego, represented by the ego that is usually misunderstood as the external condition. So, for Fichte, the goal of philosophy is to establish the creative ego or absolute ego that subsumes the universe.

The relation between natural order and human liberty is the central problem that is gaining the attention of current scholars. There are a lot of variants of this problem, such as laissez-faire or government intervention, the natural law theory or historicism. Four German thinkers attempted to answer this problem.

Friedrich Wilhelm von Schelling criticized Fichte because his teaching seemed to exclude all physical matters from the system of philosophy. To secure the original sameness of the nature and human cognition, Schelling argued that we have to start with identifying the two. He named this first principle *the absolute* and attempted to construct his philosophy of *materialistic idealism.*

Hegel argued that there is firm sameness between the being and its human representation, so the law that rules the beings in the universe is not necessarily materialistic, but idealistic. He called this fundamental law *absolute intellect, pure notion,* or *spiritual notion.* If we agree with him, the traditional problems concerning the relation between the being and its human perception disappear. We only need a system of dialectical logic that analyzes human reasoning and notions. Hegel's philosophy is called *logical idealism.*

Arthur Schopenhauer made a clear distinction between the *being* and the *idea.* Human desire is the fundamental principle of beings in the universe. Intellect plays only a minor role. When a human reflects upon his/her own mind, they find the original relationship of the external matter is not with your intellect but with your desire. Employing your intellect, you systematize various relations between the two and acquire a coherent view of the world. According to Schopenhauer, the highest intellect can finally be aware that it is oneself that causes all distress and agony in life. At that moment not only does one's desire disappear, but also the world disappears. Schopenhauer's philosophy is called *kinetic idealism.*

Karl Robert Eduard von Hartmann pointed out that both Hegel's logical idealism and Schopenhauer's kinetic idealism succeeded in clarifying the relationship between nature and human cognition, but neither was sufficient. Hartmann proposed to integrate the two, by his own concept of *unconsciousness* that includes the idea and the desire as its major attributes. For Hartmann, the world is a representation of the unconsciousness. His philosophy is called the *idealism of restoration.*

There has been continuous effort to establish the philosophy of integration in modern philosophical thought. Perhaps Herbert's pluralism was the sole exception. Herbert maintained that the universe is made of various, simple substances. The atom that constitutes the subjective world is representation. The atom that constitutes the objective world is called a monad [something that is indivisible]. His pluralism stimulates psychological studies, but it does not contribute much in terms of resolving the fundamental problems in philosophy.

As noted above, modern philosophical thought has developed in the right direction. It is going to establish a good view of life within a large worldview. Today philosophers like Wundt attempt to apply those highly abstract theories to the pragmatic problems of ethnic psychology. Friedrich Wilhelm Nietzsche struck a decisive blow to the remaining ancient-regime in philosophy. Of course there are not only German, but also French and British philosophers. But I think sociology is the greatest achievement of nineteenth-century French and British thought.

THE ADVANCEMENT OF HISTORICAL STUDIES

As philosophy has begun to study the problem of the natural order and human perception based on a stable worldview, historical study also began to address this problem. Traditionally history was understood as the reporting of a collection of past human experiences. François Pierre Guillaume Guizot (1828) and Henry Thomas Buckle (1857-1866), in their attempt to study the causal chain in historical events, gave birth to the study of the history of civilization processes. The causal relationship they wanted to discover in human history was directly derived from the modern natural sciences, especially physics. Taking a different viewpoint, Thomas Carlyle (1837, 1840, 1843) described historical causation as the accumulation of individual behaviors and conducts (see also Robertson, 1891). The development of the study of civilization is a major sign of the development of historical study.

In Germany, the historical study of the civilization process is divided into two movements: philosophy of history that tries to articulate the laws within the process, and history of civilization that focuses on the collection of major facts within the process. Friedrich von Schlegel (1829) published his description of the philosophy of history. About a decade later, Georg Hegel (1837) built his philosophy of history into his system of philosophy. This represented the typical stance of the philosophy of history when it attempted to clarify the principles or assumptions in the study of history. When Ducoudray (1888), Lippert (1885-1886), and Edith Jemima Simcox (1894) published their works, scholars began to recognize the importance of the history of civilization and the difference between this and the philosophy of history (see also Henne-am Rhyn, 1890; Honegger, 1882-1886). There are still a few debates concerning the status of the history of civilization (see Gothein, 1889; Gumplowicz, 1892a; Flint, 1893; Rappoport, 1896; Tönnies, 1894).

A third movement in the advancement in historical study is in its methodology. There has been great methodological advancement in collecting, restoring, and analyzing historical materials, and the precision has been getting better. But its impact is narrowly limited within the study of history.

The rise of the study of world history is the fourth aspect of modern development. Its best example can be seen in Leopold von Lunke's work that is highly valued as an educational textbook.

Social science, especially the field of jurisprudence and economics, has been deeply stimulated by developments in historical study, and is currently following the major trend called *historicism*. The main purpose of historicism is to exclude folklore and construct historical theory from historical evidences. But historicism sometimes tends to confuse *what is* and *what it should be*. Although it is not sufficient, historicism attempts to use positivism.

As discussed above, developments in the study of history stimulated the scientific study of society both directly and indirectly.

THE ADVANCEMENT OF ECONOMICS

Economics was differentiated from politics in the eighteenth century (see Ingram, 1888; Cossa, 1893, for history of economics). Physiocrats like François Quesnay, and Anne Robert Jacques Turgot saw economic wealth as the growth of production, especially the growth of agricultural production. They failed to evaluate the importance of transportation. Adam Smith (1776) was the first to conceptualize economy as the integrated body of production, distribution, and trade. He established economics as an autonomous branch of science. Some people abuse Adam Smith's disciples saying that they are selfish and mammonistic. *Manchesterian* is the derogatory name of Smith's disciples. I think the major problem in Smith's economics is that his methodology tends to overestimate the role of deduction. Jean-Baptiste Say (1803) in France constructed a system of economics similar to that of Smith.

The importance of distribution came to be recognized by David Ricardo (1817) and Thomas Robert Malthus (1798). Ricardo's theory of land rent and Malthus's theory of population demonstrates that economics can overcome methodological difficulties and develop as a positivistic social science.

Historicism in the field of economics arose in the first half of the nineteenth century with the work of Wilhelm Heinrich Roscher (1843). He argues that there is no universally valid, unchangeable principle to judge the political decisions toward economic phenomenon. Evaluation of one single event can be reversed as time proceeds. So we should not be content with studying contemporary economic phenomena, but we need to establish the spatio-temporal comparative study of economy, between the ancient and the modern nations.

Bruno Hildebrand (1848) and Karl Knies (1853) built on Roscher's (1843) work. It is clear that this trend is successful in at least partly reforming the methodological difficulty of economics. However, this trend in economics is directly influenced by historicism in the field of jurisprudence. The full-scale reformation of economics seems to be accomplished by *Kathedersozialismus* [cathedral or academic socialism rather than hostility to accomplish socialism. Eds.]. Actually some historicists are also the *kathedersozialist*.

Current advances in economics are closely correlated with the development of socialism. By the interrelationship with socialism, economics took shape as a science of the economic aspects of human life within a national society. Adolf Wagner (1892-1893) developed the psychological study of economy. This seems to indicate that economics can be a science that can be used to clarify what *ought to be* (see Ingram, 1888, p. 90). Schmoller, Brentano, Held, and all other leading economists of today have these characteristics. It seems that Wagner attempted to continue Adam Smith's ambition.

The founder of economics, and a major thinker of the time, Adam Smith emphasized that all economic phenomena have a certain relationship to social phenomena. This suggests that Adam Smith was one of the founders of the general unified study of society (see Ingram 1888, p. 90). It is not useful to criticize Adam Smith's work as confusing and impure. As Comte pointed out, the degree to which economics treats the economy as isolated from other human activity is the degree to which it will fail. Wagner recognized this and began the psychological study of the economy. This eloquently proves the necessity of sociology.[17]

THE ADVANCEMENT OF POLITICAL
AND LEGAL SCIENCE

In ancient times, political science and jurisprudence were simply the parts of humanity, and human knowledge was archaic. Like other branches, political science had not been differentiated (see III.1). As human knowledge became differentiated in the seventeenth century, political science and jurisprudence became autonomous branches of science. Machiavelli founded political science; Hobbes and Locke further established it. After Machiavelli, Gentilis, and Grotius founded modern jurisprudence, Montesquieu (1748) integrated those two streams of the theory of natural law and was the earliest scholar who prophesied the rise of the new trend in the study of humanity: historicism.

Over 200 years after the Reformation and the birth of the modern philosophy, Friedrich Karl von Savigny (1815-1834) began studying the history of law. At the time, the seventeenth-century theory of natural law was considered to be hackneyed, and its validity was questioned. Savigny proposed to conceptually distinguish between natural law and written law, and studied the latter in a historical perspective. Georg Friedrich Puchta (1844) was his most distinguished disciple. Sir Henry James Sumner Maine in England began a comparative study of ancient law (1861, 1872, 1875, 1883). Also, there were writers like Heinrich Aemilius August Danz (1840-1846), Otto Karlowa, (1885-1901), and Rudolf von Jhering, (1852-1878). Heinrich Brunner (1887-1892), Ferdinand Walter (1853), and Stinzing (1880-1910) were the leading scholars in German law.

In this way the scientific study of jurisprudence advanced. With help from philosophy and other sciences, it now focuses on examining the fundamental principles of law.[18] Political science has not been fully developed. Gneist (1879) and Lorenz von Stein (1852-1856, 1876) studied public administration and national law. Gumplowicz's work is closer to sociology than political science.[19] He says he realized that the study of society is required before studying politics. Heinrich Gotthard von Treitschke began his splendid academic career with the study of history (1859, 1897-1898). Today he is studying sociology and political science, but it is not very successful because he has not mastered the fundamentals of sociology. Ratzenhofer (1893a), whose work represents the most substantial advances in political science, says that political science should be applied sociology.

To sum up, both jurisprudence and political science have not been independent, autonomous branches of science. They should be integrated into a single, comprehensive branch of science.

AUGUST COMTE

As modern west European thought has developed, there have been five schools and six streams that lead the advancement of science. It was August Comte who attempted to discover the general law that governs those developments. Like Confucius and Plato, Comte integrated all human knowledge of the time, and tried to give an answer to the ultimate question of human life and apply it to improve society.

Today some people say Comte is just a founder of scientific sociology but this is not accurate. Comte looked through all branches of human knowledge and found that the system of science lacked an important subject—society. In a sense Comte was first to discover society.[20] However, Comte did not just found sociology, he established a new system of philosophy, called positive philosophy. Just like Confucius and Plato, Comte can be considered both a philosopher and sociologist. Comte's main teachings can be summarized as follows:

Unified science. There are many ways to aim toward the goal. But the goal itself must be the same. The goal of science is to improve human life. To achieve this goal, Comte projected to unify all branches of science. The universe is a single body that integrates objective matters and subjective matters. The basic motif of Comte's system of positive philosophy is establishing a single, unified body of science.

Systematic science. The system of positive philosophy as a unified science does not allow any omission. It is differentiated into subsystems like mathematics, astronomy, physics, biology, and sociology, according to the distance from the goal of science and the logical relationship with the characteristics of its subject matter.

Positive science. Comte insisted that the concept of *positive* must be real, useful, certain, and precise. Those characteristics distinguish positive philosophy from other systems of philosophy. Comte proposed his positive philosophy as a unified science that balances the deduction and induction theories and integrates the subjective and objective viewpoints. Its method should conform to the third stage of advancement.

Humanitarian science. In a single word, his proposal of a new science was humanitarian, as Comte's religion of humanity insists on benevolence, order, and progress.[21] According to Comte, there are two aims of his positive philosophy: (1) To make the social or moral science positive; (2) To systematize all concept of positivism from a humanitarian viewpoint. Humanitarianism is the starting and ending point of the new science.

Comte's new science is on a grand scale and full of aspiration. In the system of science sociology occupies, for Comte, the highest position.[22] Among Comte's writings, the most important one is *Cours de Philosophie Positive* (1830-1842) which provided the essence of his academic views. *Systeme de Politique Positive* (1851-1854), his second most important work, focused on the application of his positive philosophy to practical problems. Other writings provided additional elaborations of the above two.

The emergence of sociology, as described above, was extraordinary. I surmise that not only its past, but also its future shall be extraordinary.

SOCIOLOGY AFTER COMTE

To treat the history of sociology after Comte, we have two methods. One is chronological and the other is national. The chronological method is suitable for describing the general trend, but sociology only has a fifty-year history. The substantial relationship between sociologists is best discussed by placing them in their national context. Therefore, we will examine the contributions to sociology within a national context.

In a single word, the development of sociology after Comte has been partial. Just like Confucianism after Confucius and Platonism after Plato, sociology after Comte lost its original scale, although it has been adding partial annotations. Generally speaking, we have to say that the history of sociology has been progressing in quantity but regressing in quality.

In France, immediately after Comte, Adolphe Quételet adopted his statistical concept of *homme moyen* (average man) to sociological study in an attempt to discover the laws of social phenomena.[23] He believed that the laws of social evolution could be clarified by quantitative research. He misunderstood Comte's positivism as materialism. Frédéric Le Play developed a statistical method combined with a descriptive method, which he used to discover social laws and apply them to social reform.[24] His suggestions for practical issues were not successful, but he made a great contribution to the development of methodology. Charles Letourneau cultivated the descriptive method and produced many basic research materials.[25] Ambroise Clement (1867) attempted a normative description of the ethical and civil issues and other social phenomena. Although it is poorly written, it contains brilliant insights.[26] Durkheim wrote about sociological methodology and recently investigated specific social phenomena. Tarde has been investigating the psychological laws of social phenomena, although his originality often twists the argument.[27]

Russian scholars often write in French and have close connections with French scholars. Paul von Lilienfeld, the reigning scholar of Russian sociology, has been a guardian of the theory of social evolution. [Takebe did not specify the titles. Lilienfeld published at least seven books which are listed in the references. Eds.] Jacques Novicow (1886, 1893, 1894a,b, 1895, 1897), Eugène de Roberty, and Maksim Kovalevsky belong to the younger generation. Novicow's study of international struggles (1886) is quite unique. De Roberty (1881, 1891) analyzes the major characters of sociology. Kovalevsky (1890) has been studying the development of the family system, which is quite interesting. Lothar Dargun (1883, 1884, 1886, 1892), who published in German, has been studying social institutions and social statics.

Unfortunately, we do not know much about Russian scholars who publish works in their native language, except Tcheko (1884) who defined sociology as the science of human fate. In addition, Johann von Bloch (1899), a Polish journalist, wrote a series of books concerning the war and became a leader of the Russian pacifist movement. Constantine P. Pobedonostzeff (1897) drew a lively picture of contemporary Moscow in his book.[28]

In Italy, sociology has been embraced by criminologists such as Enrico Ferri (1892, 1895a,b), Raffaele Garofalo (1895), Cesare Lombroso, and more recently Napoleone Colajanni (1889, 1898). Non-criminological sociology has been developed by Achille Loria (1900), Giuseppe Vadale-Papale (1882), Icilio Vanni (1888), Angelo Majoranna (1891), and De Bella (1895). Sociology has also been acknowledged in the southern side of the Pyrenees. For example, books by Adolfo Posada (1896) and Eduardo Sanz y Escartin (1893, 1896) have been translated and published in France. Vincente Santamaria de Paredes (1896) is also becoming known in the field. I would also like to add Ovijilo Figuerra, an Italian-Chilean sociologist, in this group.

Now let us turn our eyes from the Latin to the Anglo-Saxon scholars. In Britain, Spencer is the most influential sociologist; a detailed explanation is not needed. Sir John Lubbock (1870, 1872), John McLennan (1876), Lewis Morgan (1877), and Edward Tylor (1873) wrote enduring works on primitive societies.

Robert Flint's (1874, 1893) work on the history of civilization made a contribution to sociology. Ernest B. Bax, Jan H. Ferguson, George Harris, Thomas H. Huxley, George C. Lorimer, and Thomas Mackay have been attempting to popularize sociology.[29] William Jevons (1883), who inherited the legacy of Mill, Maine, and Carlyle, is now being acknowledged as an authority on logic and economics. John Mackenzie (1890), a disciple of Jevons, has attempted to articulate the future course of sociology.

In North America, Franklin Henry Giddings (1896, 1897, 1901) stands out as an analytical and psychological sociologist. Actually his theory is an epoch-making one. Lester Ward (1893, 1898), who had attained academic fame by his book *Dynamic Sociology* and recently wrote *Pure Sociology* (1903), has attempted to revise his system in the modern style. Albion Small and George Vincent (1894), Charles Richmond Henderson (1898), and Edward Alsworth Ross (1901) have not published masterpieces yet. But each has an excellent reputation as a teacher and a scholar of sociology. Arthur Fairbanks (1896), John Bascom (1895), and John Franklin Crowell (1898) are considered to be weak by other scholars. Henry Charles Carey (1858-1867, 1872) is the most faithful follower of Comte's teachings.

Although Germany and German-speaking countries are in the forefront of science in general, they slight sociology.[30] I think this is surprising. The Swiss sociologist Ludwig von Stein suggests two reasons for this.

1. The German scholars are afraid that French sociology has often been daydreaming; otherwise it has a close relationship to political radicalism.
2. They do not see essential difference between philosophy of history and sociology. They attach greater importance to their own national legacy of Herder, Kant, Fichte, Hegel, and Marx, than they do to foreign thinkers. But Stein thinks they are wrong (see Stein, 1842, 1850, 1897, pp. 23-24). In fact philosophy of history and sociology share a major theme: the development of society. But there are many methodological differences between the two, to treat the same theme.

I agree with Stein. But I'd like to add one more point. As German scholars have made great contributions to the establishment of the modern German Empire, they have been slandered by saying that they are scholars under the government's thumb. I think this is unjust abuse, even though it is true that they tend to be chauvinistic. The German scholars are not indifferent to sociology, but afraid of the contemporary affinity of sociology with social democracy. So, in absorbing foreign sociology, they have been employing their own philosophy of history, history of civilization, comparative ethnology, comparative linguistics, and so on. In short, they have been choosing substance over appearance. Stein enumerated the effective sociologists. But there are many other contributions to sociology from the history of civilization.[31]

Austria produced distinguished sociologists such as Gumplowicz and his disciple Ratzenhofer. The Swiss produced Ludwig Stein. Social psychologists like Gustav Adolf Lindner, Moritz Lazarus, Heymann Steinthal, and Wilhelm Max Wundt are improving the international status of German sociology. Sociologists in other countries include Carl Nicolai Starcke (1888) in Denmark, Tomáš Garrigue Masaryk (1899) in Hungary, and Dalmarng in Bruxelles (also see Fedor Schmidt-Warneck, 1889).

Generally speaking, classes in sociology are found in almost all colleges in the West. Sociological organizations exist in almost every city. The biggest organization is the International Institute of Sociology (IIS), based in Paris. Under the IIS, there are dozens of branches that have journals that publish the results of their studies.[32]

This is the status quo of sociology. And it is not difficult to foresee the future of sociology.

III.4

The Future of Sociology

Tongo Takebe

THE MEIJI ERA

We have examined the genesis, the formation, and the current situation of sociology. Now we turn our eyes to our own age, especially in the Japanese context. What is the major character of our age? How can we grasp it in a scientific way? As Meiji scholars, we should not neglect those questions.

Under the unbroken lineage of the majestic Tenno, by geographical and ethnic characteristics, Japanese society had been developing naturally and independently for 2,500 years. Throughout the long medieval era, Tenno's power had declined. Go-Daigo Tenno (1288-1339) made a desperate effort to restore the power of Tenno by subordinating the samurai clans (Kenmu no Chuko, 1333), but he failed. In the decadent era of the Muromachi government (1336-1573), people wanted to live in luxury but were tossed about by the Ounin War (1467-1477).

After the long war-torn period, the Tokugawa clan succeeded in establishing a stable regime of the shogunate (1603-1867), but this resulted in a big problem regarding Tenno's political and legal status. Even the Toshogu shrine failed to resolve the problem. Ieyasu Tokugawa (1543-1616) gave 100 instructions to his descendents on how to maintain the regime, and actually it was quite effective.[1] But among those instructions were some articles that declared the shogun's supremacy over Tenno. In the nineteenth century, the big wave of West-

Japanese Family and Society
© 2007 by The Haworth Press, Inc. All rights reserved.
doi:10.1300/5840_10

ern materialistic civilization had far-reaching effects on Japanese society. And now, our society is entering into world history.

There have been many popular movements to protest against the King's abuse of royal prerogative in modern European history. These appear to be similar to the 1850-1860s Japanese movement of advocating reverence for Tenno and the expulsion of the Tokugawa regime. But it is not the same. The Western society does not know the optimum point that should be achieved, whereas the Japanese society knows it. The Japanese society had once completely collapsed at the Ounin War. But from that point until today, Japanese society has been getting closer to the optimum balance between the physical power of the government and the spiritual power of the Tenno. Today the Japanese people recognize that the Tenno's authority is necessary for controlling the government's force. It is quite different from the contemporary western problems regarding sovereignty.

The Tokugawa Confucian scholars did not neglect this long existing tendency of Japanese society. From Mitsukuni Tokugawa (1628-1701) and his school in Mito located 100 km north east of Tokyo, Ansai Yamazaki (1618-1682) and Soko Yamaga (1622-1685) in Kyoto, and Banzan Kumazawa in Bizen (150 km west form Kyoto), Confucian scholars tacitly attempted to resolve the problem.

Hakuseki Arai (1657-1725), in his *Tokushi Yoron,* explicitly analyzed this problem and presented a system of philosophy of history. Considerably earlier than Arai, in the Kenmu period, Chikafusa Minamoto (1293-1354) made a similar attempt to reflect upon the past and articulate society's future direction. About 100 years after Arai, San'yo Rai (1780-1832), during a period of conflict between Tenno and shogun, tried to resolve the problem. In addition, Masayuki Takayama (1747-1793), and Shikibu Takenouchi (1712-1767) also tried various ways to resolve the problem. These were the main streams of sociological thought in the Tokugawa era.

There were two sub-streams of sociological thought that related to the central problem of the social constitution. One social problem concerns class relationships—the gap between the rich and the poor. It was already seen in Banzan Kumazawa. Chusai Oshio (1793-1837) strongly argued for solutions to this problem and died a martyr. But his ideal was not consistent with the social constitution of that time.

This problem should have been resolved after the central problem of the social constitution came to an end.[2]

Another issue is international problems concerning trade. In the early phase of the Tokugawa era, Date Masamune (1567-1636), a lord of Sendai (280 km north from Tokyo), sent envoys to the Vatican. In addition, in this short period of free trade, a considerable number of the southwestern Japanese merchants immigrated to the South Pacific seas. But attempts to communicate with the outer world were a temporary and not a widespread phenomenon. As the western merchants expanded their power in southeast Asia, those movements dispersed like mist. It was the main cause of Tokugawa's national seclusion policy, but the policy was also necessary to cover its crucial problem, which was the growth of the Western super powers. Banzan Kumazawa, in the seventeenth century, already predicted the great transformation of international relations in and around Japan. Kon'yo Aoki (1698-1769), Kazan Watanabe (1793-1881), Shihei Hayashi (1738-1793), and Choei Takano (1804-1850) continued Kumazawa's legacy.

In the middle of the nineteenth century, the above problems finally squeezed the Tokugawa regime to death. The U.S. Commodore Matthew C. Perry's (1794-1858) visitation triggered the upheaval. Many scholars stopped analyzing the situation and took direct political actions. Among those, Shoin Yoshida (1830-1859), Shozan Sakuma (1811-1864), Toko Fujita (1806-1855), and Shonan Yokoi (1809-1869) were exceptional (see Fujita, 1884; Yoshida, 1868). They integrated the sociological thoughts of the Tokugawa Era and designed the framework for the new regime.

The Meiji Restoration resembles the French Revolution, although there is a clear difference in their consequence; while Japan immediately reached the stable condition, French political unrest persisted. After the Revolution, Auguste Comte tried to foresee the future by studying the past and present thought. We should also look through the brief history of Japanese thought after the Restoration.[3]

Yukichi Fukuzawa's (1835-1901) materialistic utilitarianism[4] and Jo Niijima's (1843-1890) Christian spiritualism[5] were the most influential thoughts circulated among the Meiji people. Concerning politico-economical issues, there were four strands of thought: (1) The French liberal egalitarianism was advocated by Taisuke Itagaki (1837-

1919) and Tatsui Baba (1850-1888); (2) Shigenobu Okuma (1838-1922) and Azusa Ono (1852-1886) promoted the English orderly progressivism; (3) Hirobumi Ito (1841-1909)[6] absorbed the German nationalism; (4) Some Christian thinkers advocated the American democracy.

The different factions disagreed with each other and Setsurei Miyake (1860-1945), Katsunan Kuga (1857-1903), and Tateki Tani (1837-1911) greatly disliked all those Europeanized thinkers who proposed a conservative nationalism. This awakened a consciousness of nationality in the Japanese and stimulated the study of the national language and national history. Also a full-scale investigation of Asian literatures and philosophies began. However, it seems to me that the current national conservatism has been quite passive. It does not yet have an independent feature.

It cannot be said that sociological ideas are fully expressed in the Meiji academic writings. This is because the effects of the Restoration have not been fully put in place. Similar to other aspects of Japanese life, in the academic world the productive usage of the new institutions has not yet appeared. So, most scholars and poets maintain their status by absorbing and introducing west European knowledge. Fukuzawa's book is famous because the price of paper increased considerably in Tokyo as a result of the publishing company's production of a large number of copies. However, it had very little influence on the academic world. Masanao Nakamura (1832-1891) was a man of character, but he did little more than encourage private self-cultivation.

Amane Nishi (1829-1897) contributed to deciding on the Japanese terms to translate the Western academic terms, but today there is no one to succeed him. Shigeki Nishimura (1828-1902) devoted all his life to moral education, but his influence is limited to the narrow area of encouraging personal self-cultivation. It is strange and deplorable that Kiyonori Konakamura's (1821-1895) draft of *Koshitsu Tenpan* [Rules Governing the Imperial Household][7] was the only substantial contribution to the advancement of Japanese society, which the Meiji scholars made.

On the contrary, the German movement for independence and integration started from the study of their own traditional laws and customs: Goethe, Herder, Friedrich Gottlieb Klopstock, Hegel, and Wagner were the best examples. They developed the modern framework of the legal system. Kaiser Otto von Bismarck and Helmuth Karl von Moltke carried it out.

Hiroyuki Kato (1836-1916) was familiar with the leading German theories. He considered himself to be a sociologist and published his theory of human rights in Europe. But I think it is too early to know the impact of his work. We first need scholars who can contribute to developing Japanese sociology. I think the worldwide academic contribution should be made through the study of some particular country's situation.

Masakazu Toyama (1840-1900) diligently taught sociology for twenty years at the University of Tokyo. He wrote several essays on ancient Japanese women and religion. Although he did not publish any major sociological work, his efforts in education shall soon bear fruit. In addition, Toyama encouraged people to distinguish sociology from socialism when socialism was equated with anarchism and terrorism.

In a sense it was unfortunate that he was appointed Minister of Education in 1898, because he was then forced to resign his post of professor. At that time he was writing a book concerning social evolution theory and current sociology. He died in 1900, so we lost the opportunity to gain from his knowledge.

Tetsujiro Inoue (1855-1944) has been emphasizing the importance of studying Eastern philosophies, and he has presented lively comments on current issues like the Alien Law and the conflict between education and religion. Inoue is a positivist who advocates Japanism. However, he has not yet published his academic masterpiece. Its effect in the future may be equal to that of Hegel's influence in Germany, although the national conservative movement had already influenced the government.

Setsurei Miyake, besides being a famous critic and public educator (see 1855-1858), published two works concerning ethnic psychology: *The Japanese: Truth, Good, and Beauty* (1891a) and *The Japanese: False, Evil, and Ugly* (1891b). These books express his personal impressions of the Japanese people and provide a proper introduction to the study of ethnic psychology. His criticism of academicians seems to be fair and productive. However, he is not interested in constructing a theoretic system. It seems to me that his stance is between Christian Wolff and Kant.

Nagao Aruga (1860-1921) seems to be the best sociologist of Meiji Japan. He wrote *Of Social Evolution* (1883), *Of Familial Evolution* (1884), and *Of Religious Evolution* (1883). These contributed considerably to the development of Japanese sociology, although he borrowed much from the western scholars. His profound knowledge of sociology is reflected in *An Outline of the Japanese Imperial History* (1897).

Aruga is a man of extraordinary versatility. He started his academic career as a philosopher, psychologist, and pedagogic. But after he gained a reputation with sociological works, around the Sino-Japanese War (1894-1895), he distinguished himself as a jurist and a diplomat. The Japanese academic world is now longing for his return to sociology.

Recently some economists, who are eager to expand the study of economic-based social problems, established the Society for the Study of Social Policy (SSSP) (1897). They are trying to apply scientific knowledge to current social problems. This represents a wholesome development of the Meiji social science. A few Christian socialists exist in the SSSP, but their influence is limited.

Fourteen years passed since the Imperial Congress was established in 1890. Various problems still remain to be fixed. Even the elders of distinguished service are still worried about the future of this country. In such a situation, there are people who corrupt public morals. But the younger generation under Toyama, Inoue, and the wise guidance of other teachers are not content with just studying metaphysics. They use sociology to address practical problems. Already there have been numerous results. But their efforts shall be rewarded in the near future when they proclaim the independence of the Meiji Japanese academic world from Euro-centrism.

Unlike Germany, the Japanese society does not have prejudice against sociology. Unlike France, we did not develop in reaction to radical events. Unlike western Europe in general, we do not have a religious bias. Therefore, the Japanese situation has many advantages that will be useful for future advances in sociology.

LIMITATION IN THE CURRENT STUDY OF HUMANITY

The particular primitive religion of western European society has found a new means of survival in subjective thinking. Even the leading scholars do not recognize it, so they tend to fall into the Aryan-centric belief that the Western nations are the most superior and therefore the other regions of the world should be subordinate to them.[8] At the same time, the Chinese praise themselves as civilized and look down on the Japanese as savage. Those are not fair claims.

Among European scholars, no one adopts Comte's work in its entirety. There have only been partial advances of Comte's work. Nevertheless he intended to establish a new integrated science that has a bird's-eye view of science in general. In the worst case scenario, the genuine study of sociology will decline, as the study of sociology by dilettantes increases. There are a lot of planets and satellites, but in the latter half of the nineteenth century there seems to be no sun in the scholarly system. This is a necessary consequence of the division of labor, and results in a critical limitation of the times.

Today the term *scientific study* means partial inquiry. In fact in the study of physics, various partial inquiries can be smoothly integrated into a general theoretical system. But in the study of humanity, we do not have an optimistic view. De Roberty (1881) repeatedly referred to this point. As a result, human science and practical science have reached a deadlock.

The tendency toward social differentiation has resulted in prejudice between the occupational classes. The widening gap between social statuses further amplifies mutual dislike. People take this tendency for granted. Many economists, in arguing for reform of problems, support the laissez-faire doctrine which actually promotes further division and differentiation.

The tendency toward social differentiation causes various conflicts and contradictions. No one can settle those debates. Our society is filled with this kind of conflict between laws and morals, science and religion, politics and society, art and morals, education and religion, and so on. Those are the consequences of the division of labor. People leave everything in the specialist's hands, and the specialists disagree with each other. Society, in the first place, must be a single, unified body. The existing conflicts suggest that our society is imperfect. So, it is deplorable when scientists do not look squarely at this reality and instead run into the safety zone of partial studies.

The tendency toward the division of labor has also had a serious effect on international relations. The international division of labor and the promotion of trade should be reciprocal and cooperative, but in reality it is often transformed into invasion and destruction. The intelligentsia should reconsider the relationship between the ultimate goal of civilization and the free trade doctrine.

I think those serious side effects come from the basic character of Western civilization and its developmental process. First, they left their own primitive religion as it was. Second, their natural environment has not been fertile enough. Third, they constantly suffer from serious international conflicts. Fourth, their hierarchical system of classes results in problems. Our civilization shall be completed when we truly integrate the Western and Eastern civilizations.

THE FUTURE OF SOCIOLOGY

Throughout the latter half of the nineteenth century, the worldwide tendency toward differentiation proceeded, and its negative effects have been getting more serious. The leading scholars did not just look on with their arms folded. Four new sources of influence have been developing.

The notion of "the world" has become a reality. As mentioned before, the nineteenth century physics notion of the universe developed remarkably. In addition, throughout the latter half of the nineteenth century the notions of *mankind, world history,* and *civilization* also developed as have the effects of the expanded and deepening political-economic communication. The Western knowledge of the East is not greater than the Eastern knowledge of the West. And the Western knowledge of itself is equal to the Eastern knowledge of itself.[9] Therefore, the East, especially Japan, is in the most advantageous position to understand the twentieth century world. The Japanese scholar can be a leader of the world of science.

International cooperation has progressed. Since the establishment of the International Committee of the Red Cross at the Geneva Convention Treaty of 1864, various international groups have flourished.[10] These include the conference on the currency exchange, labor unions, the expositions, academic associations, the Universal Postal Union in 1878, and so on. Each of them has particular importance, but no one can participate in all such associations. I think the most advanced system of international cooperation can be seen in the Hague Peace

Conference in 1899, conducted by the Russian Emperor Nicolai II. Those movements shall be more influential in the twentieth century.

Socialism has advanced. Formerly socialists insisted on the equalization of individual freedom and welfare, but today they attach greater importance to the equalization of ethnic rights. The current international socialist movement shall bear the fruit of universal peace.

Science and humanity have advanced. As mentioned in the former chapters, natural sciences, philosophy, history, economics, and politico-legal sciences have been advancing at different rates.

The need for sociology will continue to grow and the field will be expanded. The status of sociology will be improved. In the twentieth century, sociology may be the leading science to guide mankind in the right direction. Whether it will be realized or not, depends on the sociologist's will and diligence. This is especially true for the young Japanese students who shoulder the future of the Japanese Empire and mankind.

PART IV:
FAMILY ORGANIZATION

IV.1

The Family

Tongo Takebe

FOREWORD

The structure of a well-organized society can be analyzed as three elements. First, there is the family system that constitutes the order of natural society (clan society). Second is the state system that constitutes the order of man-made society (village, city, and state). Third is the international system which constitutes the order of international society—that does not exist yet.

The family system is the basis for the organization of the state system, and the state system is the basis for the organization of the international system. This inference leads us to a unified, general theory of human society.

Part IV is from Tongo Takebe, *Social Statics* (1909), pp. 79-155. Tokyo: Kinkodo Press.

Japanese Family and Society
© 2007 by The Haworth Press, Inc. All rights reserved.
doi:10.1300/5840_11

Usually the sociologist uses the concepts *social condition* and *social phenomenon,* to inquire about the *forms* of social organizations and their *functions.* All sociologists who explore the themes of social statics, such as Herbert Spencer and Guillaume De Greef, do this without exception.

Social analysis has made great advances by distinguishing between forms and their functions. Social phenomena are too complex to classify by single measures, so there must be at least a two-dimensional table in which the type of organization forms the x-axis, and the types of function forms the y-axis. Thus, in this book, I have discussed these as separate sections for the theory of social organizations and the theory of social functions.

Family ties form the initial social system, made from the overlapping of family relationships and clan relationships (Ferguson, 1876; McLennan, 1876; Morgan, 1871). The family relation consists of husband-wife, parent-child, and brother-sister relationships. From the ontogenetical point of view, the husband-wife and parent-child relationships are original, and the brother-sister relationship is derivative.

The major developments in the study of family organizations were made by scholars such as John Ferguson (1876), Alexis Giraud-Teulon, (1884), Friedrich von Hellwald, (1889), Henry James Sumner Maine (1861), Charles Letourneau, (1888), John Lubbock, (1870, 1872), John McLennan (1876), Lewis Henry Morgan (1871), and Edward Burnett Tylor (1873).[1]

There are two theoretical perspectives with which to view family organizations— paternalism and non-paternalism. I think it is dangerous and unnecessary to hastily conclude which is true and which is false, since we do not yet have enough data to judge it. At present, we should be content with classifying various forms of family organizations. Josef Kohler (1897), Ernst Grosse (1896), and Heinrich Cunow (1898) provide the general theories of family. Friedrich Engels (1891) and Adolfo Posada (1896) provide an important analysis of this polemic.

There is a theoretical debate concerning the relationship between the family system and society and what is the fundamental unit of society. René Worms outlined the history of the debate between collectivism and individualism (Worms, 1895b, p. 114). According to Worms, Le Play's disciples mistakenly argue that their master was the first advocate of collectivism. Prior to Le Play, Comte already gave a collectivist answer in his *Cours de Philosophie Positive* (Comte, 1877, vol. 4, p. 398). Every system is made from parts that share the same essential nature with the whole system. An individual's system does not share the essential nature with the social system that he/she lives in. The fundamental unit of the social system is family organization, or male/female relationships, since reproduction is based on this. From his/her birth until adulthood, every gratification of basic desires depends on the parents' care (Comte, 1877, vol. 4, p. 339). This argument is exactly the same as the basic assumption of Le Play's social theory.

Although Le Play was solely interested in the economic aspects of family and society, he observed each family as a miniature copy of the state society. Recently Fustel de Coulange has taken the collectivist stand. Worms takes an individualist stand, and argues that the major characteristic of modern French society is the instability and vulnerability of the family bond, just as Le Play himself noticed. This seems to be a major consequence of the modern state system that is based on individual rights and duties and is not dependent on family organizations.

The theory of family systems should include the classification and analysis of various family organizations. In addition, it should include two components; the study of the relationship between family system and social system, and the study of women's social status or position in the society.

FORMS OF MARRIAGE

There is a difference in sexual relationship between male and female depending on whether or not they are married. This sociological definition of marriage is quite broader than that of ordinary language. In ordinary language, spousal relationships exist only when the participants are conscious that their relationship is different from other relationships. There are many forms of spousal relationships according to the variety of the forms of marriage. We can examine spousal relations by clarifying the forms of marriage, the relationship between husband and wife, and the functions of marriage.

Usually sociologists do not consider analyzing the spousal relationship as important. They take the totality of the family system for granted. But this stance is dangerous since the family system cannot exist without the spousal relationship. Furthermore, we do not have enough data to decide which type of family system corresponds to which stage of social evolution.[2] Given our current state of knowledge, we should be content with drawing the forms and functions of marriage and their logical relationships. Marriage can take the following five forms:[3]

1. *Temporal marriage.* In the primitive stage of society, humans meet and part, and do not establish a stable relationship. They satisfy their sexual desire as the opportunity permits, so their marriage is quite short-lived. This form of marriage can also be called *desire-ruled marriage.*[4] This is the initial, the most primitive form of marriage, and it cannot produce stable spousal relationships.

2. *Marriage by capture.* In the next stage, human society had not yet progressed to a more complex level and it operated on the basis of the stronger oppressing the weaker. In most cases males capture the females. This form of marriage flourishes under the circumstance in which people know who their friends are and who their enemies are. In this stage a male obtains his wife through assaults and abductions of females. There are two types of abduction. One is to attack for the purpose of capturing females. The other is to abduct females because that is your right as winner of a battle. This can be achieved either by the winner's plunder or by the loser's donation.

3. *Marriage by purchase.* As a result of the repeated conflicts, females were seen as a commodity.[5] The more society becomes developed, the more society is forced to supply females from another society. If the group prefers a peaceful way to supply females, they purchase females from other societies. In the familial or tribal society, the patriarch is the one who holds the purchasing power. Matrimonial societies rarely take this form of marriage.

4. *Marriage by servitude.* Marriage by capture and marriage by purchase, described above, are the forms of marriage between two societies. In this stage of social evolution that is not yet civi-

lized and has no clear social order, there is a form of marriage between males and females who belong to the same society. In this form the weaker obeys the stronger—the female obeys the male. Thus, it is marriage by servitude.

5. *Marriage by agreement.* Once society has become more cultivated and the social order established, the concept of the stronger suppressing the weaker is no longer acceptable. As social differentiation proceeds, the gap between the stronger and the weaker narrows. In this stage of social evolution, the male-female relationship transforms drastically and mutual agreement is understood as the foundation of marriage. This form of marriage is called marriage by agreement.

Generally speaking, marriage by capture and marriage by purchase are the forms of exogamy (marriage outside the group), and marriage by servitude and marriage by agreement are the forms of endogamy (marriage within the group). Exogamy and endogamy have two stages: the primitive and the civilized. Endogamy in the most primitive stage seems to have no taboos. Through the process of civilization, humans gradually came to avoid lineal parents, brothers, sisters, and cousins. At the more civilized stages, there may be the taboo not to marry a brother's widow, or a taboo not to marry a deceased wife's sister.[6]

There are three reasons why the transformation of marriage from primitive endogamy to primitive exogamy occurs. First, because of human nature, endogamy is not preferred.[7] The primitive society is heavily influenced by instinct, so endogamy was soon abandoned. Second, because society is initially small and homogeneous, mates must be selected from the group. In the later stage society grows and becomes more complex, and members no longer know each other as well. Third, because of the relative ease of invasion[8] in a primitive stage a society easily invades other societies. So they have many chances to plunder females from these other societies. In this way marriage transforms itself from the primitive endogamy (marriage within the group or tribe), to the primitive exogamy (marriage outside the group or tribe). The human instinct to prefer exogamy seems to be unchangeable. But as social evolution proceeds, the second and the third factors gradually waned. At this point, civilized endogamy arises, and marriage by agreement is established. After that, the civilized exogamy emerges. I think it is needless to forecast the future collapse of the civilized forms of marriage.

Spencer, McLennan, and Morgan discussed endogamy and exogamy in great detail. Spencer sees exogamy as the primitive form of marriage that is characteristic of peaceful social life. This looks right, but we should be cautious that endogamy is not synonymous with primitive society. The distinction between endogamy and exogamy is useful as a secondary analysis of the above five forms of marriage (McLennan, 1876; Morgan, 1871; Spencer, 1876-1896, vol. 3).

Marriage is the central issue of family study; so all scholars address it. Edward Westermarck's work (1893) is voluminous and insightful, but it is also complicated. Tillier's recent book (1898) is systematic and concise. Tillier classifies the types of marriage according to the following five dimensions:

1. Number of persons who form the marriage.
2. The ways in which the male acquires the spouse.
3. The form of the relationship between the individual and the social group, that is, endogamy or exogamy.
4. The length of time that the marriage is expected to continue.
5. The social status of the female. The social status is determined by the way in which the wife became a spouse: contract, capture, servitude, or agreement.

Hellwald (1889, pp. 273, 323, 366) provides an explanation of the evolution of marriage and family from the physiological point of view. He examined kissing and hugging behaviors as the physiological and social expressions of sexual instinct. Then he refers to the rise of clan organization from the exogamy and classifies the forms of marriage. Finally, he examines how patriarchal society arose.

THE FORMS OF MARITAL RELATIONSHIPS

The form of marital relationships consists of the status of male as husband, the status of female as wife, and their relationship. The variation in the forms of relationships between spouses comes primarily from the number of people who form the relationship and how long the relationship continues. From the viewpoint of the number of people, there are four forms of a spousal relationship.

1. *Promiscuity.* Some males have sexual relationships with females, and there are no steady relationships involved.[9] Promiscuity can take two forms: *unlimited* and *limited.* It can also be classified into the homogeneous and the heterogeneous. As I noted in my earlier discussion of promiscuity, if the relationships have clearly defined hierarchical social roles, for example, primary partner and secondary partner, this can be called heterogeneous promiscuity.[10] If there is no such differentiation (sex with many persons), it can be named homogeneous promiscuity. If some of the patterns are based on rules defining who must be avoided, for example, based on age, parent-child relationships, or brother-sister relationships, it can be named the limited promiscuity. If there is no such avoidance, it can be named the unlimited promiscuity. The heterogeneous and unlimited promiscuity is an initial sign of the evolution of marriage.

2. *Polyandry.* Polyandry is a form of spousal relationship consisting of one wife and plural husbands. Polyandry is a more distinct form of spouse relationships when compared with promiscuity. There are three characteristics of polyandry. First, it is a burden on the wife, so it is difficult to maintain this relationship for a long time. It is relatively difficult to identify the father of each child, but it is quite easy to identify who is one's brother or sister. Polyandry is rare in reality. This is because the husbands are often sons of the same father, although those brothers could be hierarchically ordered.[11]

3. *Polygyny.* Polygyny is a form of spousal relationships consisting of one husband and plural wives. Compared with polyandry, it is relatively easy to maintain this relationship for a long time because there is very little burden on the husband, and it is quite easy to decide who is the father and the mother of each child. Thus, polygyny is not only a form of a spousal relationship, it is also an autonomous form of a family system. In comparison with promiscuity, it is relatively easy to decide who is one's brother or sister. It seems that polygyny is a phase in the evolution of spousal relationships that every human society has experienced.

There are two types of polygyny: natural and artificial. Artificial polygyny is often established in a society in which inheritance is based on the male for the purpose of maintaining the lineage.[12] Therefore, it is important for the husband to produce a male heir. Even in societies that have the norms of monogamy, vestiges of polygyny still remain. Among these societies, there are rare cases in which the wives are blood-related sisters[13] which functions to make close ties among their children.[14]

4. *Monogamy.* Monogamy is the form of spousal relationship consisting of one husband and one wife. In monogamy, society achieves the most constant and stable marital relationship and there is little doubt in identifying who is the mother and father or who is one's brother or sister.

From the evolutionary viewpoint, monogamy seems the most civilized form of marital relationships. But if we understand that the goal of marital relationships is reproduction, monogamy has a big problem in comparison with polygyny since monogamy lowers the probability of reproduction.[15]

We can distinguish three types of spousal relations according to how long the relationship continues. Passing relationships are those that are established only to gratify the sexual desire and are often seen in promiscuity. It is the most primitive form of spousal relationships. Limited relationships must last for a sustained length of time and are often seen in polyandry and polygyny (Letourneau, 1888). Unlimited relationships are sustained until the partner dies. This form is often seen in the refined form of polygyny and monogamy. Today, although the unlimited relationship is endorsed by legislation, religion, and morals, it is not done in practice. And there are many unpleasant outcomes concerning this norm.[16]

FUNCTIONS OF MARITAL RELATIONSHIPS

We can articulate the functions of spousal relationships by observing the aims of the relationship. There are at least two aims of spousal relationships: marriage and reproduction. When the goal of couples is to marry just for their own satisfaction, reproduction is often an unexpected consequence. On the other hand, if the goal is to have children, then marriage is just a means to achieve it. Even today there is a clash of opinion between those two positions. Some people argue that the marriage itself is meaningful and it represents the maturity of the individuals' social personality. Just as the individual develops from a baby to an adult, it is an advancement of the social personality to live your life with the opposite sex. Reproduction is almost necessarily derived from marriage, but the goal is the marriage itself.

Others insist that reproduction is an obligation of humans to maintain society. To meet this obligation, the stable marital relationship may be useful but not necessary. The marital relationship is not the primary goal. It is a means necessary to maintain society which is the important goal. Although it may appear that the aim of marriage is reproduction, marital relationships with the focus on marriage itself, is universally observed regardless of the stage of social development. On the other hand, it seems that marriage with a primary goal of reproduction can only exist in the relatively advanced stage of social evolution. The above is a formal description of the goals of marital relationships. In the real world those two goals are mixed. Even today there are some vestiges of savage unconsciousness and aimlessness in contemporary marital relationships. Today, there are a few radicals attempting to exterminate such vestiges. Then, from the functional viewpoint, spousal relationships can be subdivided into two types: natural (biological) marital relationships, in which the function is to marry, and fictive marital relations, in which the function is to reproduce offspring. Natural marital relationships functions in the following four ways according to the female's status.

1. *Sex-driven relationships.* They do not have a steady relationship, only haphazard sexual intercourse. This is similar to temporal marriage (as a form of marriage) and promiscuity (as a form of spousal relationships).
2. *Possessive relationships.* The female is perceived as a possession of the male. Compared to the sex-driven relationship, this results in a relatively stable relationship. This is similar to marriage by capture and marriage by purchase (as forms of marriage) and polygyny (as a form of spouse relationship).
3. *Subordinate relationships.* There are two types. In the first type, the husband sees his wife as a person (not as a property) but the

relation is not yet equal. In the second type, the wife sees her husband as a person, but the relationship is not yet equal. These relationships are found in marriage by servitude, polygyny, and polyandry.

4. *Equal relationships.* The husband and the wife acknowledge each other's personality and interact with each other on equal terms. They differentiate their roles according to their natural aptitude, without hierarchical order. This would occur in marriage by contract and monogamy.

The artificial spousal relationship also has two types based on the degree of complexity. It differs from natural spousal relationships, and occurs at a relatively higher stage of evolution since it requires human consciousness and intention. The first type is *simple relationships* with the goal of reproduction. It corresponds mainly with the marriage by servitude or higher form of marriage, although it can also be seen in the elementary form of marriage. The second is *complex relationships* where the goal is not only reproduction but also maintaining the family. In *artificial-complex relationships* the husband and the wife collaborate on running the household and caring for children. This type of relationship can be further subdivided into two types, according to the scale of family that is to be maintained. The first type is the *elementary-complex relationships,* which has the goal of maintaining the nuclear family. In the second type, *advanced-complex relationships,* the goal is having the various clan lineages work together to maintain the most important lineage. The most highly developed *advanced-complex relationship* can be seen in the state system based on hereditary rule. In some cases this type of clan society can be maintained in modern, public law-guided state systems. The Japanese *Imperial Household Law* is the most well-known example of this.

Spencer and other Western scholars neglected the functional aspect of spousal relationships. As a non-Westerner, I know that a large cultural difference exists in the functions of spousal relationships between the West and the East. In this section I intended to draw a rough sketch of the West-East difference. The following Figure IV.1 illustrates the three sections.

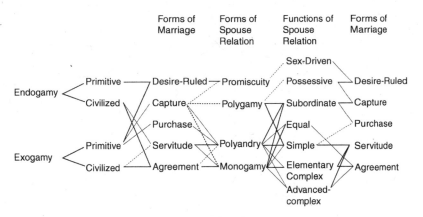

FIGURE IV.1. Summary of Forms of Marriage, Spousal Relationships, and Their Function

FORMS OF PARENT-CHILD RELATIONSHIP

Compared to the observation of the spousal relationships, the parent-child relationship is relatively easy to analyze, and we can more easily clarify the forms and functions of parent-child relationships. The forms of parent-child relationship can vary according to the parent's status, the child's status, and the combination of the two. The relationship between parent and child cannot be equal, since the child is subordinate to the parent from his/her birth until maturity. There are five forms of parent-child relationships based on who is recognized by the child as the head of the family.

1. *No-head relationships*. At the most primitive stage, there is no distinct relationship between the parent and the child, except the natural fact that they are the parent and the child. But this is just a logical abstraction. Even in a quite primitive stage of natural society the child must be nursed and cared for by the parent.
2. *Mother-oriented relationships*. The parental authority is assigned to the mother. In the early stage of the child's life he/she cannot live without the mother. In addition, in the primitive stage of so-

cial evolution, the father has a relatively weak tie with the child when compared to ties with the mother. But the primitive forms of marriage, the temporal, capture, and purchase forms, and the promiscuity and polygamous forms of spousal relationships, often obstruct the mother-child relationship. Polyandry is probably the best-suited form of spousal relationship for maintaining a stable mother-directed relationship. In polyandry, the family name is often the same as their totem and is inherited according to matrilineal order. Polyandry usually gives rise to political matriarchy. But it seems that there is no causal relationship between matrilineal inheritance and political matriarchy.

3. *Father-oriented relationships*. The parental authority is mainly assigned to the father. Usually this does not mean deprivation of the mother's authority.[17] The father-directed relationship is suitable for all forms of marriage and spousal relationships other than polyandry. The father-oriented relationship is established at the higher stages of social evolution. The more social evolution proceeds, the more character-building becomes important. In the father-directed society, the family name is inherited according to patrilineal order. This succession often accompanies ancestor worship. As a historical fact, patrilineal inheritance and patriarchy seem to occur together.

4. *Parent-oriented relationships*. The father and the mother equally have parental authority toward their child. This seems to arise only when the society adopts monogamy as a form of marriage. It is difficult to maintain the parent-directed relationship in polygamous and polyandrous circumstances.

5. *Family-oriented relationships*. In the advanced-complex, artificial relationships, people consider the family, not the separate members, to be most important. This can also be called *state-oriented relationships* when the society reached to the evolutionary stage of a national society that maintains a hierarchical system of lineage, as Japan does today.

Now we have completed the description of the five forms of parent-child relationships. As noted, every form has strong correlation with the spousal relationship forms. Every moral viewpoint and legislation concerning family is derived from the forms of family relationships described above.

Alexis Giraud-Teulon (1884) described the forms of family relation-tion as follows. At the beginning, there might be the system of com-munal family and no-head relationships based on promiscuity. As social differentiation proceeded, a system of marriage arose. The mother-oriented relationship has strong affinity with brother-sister marriage. The origin of the father-oriented relationship was often ful-filled through the mother's lineage with the uncle fulfilling this role. According to Giraud-Teulon's theory, there are quite a few rules set by the natural order concerning the human family.

Kovalevsky (1890) does not agree with Giraud-Teulon, and he almost negates the historical existence of promiscuity and no-head relationships. At the same time he criticizes Maine for not recogniz-ing that Semites also experienced the era of the mother-oriented rela-tionships. The vestige of this can be found in the oldest code of Hammurabi and the various records of the Moors of that era. Accord-ing to Kovalevsky's theory, the mother-oriented relationships were universally observed in every ancient society without exception. He proposes a three-stage theory of the evolution of the family: the mat-rimonial system, the patrimonial system, and the individualist sys-tem. The individualist system is the family system that is based on marriage by agreement and monogamy. And he warns that today the individualist system of family destroys the blood-bound and the territory-bound systems in the Western societies (see Kovalevsky, 1890, pp. 37-138).

Lippert (1884) clearly distinguishes *Mutterrecht* [political matri-archy] from *Mutterfolge* [matrilinieal inheritance], and proposes that political matriarchy developed under the matrilineal circumstance. He also believes that the mother-oriented relationship existed before the establishment of patriarchy. Ernst Grosse (1896) also distin-guished between the inheritance and the political power. His term *Gynëkokratie* [gynococracy, a society ruled by women] means the combination of matrilineal inheritance and political matriarchy.

Hellward says polyandry was not necessary in the transition pro-cess from matriarchy to patriarchy. Karl Kavtsky sees the levirate marriage, in which a man's widow marries his brother, as a vestige of polyandry. Hellward sees the levirate as an early form of patriarchy

since it often accompanies the notion of inheritance. I think the
levirate is a marital system that arose in the transitional period from
matriarchy to patriarchy.

Johann Richard Mucke has a unique view on the above issues
(1895). He criticizes the past studies as too speculative. For him the
research materials should be given not from archeological data but
contemporary primitives. He takes the research materials from contemporary Hawaii. The Hawaiian language does not distinguish between one's sister and brother. The language distinguishes brother-
sister relationships by age, but not by gender (see Mucke, 1895).

So, according to Mucke, the initial differentiation of human relationships was made not according to sexes, but ages. I think Mucke's
theory is original and interesting, but it does not have sufficient power
to overthrow the standard theories.

FUNCTIONS OF PARENT-CHILD RELATIONSHIPS

We can distinguish the functions of parent-child relationships into
four types.

1. *No relationship.* There exists no stable relationship except the
   biological fact that there is a blood relationship. This might be
   seen only in the early primitive stage of promiscuity and the no-
   head relationships.
2. *Possessive relationships.* The parent sees the child as a kind of
   property. In the possessive relationship, the parent rules the child
   in all aspects of life. This corresponds to the mother-oriented relationship and the father-oriented relationship. It is not suitable
   for monogamy, the parent-oriented relationship, and the family-
   oriented relationship.
3. *Ruling relationship.* Unlike in the possessive relationship, the
   parent rules the child in some aspects of life. This is not similar
   to the no-head relation, but it does correspond to the mother-oriented and the father-oriented relationships. The parent-oriented
   relationship may also be consistent with the ruling relationship,
   but it is rare. The family-oriented relationship is not compatible
   with the ruling relationship.

4. *Egalitarian relationship.* The parent recognizes the child as a person; the child can develop his/her personality at his/her discretion in some degree. Of course the human personality is developed through the gradual process of growth. So in reality the relationship between parent and child cannot be equal. The parent acknowledges that the child shall acquire his or her personality some day. This is not consistent with the no-head, mother-oriented, or father-oriented relationship. This corresponds to the parent-oriented and the family-oriented relationship.

The parent-child relationship transforms itself according to the growth of the child. When the child becomes equal to the parent, the parent emancipates the child. It is often the case that society makes a legal distinction between childhood and adulthood.

I think that past family studies were in error for focusing on the debate between paternal and nonpaternal theory, without a systematic analysis of marital, spousal, and parent-child relationships. The debate had many defects. Sometimes it neglected the basic difference between natural and artificial relationships and rushed to conclude that the evolution of relationships was based on exogamy and endogamy. In addition, no attention was given to the difference between the parent-oriented and family-oriented relationships. I think those defects have resulted from the westerner's lack of knowledge of Eastern cultures.

It seems that the basic historical assumption of Christian creation theory has been penetrating the westerner's mind, even the scholar's mind. Their sociological theories of family reflect this. I also do not understand why they try to explain ancient social conditions directly from the life of contemporary primitives.

I consider it to be unacceptable that Westerners look down on polygamy and polytheism as uncivilized, regardless of the fact that the ancient Greeks, their spiritual ancestor, practiced these customs. I need to note that their mental view of the wall between the pre-Christian (the savage) and the post-Christian (the civilized) is now duplicated in their views toward current relationships between Christian and non-Christian societies. This is not appropriate for academic discussions. I'm afraid that this tendency shall be rather enforced by their studies of contemporary Japan and China.

BROTHERHOOD (SIBLING RELATIONSHIPS)

The forms of brotherhood can be classified into two kinds: natural and artificial. And each kind can be subdivided into two types: equal and unequal.

1. *Natural-equal relationships.* Without any distinct system of family, there might not be any clear form of brotherhood. This corresponds to promiscuity and no-head relationships between parent and child.
2. *Natural-unequal relationships.* As the spousal system and parent-child system become more distinct, the brotherhood becomes more differentiated according to age and gender. This corresponds primarily to polyandry and polygyny (Mucke, 1895), and this inequality results in conflict among brothers and sisters.
3. *Artificial-equal relationships.* After the establishment of the family system and parent-child relations, the simple equality among brothers/sisters arises. This often corresponds with the parent-oriented relationships because among brothers and sisters the traditional rules of power based on gender and age do not operate.
4. *Artificial-unequal relationships.* Among brothers/sisters, the specific age and gender is important. This corresponds to family-oriented relationships.

There is another classification of brotherhood: brotherhood by different father, brotherhood by different mother, and perfect brotherhood that corresponds to monogamy. The functions of brotherhood can be classified into four kinds according to the forms of brotherhood.

1. *No relationship.* There exists no stable relationship among children except that they are biologically related. There can be no inner-brother/sister conflict.
2. *Self-directed relationships.* Each child attempts to maximize his/her advantage in family matters.
3. *Autonomous relationships.* In the artificial-equal relationship, children become aware of the equality among them.
4. *Orderly relationships.* Sharing the goals of the family—that is, maintenance of the lineage—is an area in which children cooper-

ate with each other. This is the most organized, systematic brotherhood. The brotherhood functions as a branch of the family and clan system.

CLAN RELATIONSHIPS

The clan relationship and its system develop from brotherhoods. As the generations proceed, they branch off from the original lineages and become complex. Finally they see each other as if they do not share blood, and get married. The clan relation can be classified into two types.

Natural relationships. This is an extension of brotherhood and it has no definite form of relationships or hierarchical order among lineages. As the human consciousness develops, the artificial relationships are established on the foundation of the natural relationship.

Artificial relationships. In this form of clan relationship, people consciously maintain the lineage and the clan. Artificial relationships can be classified into two types: equal relationships and unequal relationships. In the equal relationship, lineages communicate on equal terms. This type of relationship does not result in further differentiation of society. However, in an unequal relationship further social differentiation occurs, but because they share the goal of maintaining the most important lineage, they cooperate with each other.

As a historical fact there is scarce evidence to prove the existence of the clan society that is in the artificial-equal relationships. It seems that equal relationships dilute the clan society itself. Society seems to grow and differentiate itself often with hierarchical inequality. In the artificial-equal clan relationships, the various lineages communicate with each other voluntarily and on a temporary basis. In artificial-unequal clan relationships, each lineage has its own task and obeys the ruling lineage. The complete artificial society is one in which the state system arises from the development of the artificial-unequal clan relationships.

Today the study of clan and tribe has just begun. As Engels and Morgan observed, the Ancient Roman *Gens* was a medium of family system and state system. The observation of the Eastern society and the comparative study of Western-Eastern cultures will contribute considerably to this scholarship.

THE RELATIONSHIP BETWEEN FAMILY
AND SOCIETY

Above we have completed the classification and analysis of family systems. In this section we will clarify the relation between family and society.

The analytical unit of society is not the individual but the family. This is a universal truth in all societies at all stages of societal evolution. The individual is of course an important element of society. But simple accumulation of individuals cannot constitute society. It is false to think that future social evolution will lead to the dissolution of the family system and the rise of the individual. There are four reasons for this position.

1. Society cannot sustain itself without sexual reproduction. And it is a major function of the family system, the various forms of marriage, the spousal system, and parent-child relationships, to control reproduction. A society that does not adequately support reproduction can not avoid extinction. In this respect, the evolution of the family system is equal to increasing the probability of reproduction. Thus, the family system can transform itself, but the family system in general will not become extinct.

2. In the cultivated forms of society, a major function of family system is to raise the children. Highly differentiated society can provide certain subsystems other than family to bring up the child, for example the temple and the orphanage, but even today those are understood as substitutes for the family system. In this respect, the family system endures the advancement of society.

3. The family system has long been a major stage for sex role differentiation and collaboration. Sexual difference is the most distinct natural difference among mankind,[18] so it seemed to contribute to the initial differentiation of social roles. As civilization proceeded, sex role differentiation, like many other modes of role differentiation, became more distinct, more complex, and more harmonious. Later development tended to abolish some parts of the sex role differentiation in the family system.

4. As a historical fact, society could not maintain itself without the family system. From natural society to consent-based society,

from village to city, societies of all types are maintained through their family system. Although in the future there may be something not yet experienced, the family has long been a major system that functions to maintain society.

Therefore the analytical unit of society is the family. Without the family system, society could not arise and develop. The development of society stimulates the development of the family system, and vice versa. The development of the individual is, of course, a major effect of social evolution. But it does not mean the individuals can constitute society without sex role differentiation and collaboration in the family system. Individualism is a fallacious fantasy.

Comte, Le Play, and Coulange see the family as the analytical unit of society. Worms takes the individualist stand. Spencer and Maine argue that society transforms itself from family-based to individual-based. Engels pointed out that women could not be emancipated until they not only took part in the household but also in the labor market (Engels, 1886, p. 126). The social status of women is a big issue that occupies a major part of family problems. This will be explored in the next section. Is it possible to emancipate women while maintaining the family system? Does the improvement of women's social status necessarily accompany the decline of the family system? My answer differs from that of Spencer and Maine.

THE SOCIAL STATUS OF WOMEN

Women's social status is closely correlated with the forms of family system such as the forms of marriage, spousal and parent-child relationship. Under polyandry and mother-oriented conditions, the status of the female was quite high. But generally speaking, throughout human history, women's status has been lower than that of men because of the differences in physical ability. However, today, under monogamous and parent-oriented or family-oriented conditions, we need to address to the problem of how to improve the social status of women.

The social status of women is determined by two conditions: a priori and a posteriori. The a priori condition consists of physical, mental, and social factors.

Compared to men, women have the following nine physiological characteristics:

1. Women mature physically sooner than do men.
2. Womens' bodies are more flexible. Their small muscle control is greater, but they are not as strong.
3. Women have a smaller appetite.
4. Women have sensitive nerves, so they tire sooner than do men.
5. Women have a considerably heavier reproduction burden than do men.
6. Women's reproductive organs mature earlier and cease functioning earlier than do men.
7. Women live longer than men after the reproductive period ceases.
8. Women have mammary glands so are able to nurse their babies. Men cannot suckle the baby.
9. Throughout their reproductive period, women menstruate.

Those are women's inborn physiological characteristics. Men should respect women's physiological characteristics.

From a psychological perspective, women's intelligence develops sooner than men's. They have a good memory and imagination, but are weak in calculation and reasoning. Their moral sentiment is quite strong, but their will power is often weaker. In sum, they are weaker in controlling feelings, but they are superior in expressing them. The social characteristic of women is based on their sex roles. Men and women have differentiated social roles and collaborate with each other. First, the most important goal of their collaboration is reproduction. There are big differences among societies in the forms and status of the reproductive collaboration, based on their degree of social development. But no society can maintain itself without some form of the reproductive role differentiation and collaboration. Also women have a natural ability to raise children.

Women fulfill these two very important social roles in the family system. And, the family system requires the women's devotion rather than males. Furthermore, women's psychological characteristics fit very well for nursing children. From the above reasons, women have a special status in the family system. In some sense, they have been bound to the household. However, women may have a potential to fulfill some social roles other than wife-mother roles. As mentioned above, there exists a big natural difference between male and female. But it is also true that female and male have a common nature as human beings. Women's intellectual ability has gradually improved as a result of the modern general education system. In fact, women who utilize their talents for nonfamily activity are increasing. In the near future we may establish a certain social system that substitutes the mother's role entirely.

There are acquired conditions of women's social status. Occupation is the most important factor shaping a women's position in society. Today there is no restriction on women's choice of occupation. Historically, women have been relegated to occupations that have been defined as appropriate for women but as social differentiation proceeds, this is lessening. We can distinguish two types of female occupations. One is female specific, the other is universal. The universal type of occupation is disadvantageous for women, because it is clear that women cannot be given the same treatment as males in universal competition. On the other hand, female specific types of occupation are necessary for the maintenance of society. The wife-mother roles shall be kept indispensable as long as the family is the basic unit of society. So the improvement of women's status should be based on this indispensability and the diffusion of humanity.[19]

The second acquired factor is the private property right that could be seen in every civilized society. It has equal importance with occupation. If everyone belongs to a certain family, there is no need for individuals to have private property. However, in some instances people lose family members and are without kin. In these cases the individuals need to have their own resources. That is to say a female does not need her own private property as long as she has certain status among family members. But circumstances could arise that result in her need to live alone. So it is improper to negate their private property right (see Collet, 1902; Leroy-Beaulieu, 1888). Both Leroy-Beaulieu and Collet insisted that the newly arising service industries should be opened for females to establish the universal equality among sexes.

The social status of women is defined according to the above conditions and factors. Women's social status shall decline if we shut them out of their families, give them disadvantageous occupations, and put them in direct competition with men. If the emancipation of females lacks the development of their ability, they shall suffer severe consequences (Gunther, 1898; Legouvé, 1864; Rabutaux, 1851).

The equality between sexes should be accompanied with the cultivation of women's potentials. The cultivation should be harmonized with the development of the family system. Women can only be emancipated within the family system in a family-centered society. Consider that it is women who carry out two main functions of family: giving birth and nursing the child. The negative consequence of female's labor is bigger than that of male. If we mishandle this issue, not only women but also men lose chances to show their inborn ability. In sum, the male's main domain is outside the family, while the female's main domain is inside the family.

Women's social status should be equal to that of men but should not be the same. If we mistakenly expect men and women to be the same in all respects, this lessens the women's status in society. The universalization of labor should be gradually developed according to the level or depth of the division of labor. As the division of labor proceeds many new types of occupations arise, production efficiency is improved, housework is reduced, and spare time increases. Women can use this spare time in the labor force thus dividing their occupations. Once again, the equality between sexes is not the same thing as the sameness between them, and the sphere of women's labor should be expanded in accordance with their reduction in the level of housework.

There have been many Westerner's studies on the social status of women. John Stuart Mill (1870) was a dedicated scholar who wrote a book that focused on this subject. As he himself warned, this book expressed his personal belief that is derived from his experience and contemplation. He argued that legally justified oppression of women is an obstacle not only for individuals but also for the development of humanity. There must be absolute equality—without any privileges or difference in aptitude—between the sexes.

Recently, the Spanish scholar Eduardo Sanz y Escartin (1893) shows a quite moderate view on this issue. A German scholar August Bebel (1891) studied various social problems facing women. Havelock Ellis (1890) provided a brilliant contribution and noted that we do not have enough data to decide each issue. Jacques Lourbet (1900), Eduard Reich (1875), Hermann Ploss and Max Bartels (1902), and Max Runge (1896) attempted to study the inborn characteristics of females and proposed some solutions for this problem. These were great advances in methodology. They suggest the defeat of the metaphysical theory of equality (all aspects of conditions being equal), and the victory of the scientific theory of equality (a more moderate view).

Notes

PART I:
OVERVIEW OF JAPANESE HISTORY
AND SOCIOLOGY

I.1. Society and Family: A Brief Overview
of the History of Japan

1. I wish to acknowledge S. Alex Takeuchi for reviewing several versions of this chapter, locating and translating/interpreting numerous articles, and attempting to explain the various leadership roles in Japanese history. Any errors in reporting this information are those of the author.

2. The Chronicles note the first recorded contact with Japan as a country. Other older Chinese records such as *Wei Chih* had already noted contact and trade with the Japanese in some 100 small kingdoms in about 100 BCE (Kasahara, 1988). In 239 CE, Queen Himiko, ruler of Yamato, sent her younger brother to visit the China's imperial court of the Wei dynasty where he received a gold seal from the emperor (Schirokauer, 1993; Churchill, 2005).

3. Articles reporting newly found artifacts indicating habitation as early as 500,000 BCE have proven to be a hoax. See Oda and Keally (1986) for an extensive review.

4. Soga and Mononobe were separate ruling clans. During the Soga family's rule, the Nakatomi family emerged as a third political power in the imperial government. The chief of the Nakatomi clan, a faithful servant to Crown prince Nakano Oe, opposed the government's official adoption of Buddhism. As the supreme bishop of Shintoism under the new government's policy, he could not expect to gain more political power unless he eliminated the powerful Soga clan (and their support of Buddhism). Nakatomi conspired with Crown prince Nakano-Oe, assassinated the chief of the Soga clan (Soga no Iruka), and removed all Soga members from government positions—an event called the Taika Reform. Crown prince Nakano-Oe succeeded to the throne and Nakatomi no Kamatari, the chief of the Nakatomi clan, was promoted as prime minister of the imperial government and given a new surname, Fujiwara, by the new emperor. This is the beginning of the ruling of the Fujiwara clan that lasted into the Heian period (Churchill, 2005; Kasahara, 1988, 2001).

Japanese Family and Society
© 2007 by The Haworth Press, Inc. All rights reserved.
doi:10.1300/5840_12

5. Empresses who ascended to throne had always been considered as intermediate or temporary successors to the throne for political reasons but never as "successors of the imperial lineage." There were a total of eight empresses in Japanese history who sat on the throne; two of them served as empress on two separate occasions. The last two empresses, Meisho and Go-Sakuramachi, ascended the thrones in 1629 and 1762 respectively (Kasahara, 2001; Takinami, 2004).

6. The transformation of the position of *Seii Tai Shogun* (Shogun) into the Military Governor/Ruler of the nation did not occur until much later (Imatani, 1993; Okano, 2003). It was in 1192 when Minamoto no Yoritomo received this title and was also granted the full military and police authorities to govern the nation on behalf of the emperor.

7. A clarification of terms is useful. *Samurai* (or *bushi*) basically means "the advantage class of warriors" who ruled premodern Japan on the basis of military power. *Daimyō*, a subcategory of samurai, were the highest ranking and the most powerful members of the samurai class. During the Edo period, only members of the samurai/bushi were allowed to wear one long sword and a short sword together. *Chonin,* the merchant class, were not allowed this privilege. *Shogun* was the official military position created and authorized by the Imperial government. It was the commander-in-chief/commander general of all national military forces commission to govern the nation on behalf of the Emperor. Those who were appointed to the position of *Shogun* were among the most powerful members of the *daimyō*, who also acted as kings of their own territories (Takeuchi, October 23, 2005, personal communication).

8. Schirokauer (1993) notes that the origins of the Kemmu Restoration can be traced to the family dispute between two branches regarding the succession of the throne. The resolution to the disputed succession was to alternate the throne, but Go-Daigo wanted his family line to retain succession and this produced a split within the shogunate.

9. See Imatani (1993) and Okano (2003) for a fuller explanation.

10. In 1464, Yoshimasa designated his brother as the successor, but the next year, his wife gave birth to a son. The wife, backed by a powerful provincial governor's family wanted her son to inherit the title. Yoshimasas's brother, supported by another powerful family, wanted to inherit the title. The conflict resulted in the ten-year Ōnin War which destroyed the Ashikaga shogunate's power base.

11. The Ashikaga Shogun retained his title for an additional five years, but was deposed.

12. Chu Hsi emphasized study whereas the competing Lu-Wang approach was based on using intuition as a mechanism for cultivating the mind.

13. Other changes also occurred during the period of occupation. The basic components of the civil code radically changed and parental rights and rights of the head of the family were no longer part of the code. Primogeniture, which strengthened the position of the eldest son, was replaced with equal inheritance rights for all children. Land reforms that created independent farmers, instead of the land being held by the head of the family, weakened the solidarity of the extended family and urbanization resulted in increased social mobility (Ishida, 1971).

I.2. The Founding Fathers of Japanese Sociology

1. In 1868, the Bakufu's Research Center of the Western Literature was reorganized and renamed the Kaisei School. In 1877, the Kaisei School was merged with the Tokyo Medical School and became the University of Tokyo.

2. The systematic oil production in Niigata began in 1874. But the existence of "flammable water" was known earlier, and it was used as substitute for rape-seed oil for light.

3. Sadao Takebe's date of birth was either 1835 or 1836.

4. At this time, the University of Tokyo was the *only* university legally existing in Japan. Other imperial universities such as Kyoto, Kyushu, and Tohoku Universities were established in 1897-1911. Private universities were legally approved still later in 1918.

5. According to Comte, sociology should be the highest form of knowledge in the hierarchy of sciences. Comte sociology integrated various scientific findings— from astronomy, physics, biology to political economy, logic, and ethics—into a single system.

6. Takebe's work stimulated the writing of other scholarly works in sociology. In the 1920s and 1930s, Japanese sociology scholars produced two outstanding contributions to the history of sociological thought. Tetsuji Kada's (1928) *Kinse Shakai-gaku Seiritushi* [Formative History of the Modern Sociology] was a standard history of modern representations of society; from social contract, via market economy to crowd, mass, and race.

Ikutaro Shimizu's (1936) *Shakai to Kojin: Shakaigaku Seiritsushi* [Society and Individual: A Study on the Formative History of Sociology], dealt with the modern formation of the concepts "society" and "individual" within the seventeenth century natural law theories. Together with Tongo Takebe's *General Sociology,* I believe that these three works represent the finest classical sociological works written by Japanese scholars.

7. *Studies of Contemporary Social Problems* was comprised of the following twenty-five titles: (1) *Modern Civilization* (2) *Poverty* (3) *Labor Problems* (4) *Urban Problems* (5) *Rural Problems* (6) *The Food Problem* (7) *Problems concerning Private Property* (8) *Social Welfare in Japan* (9) *Crime* (10) *Revolution and Propaganda* (11) *Public Morals* (12) *Problems surrounding Woman* (13) *Population Problem* (14) *Health Issues* (15) *Racial Problems* (16) *Colonial Problems* (17) *Peace Issues* (18) *National Defense* (19) *Political Reform* (20) *Class Problems* (21) *Family System* (22) *Religions* (23) *The Spirit of the Time* (24) *National Society* (25) *Bibliography and Index.*

8. According to Takebe's vitae written in his own hand, he was nominated for the vice presidency of The International Institute of Sociology in 1923. But I have not been able to verify this information (T. Sako).

9. Le Bureau Interparliamentaire, 1927: *Compte Rendu de la XXIV Conference tenue à Paris,* Paris; Librairie Payot, p. 216. September 1927 issue of *Le Monde Illustré,* p. 151, reported that Takebe argued with other delegates over the major problems in the contemporary world economy and international finance.

PART II:
THEORETICAL INTRODUCTION

II.1. Society

1. Spencer's *First Principles* (1862) and especially his *Study of Sociology* (1873) is devoted to the prolegomenon. Also see the first chapter of his *Social Statics* (1851).

2. See also de Roberty, 1881; Durkheim, 1895; Giddings, 1896, 1897, 1901; Fouillée, 1880; Gumplowicz, 1885, 1892a; Lestrade, 1889; Lilienfeld, 1873-1881, 1898, Ward, 1883, 1898, 1897-1899 attached great importance to this approach; Schäffle, 1875-1878; Simmel, 1892, 1895; Stein, 1897; Worms,1895a, 1895b, 1896a, 1896b).

3. I will provide a detailed explanation of this in the next book *General Sociology* vol. 2, *Social Logic*, 1905, Part 4, Chapter 1. Considérant (1841) took the same definition and said "La société = La collection des individus qui vivent en société."

4. This is not rare. For example, jurists sometimes mistake rights for persons who hold these rights. Classical economists focused on wealth, disregarding living people. Doctors can mistake human life for the body it occupies.

5. Just as some feel comfortable when the wind blows, others find it disturbing.

6. Unfortunately, there are two ways in which the papers in the *American Journal of Sociology* lacked adequate preparation. One way resulted from authors who attempted to resolve practical problems without any theoretical grounding. It seems to me that they used very superficial evidence to hastily develop their solutions to problems. Another way resulted from Christian socialists and Christian sociologists who, in an attempt to advertise their dogmatic teaching, disguise themselves as sociologists. I think they have had the most harmful influence on the advancement of sociological study.

7. Mackenzie (1890, p. 164) categorizes the bodies into five kinds: (1) Monadism, (2) Monism, (3) Mechanism, (4) Chemism, and (5) Organism. And he defines the organism that "A whole whose parts are intrinsically related to it, which develops from within, and has reference to an end that is involved in its own nature." I think this definition is excellent. I have not addressed why mechanism precedes chemism.

8. Durkheim (1893) provided a detailed explanation of organizations. He categorized solidarity into "mechanical," "organic," and "contractual," and pointed out that society cannot be established by "contractual solidarity." He also stressed the need for a division of labor that is based on solidarité organique. Spencer was of course aware of the importance of organizations, but he tended to approve the contractual solidarity as noted by Durkheim. De Greef (1886, 1889, vol.1 p. 214) classified the social phenomena from the viewpoint of organization.

9. Adam Smith (1776) began the closer examination of the division of labor. Recently John Stuart Mill (1848) established the more general conception of "cooperation" and introduced Adam Smith's economic idea into social study.

10. Logically speaking, there is no limit to the growth of its population. Actually the climate determines the upper limit of growth.

11. There are many symptoms of social organicism in the tradition of Chinese philosophy. For instance *Yi-Jing* treated natural reason as equivalent to human reason. [Yi-Jing dates back to the twelfth century BCE compiled his information around the first to second century CE. Eds.] Much later, although not based on scientific procedures, Zhu-xi (1130-1200) and Wang Yang-ming (1472-1528) made a carefully detailed analogy of human society with living creatures. Needless to say, the intellectuals from the Tokugawa period (1600-1867) were heavily indebted to such Chinese philosophical thoughts. Ancient Japanese myths although vague, contain ideas similar to the social organicism.

12. A Spanish scholar Santamaria de Paredes directs his attention to this point. Santamaria de Paredes (1896). *El Concepto de Organismo Social*, Madrid. [Manusmriti is an oldest scripture of Brahmanism and Hinduism, compiled in 200 CE. It is composed of twelve chapters, 2,684 articles describing cosmology, religion, morals and legislations, each caste's rituals and customs. For the translated version see Doniger (tr.), 1991. Eds.]

13. Leviathan is the equivalent of commonwealth state (in Latin, *Civitas*, means artificial, man-made person). Sovereign is its brain, administrators are its joints, and rewards and punishments are its nerves.

14. Spencer (1876-1896), (vol. 1, Part 2, chapter 2) pointed out the similarities between society and an organism. (1) Continuing growth. (2) Quantitative growth and differentiation of organs. (3) Differentiation of functions. (4) Systematic correlation between diverse functions. So it is not inconvenient to call society an organism. He also clarified the differences between society and organism. First, in creatures, the components are found close to each other. In society, the components are far from each other. Second, in society, transport facilities connect its components. It makes society a unified living body. Third, creatures have particular organization for sense and reason which society does not have. In society, each component has senses and reasons, so democracy must arise as an ideal of social life. I think highly of his effort to clarify the conceptual relationships between the political body and the biological body, but there are three points to be improved. First, his arguments on the social ideal are not satisfactorily connected to his functional analysis. Second, he tended to underestimate the functional differences between the political body and the biological body. We should clarify the characteristics of a political body more closely by investigating the functional differences of both. Third, his thought sometimes lapsed into unrefined analogy between some real society and some real living creature.

15. De Greef pointed out the difference between organism and super-organism in twelve points. (1) In an organism each component cannot live independently. In a super-organism it can. (2) In organisms, the life of the body is in great peril when just one component is damaged. In a super-organism it is not so. (3) The longevity of a super-organism is longer than that of an organism. (4) Society changes both rapidly and slowly. (5) Differentiation of the components is more conspicuous in society than in an organism. (6) Differentiated organizations are reconciled by the relative autonomy of each component. (7) Organism and society reproduc

and grow in their own in different ways. (8) Society grows beyond the limits that an organism has. (9) Contrary to organisms in society, the degree of internal differentiation is proportional to its degree of reproductive capacity. (10) In an organism, organizations correlate only simultaneously. In society, it is not necessarily so. For example, we can regain some once-lost information on traditions via archeological findings. (11) Components of society are not only humans, but also inorganic matter. (12) The minimum unit of an organism, the cell, is so simple. The minimum unit of society, the individual, is so complex and intelligent. See also Herbert Spencer.

16. Currently most of the other sociologists also ignore the naïve equation of organism and society. A good example can be seen in Mackenzie (1890) in England, Giddings (1901) in the United States, Ratzenhofer (1893a, 1993b) in Germany, Ludwig Stein (1897) in Switzerland, and Carl Menger (1883) in Austria.

17. I will make this point clearer later in Takebe, 1905. Society is an organism, but this fact does not indicate that all societies have complex institutions. The social body also has its own personality, but this fact does not indicate that all societies have highly developed personalities. Needless to say, primitive society has a different kind of consciousness than civilized society. In addition, it is clearly false that society has a higher personality than that of individuals.

18. Haeckel (1868) suggests that a child's consciousness not only comes from his parents' consciousness, but is also affected by society's consciousness. Fouillée understood social consciousness as the integrated consciousnesses of individuals.

19. As in China, natural sciences had not developed because they could not outgrow their dependence on the dogma of "five forces" (e.g., wood, fire, soil, metal, and water).

20. The Buddhist perspective of the Universe often contradicts the two ways (modes). One is the ordinary common sense view of the universe and the other is a philosophical view.

21. [In 1828, German chemist Friedrich Wöhler obtained urea (H_2NCONH_2) for the first time by the synthesis of ammonia compounds. Later French chemist Bertley generated formic acid (HCOOH) by pouring carbon monoxide (CO) into a hot solution of caustic potash (KOH). These examples suggest that there is no definite distinction between organic and inorganic matter. Eds.]

22. Lilienfeld (1898) noted at the opening of his *Zur Vertheidigung der organischen Methode in der Sociologie,* Chapter 1, that human races even during the primitive stage of development had social interaction with each other and acquired its physical and mental ability through social intercourses with others.

23. In Ludwig Stein's (1897, p. 481) *Die soziale Frage im Lichte der Philosophie* there is a citation in Leeds. Tarde (1890a) posed his own definition of society. And Comte's definition of society is, I think, of course, proper, but it is verbose. Comte said that there are two kinds of society. (1) From a natural basis, humans continually developed their ability through evolution, connected to each other by the tie of trustworthiness. (2) A multitude of individuals cooperate and are united to each other on the basis of universal equality, laws, and institutions which are led by the light of reason. Tarde defined society as; multitude of individuals who assimilate their behavior with each other, or the individuals who actually behave similarly. I think this definition catches the heart of society but it is too brief. Tönnies (1887) tried to clar-

ify a difference between two kinds of society—*Gemeinschaft* and *Gesellschaft*. Both are human groups composed of people who are similar to each other and cooperate with each other. However, *Gesellschaft* is constituted by isolated individuals, unlike *Gemeinschaft* which is constituted of individuals with a common consciousness. I think this is a very refined definition of the concept of society, but Tönnies could not analyze *Gemeinschaft* thoroughly.

24. Karl Wasserrab (1900) distinguished the usages of the concept of society as follows. First, there are groups of people that are not a mere crowd, but at least appear as if they share common rules. Second, there are the people who live under the protection and domination of a scripted code. Third, there are people who share certain aims and collaborate with each other. The fourth, are the social phenomena that are distinguished from the political. Finally, human intercourse can be viewed on a contractual basis. Wasserrab suggests several characteristics, but I think his discussion lacks academic rigor.

II.2. Sociology

1. [Like the German term *Wissenschaft*, the Japanese word *Gakumon* can indicate both learning in general, and learning in scientific inquiry, depending on the context used. Eds.]

2. People often dichotomize the *ideal* and the *real*, but I do not think this is proper. Ideal occurs in one's mind when he/she is not contented with the actual; that is, the ideal necessarily accompanies the volition to reform the actual. So reformation of the actual is the same thing as realization of the ideal. Here I employ the word progress to indicate the realization process of the ideal.

3. I do not want the reader to get the impression that nature and humans are antagonistic.

4. Ludwig Stein coined the word *"Wissenschaftlicher Imperativ."* From Comte onward, it has been the core of positive philosophy, and I believe it has also been the fundamental idea in Eastern thoughts. It was the great advancement in positive philosophy that Immanuel Kant employed *"Kategorischer Imperativ"* to indicate the connection between scientific knowledge and goal-attainment.

5. The ancient Chinese philosophers often spoke of the five procedures of knowing, questioning, thinking, telling, and acting.

6. Here I use the term "study" to indicate study or knowledge as a whole. As Comte said, this is the ultimate object of knowledge. Divisions of science are nothing more than human conventions.

7. The readers should note that this three-fold categorization of methodology appears as if it is derived from Hegel. But actually, I confess, it is derived from Comte.

8. Comte expressed it as "theological phase." But at that time, theology was not the sole source of human knowledge as there were also myths and fables. In this intellectual phase, society was in a primitive condition.

9. It is important to note that Westerners often overlook the harmfulness of traditional dogmatism. The intolerant dogmatism is also harmful to the advancement

of science. There are innumerable examples where religious belief, classic worship, and fanatic xenophiles have suppressed positive thinking.

10. Comte gave the name "metaphysical" to this phase of human intellectual evolution. Here "metaphysics" is roughly equivalent to "philosophy." But as Comte knew, there are some philosophical stands that overcame metaphysical drawbacks.

11. Ratzenhofer (1898) agreed with Comte and argued that the major characteristic of the metaphysical phase of human evolution is a satisfaction of one's thirst for knowledge. He also noted that fact-based investigation and pragmatic application of knowledge is a major characteristic of the positive phase. According to Ratzenhofer, Arthur Schopenhauer and Friedrich Nietzsche are the vestiges of the metaphysical phase. But he believed that Nietzsche's attempts to question metaphysics indicate the germination of positivism.

12. Ernst Haeckel (1868) eloquently criticizes the current German education system. He is concerned over the lack of harmony between idealistic education and practical knowledge. It is in the list Lacking practical knowledge, he said, theologians, jurists, rhetoricians, and historians are occupying all the important positions in the educational system.

13. [The *Six Arts* consists of *Yi Jing* [Book of Change], *Shu Jing* [Book of History], *Shi Jing* [Book of Odes], *Li Ching* [Book of Rites], *Yue Jing* [Book of Music], *Chun Qiu* [Spring and Autumn Annals]. Eds.]

14. The nine schools share the same origin, for example, the Chinese mythological stories of heroes. It is especially true in the case of Confucianism. [In the unprecedented era of cultural and intellectual prosperity during the *Spring and Autumn Period* (BCE 481-722) and the *Warring States Period* (BCE 221-403) in China, there were nine major schools of thought. Confucianism, Mohism (Mochism), Taoism (Daoism), Legalism, the School of Agriculture, Yin-yang School, Logicians School, the School of Vertical and Horizontal Alliance, and the School of Miscellaneous. Eds.]

15. Comte's disciples further expanded the two principles of "humanité" and "unité de science." Among them there are differences in the way one understands the "*méthode positive*." Littré and Carey especially paid great attention to the practical implications of study.

16. Arthur Bordier (1887) properly depicted this development. After Aristotle, sociology had been long hidden, just like natural history, by mysticism and superstitions. It was Quesnay and Mercier de la Riviére who uncovered it again. One of Condorcet's disciples, Adolphe Quételet (1848, 1869) argued that society develops according to the laws that rule the natural world. There is no essential difference between the heavenly body and human society. I think Bordier overemphasized the materialistic perspective, but he really knew that the notion of the universal consistency of reason had begun to be accepted by many modern scholars.

17. Carey (1872), especially in chapters 1-4, provided a detailed explanation on this issue. Also see Fiske (1874).

18. This is the mundane understanding of the relationship between humans and the universe.

19. Lu Hsiang-shan, as a comprehensive idealist, argued that all matter within the universe is a phenomenon that occurs in the human mind.

20. The recent unified philosophy (philosophy of integration, philosophy of unification) attempts to resolve the contradictions between those two stands.

21. See part I, chapter 1, section 8 of this book. Also, I will give a closer analysis on the concept of "evolution" in the forth volume of my work, Takebe (1918).

22. Hierarchy is not the same thing as system. Hierarchy is a kind of system.

23. I think of the technical terms of logic as subordinate, coordinate, and superordinate

24. I understand *logic* in the Kantian and Hegelian sense, for example, in its broadest sense. Also, here I understand "physics," "astronomy," "biology," and "sociology" in their broadest sense.

25. Astronomy is incapable of describing the role of life, human, and human thought in universal evolution. That is not to say astronomy is valueless. To describe the next stage of the evolution, we need another mode of thinking.

26. Comte (1830-1842 vol. 1, p. 7) drew the hierarchy of science as follows.

1. Science of inanimate things: (a) Mathematics. (b) Astronomy. (c) Physics.
   (d) Chemistry.
2. Science of animate things: (e) Physiology. (f) Social Physics.

27. Fouillée (1880, p. 411, 1896a, chap. 2, p. 18 "Hierarchie des Sciences Positivism, Pluralisme et Monisme Scientifique". Fouillée pointed out that the philosophical goal of the new science sociology is to integrate the cosmic theory and philosophy of history into single positivistic system. De Greef's (1886, vol. 1) system of science is made of the following: (1) mathematics, (2) kinetics (statics and dynamics), (3) physics, (4) chemistry and mineralogy, (5) astronomy, (6) geology, (7) biology, (8) psychology, (9) sociology. In this book (p. 5), De Greef says that when sociology is established, unquestionably it will be at the summit of the scientific pyramid. And, in this book (p. 92), he points out that sociology is a child between psychology and physiology. Coste (1899, p. 57) observed the great chain of various branches of science and the status of sociology within it. He showed the relationship between nine basic sciences by the diagram below [see table on the next page]. Coste is the former president of the Paris Sociological Association.

28. Herbert Spencer (1864). *Reasons for Dissenting from the Philosophy of M. Comte.* His system of science is as follows.

1. Sciences concerning the forms of human perception
   (a) Abstract Sciences
      (i) Logic and Mathematics
      (ii) Sciences concerning phenomenon that is perceived by human.
2. Sciences concerning phenomena
   (a) Abstract and Concrete Sciences (that deals with each part of the body)
      (i) Kinetics, Physics, Chemistry, etc.
   (b) Concrete Sciences (that deal with the body as a whole)
      (i) Astronomy, Geology, Biology, Physiology, and Sociology

29. There are numerous authors who are not worth mentioning—Simmel and Giddings are exceptions.

Subject Branches of Science	Quantity	Quality	Motion	Gravity	Molecular Motion	Affinity	Life	Society	Social Ideal
Arithmetic									
Arithmetic and Algebra	X								
Geometry	X	X							
Kinetics	X	X	X						
Physical									
Astronomy	X	X	X	X					
Physics	X	X	X	X	X				
Chemistry	X	X	X	X	X	X			
Organic									
Biology	X	X	X	X	X	X	X		
Sociology	X	X	X	X	X	X	X	X	
Ideology	X	X	X	X	X	X	X	X	X

30. George T. Ladd (1890). *Introduction to Philosophy,* New York; Scribner: chapter 1. Ladd enumerated a dozen definitions of philosophy. Formerly, Manshi Tokunaga, in *Tetsugaku Zasshi,* no.3, enumerated thirty-four definitions of philosophy by western thinkers, although this was not an academic article.

31. Spencer represents the third definition of philosophy, by distinguishing between "specified knowledge" and "unified knowledge," names the latter philosophy.

32. Even Hegel seemed to fall into this error. I regret that many contemporary German philosophers also make this error. So it is no wonder Nietzsche dealt a hard blow to them.

33. Medieval realism, as contrasted with nominalism, may be a good example.

34. It is often seen in Indian philosophy and western European religious teachings and theology.

35. Every branch of science has its own basic assumptions: for example, jurisprudence has a principle, economics has two principles, and ethics has concepts of person. Psychology has concepts of notion, the science of religion has concepts of god, and physics has concepts of matter and energy. Chemistry has concepts of atom and affinity, and astronomy has concepts of nebula and gravity. Mathematics has axioms.

36. Science and philosophy has been influencing each other.

37. Contemporary philosophy resembles sociology in attempting to provide general knowledge. But it is the result of the dissolution of philosophy into various branches of science. Today philosophy is the name for the residue of such dissolution, or else it is equated with knowledge in general. Spencer's (1862) *First Principles,* its first part *The Unknowable,* represents the philosophy as such a residue. And he understood the system of philosophy as the collection of scientific knowledge

(biological, sociological, and ethical). Comte and Hegel also follow the same line. As I discuss in this chapter, the philosophy as the residue is of no use by itself.

38. Ratzenhofer (1898, p. 5) excludes the other two. I think he oversimplifies the matter. He repeatedly emphasized the problematic relationship between "das Ich und die Menschen (the 'I' and 'human')" and places it outside the domain of sociology. However, as explained above, the concept of society includes both the 'I,' 'human,' and their relations. So our second definition of sociology is derived.

39. We should communicate the fallacy of this kind of doctrine.

40. Alfred Fouillée (1896a, chapter 2). Recently Fabreguettes (1897-1898, vol. 1, p. 369) takes the perspective of general sociology. He says, at present, sociology is just history study. However, sociology should assume as if all natural scientific studies were completed, and put certain meanings in the whole body of studies.

41. There are many other ways to classify the types of sociology. There is Mackenzie's method discussed above. In addition, there is Barth's method (not specifically identified, could be 1890, 1992, 1897a, 1897b), Novicow's method (1893), and Achille Loria's method of the classification. Among sociologists, there are few scholars who do not belong to particular sect. De Greef is its extreme example. Paul Barth wrote following articles in *L'Année Sociologique*. "Sociologie classifiante: Comte, Littré, de Roberty, De Greef, Lacombe, Wagner." "Sociologie Biologique: Spencer, Lilenfeld, Schäffle, Fouillée, Worms." "Sociologie dualistique: Ward, Mackenzie, Hauriou, Giddings."

Novicow (1897, p. 1) classifies sociology into "organic" and "ethnographic," and points out that the organic sociology had flourished for the past fifty years, but now it has declined. Ethnographic sociology has flourished, but organic sociology has declined and is not productive. Sociology is rootless without connection to the theory of organism.

Loria (1900) classifies four strands of sociology. (1) Psychologically grounded sociology. (2) Biologically grounded sociology (Lamarck, 1809, Spencer, 1864-1867, Darwin, Albert Weismann, Ammon, Benjamin Kidd, Enrico Morselli, Novicow, Gumplowicz, Vaccaro. (3) Economically grounded sociology (Karl Kautsky, Weissengrün, Adams, Bogers, De Greef, Alfonso Asturaro, Contento, Enrico Ferri, Alessandro Groppali, Antonio Labriola, Mallusi). (4) Comparative sociology (linguistic, historic, and colonial).

II.3. Problems and System

1. For example, in anthropology and physiology of the human body, anatomy and hygiene, researchers observe the same object "human," but the problems treated in each branch of science are diverse according to each researcher's own interest. So they established four different branches of science, according to the difference in the problems.

2. The term "teleonomy" has two meanings that should not be contradicted. One is literal and the other is scientific. Formerly, in *Overview of Philosophy* (1898) I criticized teleonomy in its literal meaning. In its scientific sense, teleonomy is a theoretical stand to see how things develop. Then I prefer to use the term "fatalism" to indicate scientific teleology. [In *Tetsugaku Taikan* (1989), *Overview of Philoso-*

phy, Takebe contrasts teleonomy with mechanism. Teleonomy explains the universe and its inner phenomena as having a particular design and purpose. Mechanism maintains that every motion in the universe is determined by physical laws, and there is no room for human liberty and effort. Takebe proposes a third position that is between the two, called scientific teleonomy' or "fatalism." In using the term "fatalism," Takebe seems to mean the liberty of humans to choose their future within the limits of physical laws. Eds.]

3. I mean the question of fate is constituted by *Werden* (become), and *Sollen* (ought to be).

4. These are, in other words, ontological, phenomenological, and teleological explanation of societies.

5. Schopenhauer railed at Hegel, Schelling, and Fichte as *"Pseudophilosoph"* or *"Universitätphilosoph."* In the present age, there are German college professors who are also experiencing being under the government's thumb.

6. Gumplowicz's (1892a), *Sociologie und Politik,* is not only verbose but also failed to grasp the main points.

7. In Jevons's (1874a) words, systematic knowledge·has three characteristics "adequate, clear and distinct."

8. Although mathematics, economics, and jurisprudence have been said to be systematic sciences, mineralogy and anthropology are not yet acknowledged.

9. For more detailed discussion on this issue, see II.4 in this collection.

10. History of philosophy plays a pivotal role in this. But human intellectual activities could not be reduced to philosophy. So I need the much broader term, the history of knowledge, so that the history of philosophy can be included. Lecky's (1865) *History of the Rise and Influence of the Spirit of Rationalism in Europe* and Lange's (1866) *Geschichte der Materialismus und Kritik seiner Bedeutung in der Gegenwart* are good examples of the history of knowledge in this sense. John W. Draper's (1864) *History of Intellectual Development in Europe* has a strongly systematic feature. The scholars of Chinese intellectual history should also not limit their scope to the history of philosophy.

11. This can be named Social Logic, and is correlated with Social Statics and Social Dynamics. As a prerequisite for investigating into factual social phenomena, there must be a certain principle or logic that makes the investigation possible.

12. Stuckenberg's (1898) *Introduction to the Study of Sociology,* identified the following Divisions of Sociology: I. The Principles of Sociology; II. The Historical Evolution of the Principles; III. Sociological Ethics, or the Conditions of Social Progress.

II.4. Methodology

1. Comte (1844) concisely explained the matter.

2. Frédéric Le Play (1864). Vignes (1897) is the best example of the Le Play Method.

3. See II. 3 of this book, The Problems of Sociology.

4. Comte (1830-1842, vol. 1, pp. 30-34) drew a general outline of methodology.

5. Immediately after Spencer published his *Principles of Sociology* (1876-1896), Small pointed out in *The American Journal of Sociology* that Spencer's book on sociology was just completed and true sociology has now arrived. I think Small is reading too much into the book.

6. (Durkheim,1893, Preface, Durkheim, 1895; Fouillée, 1896a, 1986b; Menger, 1883; Mackenzie, 1890.) As I noted earlier, Fouillée's thoughts had greatly changed during the twenty years after his 1880 publication. Similarly Schäffle is trying to re-evaluate Comte.

7. There are those who understand sensual intuitions as the consequences of the empirical inquiry. But in reality, the sensual intuitions are the consequences of rational inquiry. Rational sensual intuitions enable empirical inquiry.

8. The other names of these conditions could be "ontological conditions" and "logical inductive conditions." Mill, Kant, and Hegel understood logic in a broader sense, included epistemology and ontology in it. I think they were right, but here I understand logic in narrower a sense to compare the rational method and the empirical method. In short, the rational method follows the rules of deduction, and the empirical method follows the rules of induction.

9. The other name for "qualitative-descriptive method" could be "epistemological qualitative method." The other name for "quantitative-statistical method" could be "quantitative method."

10. The other name for "epistemological qualitative method" could be "descriptive method." The other name for "quantitative method" could be "statistical method."

11. For example, descriptive sociologists such as John Lubbock and Spencer are easily deceived by questionable travelogues.

12. Charles Letourneau is straightforward on this point.

13. [Takebe meant that we could distinguish between "phenomena themselves" (and human sense of them) and "causal relation between them." It is the logical essence of Comte's positivism and later logical positivism that differentiates itself from both "theology" and "metaphysics." Twentieth century logical-positivists such as Rudorf Carnap and Karl Popper demonstrated that causality belongs not to the objective world itself, but to human subjective reasoning. Eds.]

14. [The systematic study of probability was begun in the eighteenth century. Before then, philosophy used the dichotomy of "necessity" and "chance." For the seventeenth century scholar, *necessity* was the same as inevitability or a 100 percent probability that the phenomena would occur. *Chance* was the same as random or chaos. Thus, the discovery of probability theory was critical since it enabled scholars to discover regularities in random and chaotic phenomena. Eds.]

15. d = sample size (or total number of outcomes)

   t = number of outcomes corresponding to an event in a given sample

  X = population (or entire group we are interested in) minus d

  x = [number of outcomes corresponding to an event minus t] in the population d + X

t/d = sample mean (or probability of the event)

(t + x)/(d + X) = expected value (or population mean).

when x/X = t/d, t/d = (t + x)/(d + X). Therefore, my assumption is proved.

However, when x/X not = t/d, X is likely to be larger than d, the measurement of credibility should be X/d.

16. Kant (1884, p. 115) distinguishes "*die transcendentale Einheit des Selbstbewusstseins*" [the transcendental oneness of self-conscious beings], "*Anschauung*" [intuition], and "*Reine Apperzeption*" [pure perception]. Also, in the Buddhist theory of *Alaya* [consciousness], what is called *Ahankara* is identical with Kant's "*actus der Spontaneität*" [act of spontaneity].

17. Kant (1884). "*Selbstbewusstsein*" [self-conscious being].

18. Kant (1884, pp. 98-99) "*Kategorien*" [category].

19. Kant (1884). "*Wahrnehmung*" [true perception]. Buddhist philosophy has similar conception of human perception. According to Buddhist theory, (1) Perception is the image of the essence of vision, sound, and other stimuli, that reflects on the mind. (2) Cognition is the mental act of finding perception within its own mind. (3) Awareness is the mental act of finding cognition within its own mind. (4) Self-consciousness is the mental act of finding awareness within its own mind.

20. Just like the term "science," the meaning of the term "history" is also quite ambiguous because of its lack of sufficient conceptualization. Usually people use the term "history" in following four meanings and their components. (1) Fact-based historical study. According to its advocates, history is the record of past human affairs. They negate all historical views that are not sufficiently supported by preserved historical materials. (2) Hypothesis-based philosophy of history. According to its advocates, the fact-based historical study should be incorporated into certain hypothesis—that is, teleological, evolutional, etc. They often criticize the fact-based historical study's redundancy. (3) Dilettante historical study. Its advocates maintain that the excavation and the discovery of historical records and materials are in itself the most valuable. (4) History for national education. Its advocates understand history as the sacred scripture to be worshipped. Through mythic-historical education, they want to enforce the integration of the Japanese nation. The slogan of "science and history" is in vogue in the world of criticism and journalism And these in these disciplines dispute each other without examining the above ambiguity. Academics may as well grasp the trends in the secular world, because (1-3) are historical studies that scientists deal with. Later in this book, II.1, Data of the History of Sociology, I will discuss the fifth way of studying history.

PART III:
HISTORICAL INTRODUCTION

III.1. General Remarks on Historical Study

1. See II.1 of this book. We should not overestimate the capacity of the historical method.

2. They maintain that theoretical study and historical study should work together. Although their systems of sociology seem to be overcomplicated, their historical descriptions are worth reading. Bluntschli (1864) and Weitzel (1832-1833)

are older examples of the history of sociological thought. Contemporary works of other authors such as Höffding (1895-1896), Schmoller (1888), Mohl, (1855-1858), and Bouglé (1896) try to describe the history of sociology.

3. We may divide history into the subjective and the objective. Objective history refers to historical facts. Subjective history is the history written by historians. Subjective history and objective history cannot be the same because written history cannot exclude the writer's subjective bias. Sociology may articulate the rules of writing subjective history. See Takebe (1903).

4. See Gothein (1889), Lippert (1885-1886, 1886-1887), and Otto Henne-am Rhyn (1889). These books list and comment on various parties.

5. There have been many pioneering works of anthropology that contained sociological ideas. For instance the Alexandrian School tried to explain the genesis of human being by systematic perusal in the Old Testament. See Plinius, Gainus, Secundus (ca. 70). In the modern era, there has been David Hartley (1749) and Herder (1784-1791). The current ethological studies are coming closer to descriptive sociology.

6. Georg Meyer (1878) described the history of the theories of *Staatslehre.*

7. Bluntschli (1864, 1881) maintains that *Staatslehre* should be oriented toward establishing a general theory of state.

8. Recently "political science" that studies practical policy is gaining a growing number of students. Ratzenhofer (1893a) thinks of "political science" as a part of sociology.

9. Stein (1856) is a good example. At the core of his systematic study of state, he tried to understand the nature and characteristics of state in a sociological manner.

10. Ingram (1888) articulated the relation between economics and sociology. See especially p. 197 and p. 212. Some French, British, and American scholars like to use the term "*l'économie sociale*" or "social economy." German scholars like to use the term "*Nationaloekonomie*" or "*Volkswirthschaftslehre*." The term "*Socialoekonomie*" is relatively minor.

11. I would like to add the study of international problems and racial problems into this category, but we do not have enough material to discuss those. Those fields of social study need further research.

III.2. Historical Sources of Sociology

1. [Kokutai literally means "state body." *Kokutai* indicates the integration of the Japanese nation under the sovereign Tenno, when the *Meiji* regime was established. From the 1860s until the 1940s, the concept *Kokutai* had come to be used by the Japanese government as the ultimate legal ground for the regulation of the press and general mobilization orders during wartime. Eds.]

2. In an earlier work, I closely examined Japanese thought (see Takebe, 1898, Part 2, Chapter 7 and Appendix 2). See III.4 of this book for information concerning Meiji thought.

3. I will discuss this in Takebe (1918). *Shakai Dogaku* [General Sociology, vol. 4, Social Dynamics]. Tokyo: Kinkodo Press.

4. After the Sino-Japanese War came to an end (1895), many western states despised the Chinese civilization. Germany seized the Shandong Peninsula. Today, not only the general public but also scholars despise the Chinese without hesitation. It is inexcusable if the Japanese people behave like westerners and look down on the Chinese.

5. The holy emperor Yao said, "Oh you Shun. The voice of the heaven celebrates your coronation. You should keep a moderate course. The four seas (the whole world) are in great difficulty. May the grace of the heaven last" (Confucius, BCE 221-469. *The Analects of Confucius,* Book 20, Chapter 1).

6. Confucius stated that you should be a true Confucian, not a petty Confucian. Since the *Han* dynasty authorized Confucianism as orthodoxy, "petty Confucianism" flourished.

7. It is usually said that as the *Keju* (the civil service examination established by the *Sui* dynasty (581-618) to avoid the title-heredity system of bureaucrats) was established, Chinese thought declined and gradually collapsed. It is true. The main cause of the decline of Chinese thought was the increasing gap between pragmatic knowledge and theoretical knowledge.

8. I think the civilization under the Zhou dynasty was equal to that of contemporary Great Britain. The Zhou Confucian thought, especially, was equal to current English thought. approved.

9. *Zhou-shu* [Chronicle of Zhou Dynasty], *Tai-shi Shang.*

10. There have been disputes over the implications of the three principles.

11. According to *Yi Jing* [Book of Change], "heavenly movement is strong and immutable. A man of virtue should strive for being in perfect accordance with the movement."

12. ☰☰ Earth-Heaven-Secure. The fortune of peace, security, and happiness. ☷☷Heaven-Earth-Negate. The fortune of struggle, pain, and timidity. ☶☷Mountain-Earth-Strip. The fortune of betrayal and failure. ☷☳Earth-Thunder-Restore. The fortune of hope and convalescence.

13. Confucius (c 469-221 BCE, Book 17, Chapter 19) says "Does Heaven speak? The four seasons pursue their courses, and all things are continually being produced, but does Heaven say anything?"

14. *Chun Qiu* (*Spring and Autumn Annals*) encourages the rule of virtue, and hates militarism. According to *Chun Qiu,* the rule of virtue is the heavenly and universal command. Then I may say that *Chun Qiu* represents one of the earliest instances of universal pacifism.

15. There are three principles: virtue, warmth, and righteousness. And there are eight norms: observation, recognition, sincerity, justice, personal cultivation, familial cultivation, country government, and universal government. In *Li Ji* [Book of Rites], Book 31, we find the following sentence that represents the Confucian concept of moderation: "Nature is the command of the Heaven. Virtue is to follow the nature. Education is to learn about the Heavenly Virtue."

16. Among critical reviews for my book *Riku Shozan* (Takebe, 1897) I found a claim that I was too verbose referring to Lu's politico-economic thought. This critic likes to understand Lu as a traditional philosophic thinker. I think this is a harmful

influence of the division of scholarly work. [Lu Hsiang-shan (1139-1192) was a major Neo-Confucian philosopher of the *Song* dynasty. Eds.]

17. Friedrich Max Müller named it "Cathenotheism."

18. The six schools are: *Mîmâm-sâ* [which is the school of interpretation of the *Karmakân-d-a*]; *Vedânta* [the school of interpretation of the *Jñanakân-d-a*]; *Sânkhya* [the school of theoretical knowledge]; *Yoga* [the school of the discipline of achieving liberation]; *Nyâya* [the school of logic]; and *Vaishes-ika* [the school of pluralistic metaphysics]. Translation by Eds.

19. Thales represented socialism of that time. Heracleitos represented aristocracy. Aristides and Themistocles represented oligarchy and democracy of that time. The ancient Greeks conceptualized *Kalokagathia* [Nobility] as "every beauty is good." Opposing this, Plato revised the conception, as "every good is beautiful."

20. Grote, (1865, vol. 3, p. 802). This looks similar to Zisi's work (Confucius' grandson) in the fifth century BCE), *Zhong Yong* [Doctrine of the Mean], Chapter 100. Plato cooperated with King Dionysius of Syracuse, but he failed to achieve his ideal. I think this was because Plato, when compared to Confucius, was too focused on the metaphysical aspects.

21. Friedrich C. Schlosser (1844-1857). In the middle of the nineteenth century, Schlosser, the leading German world historian at the time, referred to China as follows. The Chinese lacks *Gemüt* (ethnic spirit). So the Chinese are incapable of enjoying sophisticated literature and belief. This is because they have many historians, but do not have philosophers. To acquire clairvoyance, they need to surmount history and establish philosophy. Nietzsche's "*übermensch*," and Carlyle's "hero" seem to represent the contemporary conception of philosopher-ruler.

22. Aristotle's (4th century BCE), works include *Organon, Nicomachean Ethics, Eudemonian Ethics, Magna Moralia* (a summary of the above two), and *Politica*.

23. Bluntschli (1881), p. 5 and Stein (1897), p. 332. Concerning Roman history, see Mommsen, (1854). Concerning the medieval Western society, see Dunning (1902), Gierke (1900), and Poole (1884).

24. *Philosophischer Sozialismus* [philosophical socialism], *Agrarischer Sozialismus* [agrarian socialism], *Religiöser Sozialismus* [religious socialism].

25. Thomas Aquinas understood the human as "Homo animal sociale et politicus [human (as) social and political animal]."

26. Aegidius Romanus de Colonna [Giles of Rome] (ca. 1277). Augustinus Triumphius de Anchona: *Summa de Potestate Ecclesiastica*. Stein, (1897, p. 241) pointed out that Christianity substituted "*Gottesstaat* [state of God]" for the Stoic "*Weltstaat* [state of the earth]." Theocracy is not the most advantageous climate for the development of questions of social philosophy.

27. Here I mean the tendency of the world history; not the tendency of the each state history.

28. The Renaissance movement may be summarized as below.

    1. The discovery and study of the classics
        (a) The revival of Platonism. George Gemistos Plethon (Constantinople). Tohannes Bessarion (Plethon's disciple). Giovanni Francesco Pico della Mirandola (Marsilius Ficinus' disciple). Johann Reuchlin (German Humanist).

19. Gumplowicz wrote several books on jurisprudence and politics (1885, 1892b, 1902). However his 1892a work is the best example of jurisprudence and political science based on sociology.

20. [Takebe lists all Comte's works (1848, 1852, 1868, 1870, 1883, 1895) and works of scholars who wrote about Comte (Caird, 1885; Eucken, 1887; Gruber, 1889; Levy-Bruhl, 1900; Lietz, 1891; Littré, 1863, 1868; Martineau, 1894-1895; Rigolage, 1897; Robinet, n.d.; Sommer, 1885; & Waentig, 1894). Eds.]

21. Written in the title page of Auguste Comte (1856) *Synthèse Subjective: ou, Système Universal des Conceptions Humaines à l'Etat Normal de l'Humanité*, Paris; Fonds typographique de l'Execution testamentaire d'Auguste Comte.

22. Ingram (1888, p. 197) summarized Comte's principles.

23. Quételet borrowed the term *"physique sociale"* from Condorcet. They employed the term to emphasize that the laws of society have same nature as the physical laws. Also see Arthur Bordier (1887, introduction).

24. [Takebe provides a complete listing of Frédéric Le Play's works (1864, 1874, 1876, 1881) as well as books written about his works (Curzon, 1899; Ribot, 1882; Vignes, 1897). Eds.]

25. [Takebe provides a complete listing of Charles Letourneau's works (1876, 1887, 1888, 1889, 1891a, 1891b, 1892, 1895a, & 1895b). Eds.]

26. Fouillée (1889) and Courcelle-Seneuil (1862) inherited Comte's positive method and are now trying to establish a logical foundation of sociology. Malon (1879, 1890) is leading the practical movement of socialism, using his pen, tongue, and power. Recently Fouillée seemed to revise his theory. His academic desire has not declined with age. Among the younger generation, Emile Durkheim, Jean Gabriel Tarde, Arthur Bordier (1887), and Combes de Lestrade (1889) are promising, although the latter two are not acknowledged enough. [Takebe lists the works of Emile Durkheim (1893, 1895) and Jean Gabriel Tarde (1890a, 1890b, 1895a, 1895b, 1898a, 1898b, & 1899). Eds.]

27. Le Bon (1894, 1895) concentrates on psychological study. Izoulet's (1894, 1898) argument is too complex. Opposed to Letourneau's view, Giraud-Teulon (1884) gathers evidence of the process of evolution. Worms (1895a, 1895b, 1903-1907) is acknowledged although he has not yet written a major book. In Belgium, Emile de Lavelaye (1874, 1881a, 1881b, 1891) is famous as both an economist and a sociologist. Guillaume de Greef wrote some treatises on methodological issues. Even though his writings have not been systematic, he is promising. [Takebe lists De Greef's writing (1893, 1895a, 1895b). Eds.]

28. G. Lauroff is a Russian pioneer of the subjective method (See Bloch, 1899; Pobedonostzeff, 1897; Stein, 1897; Tche-k, 1884). Pobedonostzeff work was originally published as *Recueil de Moscou* in 1896.

29. Ernest Belfort Bax (1886, 1891, 1897), Jan Helenus Ferguson (1889), George Harris (1896), Thomas Henry Huxley (1891), George C. Lorimer (1886), and Thomas Mackay (1896).

30. At the 1900 Paris Congress of the International Institute of Sociology, Wilheim von Lexis said that sociology is a science that Germany needs most urgently. In Germany, scholars are skeptical regarding the value of sociology, its subjects, and its methodology.

31. Rudolf Rocholl (1893) and Lippert (1883-1884, 1884, 1885-1886, 1886-1887) from economic history; Goerg Hanssen, August Meitzen, Karl Theodor von Inama-Sternegg, Georg Friedrich Knapp, Karl Lamprecht, and Gustav Schmoller from *staatswissenschaft*; and Robert von Mohl, Lorenz von Stein, Rudolf von Gneist, from comparative jurisprudence. Moreover, prominent scholars such as Albert Eberhard Schäffle (1875-1878) and Krohn (1880), who fit between sociology and those individual sciences, became leaders of the academic world. In addition, among the younger generation, Ferdinand Tönnies and Georg Simmel (1890, 1892) clearly identify themselves as sociologists.

32. There are the following journals of sociology: *American Journal of Sociology, Institut des Science Sociale Annales, Année Sociologique, Institut international de Sociologie Annale, Revue Internationale de Sociologie, La Réforme Sociale, La Science Sociale suivant la Methode d'Observation, Zeitschrift für Sozialwissenschaft, Soziale Praxis,* and *Zeitschrift für Social-und Wirthschaftsgeschichte.*

III.4. The Future of Sociology

1. [Ieyasu's Hundred Instructions was a secret document of the early Tokugawa government. Only high officials of the central government were permitted to read it. Toshogu has been taking custody of it, and, until today, it has been out of public inspection. Eds.]

2. [Kumazawa, a prominent pragmatic thinker of the seventeenth century, proposed a practical measure to resolve the structural problems of the Tokugawa regime. Chusai Oshio is a social reformist of the late Tokugawa period who organized a rebellion against the wealthy merchants in Osaka. Eds.]

3. I have only presented an outline of Japanese thought. For more details see Takebe (1897, 1898, Appendix 2).

4. [Fukuzawa, a leading enlightenment thinker of the Meiji period who, unlike prior generations, rejected Confucian philosophy and introduced the Western human rights theory and social contract theory. Eds.]

5. [Niijima, a Christian thinker and educator of the Meiji period, who graduated from Amherst College, established the Doshisha English School in Osaka, which later became Doshisha University. Eds.]

6. [Ito, one of the most powerful politician of the Meiji period, shaped Japanese legal, political, and administrative systems in the Western style. Eds.]

7. [*Koshitsu Tenpan* (Rules Governing the Imperial Household, Imperial House hold Law) was validated in 1889. Konakamura insisted that female descendants belonging to the lineage of the Imperial Family could succeed to the imperial throne, as historical evidence for this. But his suggestion was rejected. At last, the first article of *Koshitsu Tenpan* was revised as follows. "The imperial throne shall be succeeded to by male descendants who belong to the paternal lineage of the Imperial Family." On September 6, 2006, the first male heir to be born into Japan's royal family in more than four decades ended the debate on allowing women to ascend to the throne. [ds.]

8. Pierre Laffitte, a Western scholar who studies Chinese society, recently avoided using the term "Christendom" and instead used the term "Westerndom." I

think it is quibbling as there is no difference and the meaning is the same. I have to say that Laffitte exemplifies another version of Pan-Aryanism.

9. For the past ten years this tendency has been getting worse. I am worrying about Japanese students who go to Europe without a Japanese education. They tend to believe that the Japanese culture is an obstacle when we enter the civilized world. It is pitiful if they experience the same feeling as a criminal who appears in Hegel's early writing. On the other hand, the average westerners do not understand the East, although the reformers and intelligentsia and other leaders of society are quite different. [Hegel noted that a thief found that he injured not only the victim, but also himself. Then, what Takebe meant here may be as follows. Today young Japanese students go to Europe without understanding the significance of what they observed. They may carry back certain Western knowledge to Japan, but they will soon recognize that it is worthless. Eds.]

10. "Internationalism" is the generic name for this aim and the projects based on this spirit. In various international congresses held at the Paris World Exposition 1900, I witnessed the rise of internationalism.

PART IV:
FAMILY ORGANIZATION

IV.1. The Family

1. Recently Fustel de Coulange (1900), A. River (La Famille au Droit romain, 1893) [He may be referring to Alphonse Rivier (1835-1898). Eds.], Maxime Kovalevsky (1890), Arthur Bordier (1887), and Julius Lippert (1884) made brilliant contributions.

2. Even Spencer and Freidrich Engels did nothing more than guess at the evolutionary order of the forms of spousal relationships. Engels (1891) proposed a three-stage theory of family evolution as follows. (1) *Blutverwandtschaftsfamilie*. (2) *Punaluafamilie*. (3) *Paarungsfamilie*. It looks reasonable, but it is derived from only a few historical facts, so it is not a sufficiently reliable theory. At this time, there is no theory of family evolution that has equal reliability with the theory of biological evolution or the theory of astronomical evolution. Every scholar has his/her own schema, which is harmful and useless. So I will propose that we stop assuming the evolutionary process of the family. It should be done after establishing the social ideal.

3. I use the term "marriage" in a sociological way. In jurisprudence, the concept of marriage does not have such a broad sense.

4. "Desire-ruled marriage" is a tentative name. There might be a better name.

5. Hellwald (1889) described how females came to be understood as a commodity in the context of marital arrangements. He notes that females were enslaved, and this gave rise to polygamy which weakened the spousal relationship.

6. Letourneau (1892: 327). The root of the term *"revirat"* is the Latin noun *"levir"* that means sworn brother. According to Letourneau, Levirat was suited for

primitive societies because the female's reproductive period is quite short. Engels (1886) in *Blutverwandtfamilie* he elaborate further and notes that people avoid the marriage with their lineal parents. In *Punaluafamilie* he notes that they also avoid their brothers/sisters. In *Blutverwandtfamilie* brother (sister) was an equivalent of husband (wife). Morgan and Engels argued that there is some evidence to prove the existence of *Blutverwandtfamilie* in Hawaii and the Oceania islands.

7. It is said that the incest results in hereditary problems. Those societies who did not know the incest taboo seemed to ruin themselves

8. I think that Spencer overestimated the role of conflict.

9. Spencer (1876-1896, section 297) thought that promiscuity is a combination of unlimited polyandry and unlimited polygamy. He observed those three types of marriage from three viewpoints, that is, maintenance of society, child nursing, and the adult's behaviors.

10. See Giraud-Teulon (1884) and Morgan (1871). The marriage between the elder brother and the younger sister has a long history. In Arabia, Persia, and Madagascar, it has been done even in the historic era. In Persia and Madagascar royalty were obliged to marry with his/her brother/sister. In Japan, there existed a similar custom. Prior to Taiho period (CE 701-704) it was an obligation of the Tenno family to present a member of their family to be the queen. It was to keep the sacredness of the political ruler.

11. Spencer (1876-1896, section 297 and 298) made a distinction between lower polygamy and higher polygamy. The lower is the mixture of polyandry and polygamy. The higher is pure polygamy.

12. For the aim of maintaining the lineage, under the patrilineal heritage, polygyny is the best form of spousal relationship. Under the patrilineal-polygamic condition, family relation is oriented mainly by the parent-child relation rather than the spousal relation. In the next section I will give a further explanation. In most cases, polygyny accompanies wives' hierarchical rankings. If one's first wife has a child, the lower wives and their children could not inherit the property. This may suggest the earliest form of monogamy.

13. Even in highly civilized societies, this type of polygamy seemed to remain. For example it could be seen in ancient China. But it finally became a taboo, to some degree, in medieval China.

14. Spencer, (1876-1896, section 304). Spencer pointed out that there is considerable evidence that males prefer polygyny but fail to do so because they cannot afford it. He argued that there is no natural ground to limit polygamy, only culture and resources set limits. He also argued that polygamy is especially preferred under conditions in which the ratio of males to females is lower than one. Polygamy is quite advantageous in the war situation, because the number of males may rapidly decrease. Those suggest the compatibility of polygyny with monogamy.

15. Physiologically speaking, females as compared to males are severely limited in terms of the number of children they can bear. So, for maintaining the lineage, polygyny is more favorable than monogamy. Spencer (1876-1896, section 311) thought that monogamy prevailed when the notions of property and contract was established. In its effect, he argued, the male-female ratio became close to one.

16. It seems that religion has a special role in maintaining monogamy. Among western Christian societies, there exists strong, religious prohibitions against divorce which results in a large number of people who are forced to live a life of agony. As a result, some people commit adultery.

17. It is a custom known as *Couvade*. In a *Couvade* ceremony, the father wins the child rearing rights from the mother. This may be a transitional form of the parent-child relationship from mother-oriented to father-oriented. However, the hostility between husband and wife, as seen in *Couvade*, is an anomalous phenomenon. So it should not be considered to be a necessary transitional form from mother-oriented to father-oriented.

18. Ellis (1890) notes that in European languages, the etymological root of the word "lady" was derived from "lafdi" (one who kneads bread). Thus, the female has had this particular profession for a long time. Ellis says that there existed some cases where professions that had been considered as female professions were invaded and finally occupied by males.

19. Today women are entering the professions of teaching, medicine, and law. I do not know how much and what kind of effect this has on women's social status. If women go into the fields of politics and military, it will improve the women's status.

References

Abramowski, Edward (1897). *Les Bases Psychologiques de la Sociologie.* Paris: Giard & Briere.

Aegidius Romanus de Colonna (Giles of Rome) (ca.1277). *De Regimine Principum Hieronymum Samaritanium* (Ed.) Aalen.

Alberti, Valentin (1678). *Compendium Juris Naturae Orthodoxae Theologiae Conformatum.*

Aristotle (n.d.) *Organon.*

Aristotle (350-340 BCE) *Nicomachean Ethics, Eudemonian Ethics. Magna Moralia* (a summary of above two).

Aristotle (335-323 BCE) *Politics.*

Aruga, Nagao (1883). *Shakai Shinka-ron* [Of social evolution]. Tokyo: Toyokan Press.

Aruga, Nagao (1883). *Shukyo Shinka-ron* [Of religious evolution]. Tokyo: Toyokan Press.

Aruga, Nagao (1884). *Zokusei Shinka-ron* [Of familial evolution]. Tokyo: Toyokan Shoten Press.

Aruga, Nagao (1885). *Kyoiku Tekiyo Shinrigaku* [Psychology of education]. Tokyo: Makinoshobo Press.

Aruga, Nagao (1888). *Tsushin Kyoju Kyojuho* [The correspondence course in education]. Tokyo: Tsushinkogakukai.

Aruga, Nagao (1888-1890). Shakaigakushi Ryaku [A summary of the history of sociology], *Tetsugakukai Zasshi* [*Philosophical Society Bulletin*], no.19, 21, 27, 33, 43).

Aruga, Nagao (1889). *Kokkagaku* [Theory of state]. Tokyo: Makinoshobo Press.

Aruga, Nagao (1890). *Daijin Sekininron* [Responsibility of the ministers]. Tokyo: Myohodo Press.

Aruga, Nagao (1894). *Bankoku Senji Koho* [The international law of war]. Tokyo: Rikugun Daigakko.

Aruga, Nagao (1897). *Teikoku-Shi Ryaku* [An outline of the Japanese imperial history]. Tokyo: Hakubunkan Press.

Aruga, Nagao (1898a). *Kinji Gaikohshi* [Current diplomacy]. Tokyo: Waseda-daigaku Press.

Aruga, Nagao (1898b). *Teikoku Kenpo Kohgi* [Lectures on the constitution of the Japanese empire]. Tokyo: Kohokai.

Augustinus Triumphius de Anchona. *Summa de Potestate Papae.*

Japanese Family and Society
© 2007 by The Haworth Press, Inc. All rights reserved.
doi:10.1300/5840_13

Baerenbach, Friedrich von (1882). *Die Socialwissenschaften: zur Orientirung in den socialwissenschaftlichen Schulen und Systemen der Gegenwart.* Leipzig: O. Wigand.

Barth, Paul (1897a). *Die Philosophie der Geschichte als Sociologie: Grundlegung und kritische Übersicht.* Leipzig: Reisland.

Barth, Paul (1897b). *Einleitung und Kritische Übersicht.* Leipzig: Reisland.

Bascom, John (1895). *Social theory: A Grouping of social facts and principles.* Boston: T. Y. Crowell.

Bax, Ernest B. (1886). *The religion of socialism: Essays in modern socialist criticism.* London: Swan Sonnenschein.

Bax, Ernest B. (1891). *The ethics of socialism: Being further essays in modern Socialist Criticism.* London: Swan Sonnenschein.

Bax, Ernest B. (1897). *Outspoken essays on social subjects.* London: William Reeves.

Beasley, W. G. (1972). *The Meiji restoration.* Stanford, CA: Stanford University Press.

Bebel, August (1891). *Die Frau und Sozialismus.* Stuttgart: Diez.

Becker, Howard (1936). Sociology in Japan. *American Sociological Review, 1,* 455-471.

Bernstein, Eduard, Hugo, C., Kautsky, K. Lafargue, P., Mehring, F., & Plechanow, G. (1895-1897). *Die Geschichte des Sozialismus in Einzeldarstellungen.* 5 Bds., Stuttgart: J.H.W. Dietz.

Bloch, Johann von (1899). *Der Krieg.* 6 Bds., Berlin: Puttkammer.

Bluntschili, Johann C. (1864). *Geschichte des allgemeinen Staatsrechts und der Politik.* München: Cotta.

Bluntschili, Johann C. (1881). *Geschichte der neueren Staatswissenschaft: allgemeines Staatsrecht und Politik.* München: Oldenbourg.

Bodin, Jean (1576). *Les Six Livers de la Republique.*

Bonhoff, Carl (1900). *Christentum und sittlich-soziale Lebensfragen. 4 volkstümliche Hochschulvorträge.* Leipzig; Teubner.

Bordier, Arthur (1887). *La Vie des Societétés.* Paris: Reinwald.

Bouglé, Charles (1896). *Les Science Sociale en Allemagne: Le Méthodes actuelles.* Paris: Alcan.

Brinton, Daniel G. (1902). *The basis of social relations: A study in ethnic psychology.* New York: Putnam.

Brunner, Heinrich (1887-1892). *Deutsche Rechtsgeschichte.* 2 Bds., Leipzig: Duncker & Humblot.

Buckle, Henry T. (1857-1866). *History of civilisation in England.* 2 vols., London: Longman.

Caird, Edward (1885). *The social philosophy and religion of Comte.* New York: Macmillan.

Carey, Henry C. (1858-1867). *Principles of social science.* 3 vols., Philadelphia: Lippincott.

Carey, Henry C. (1874). *Principles of Social Science,* vol. 1, Philadelphia: Lippincott.

Carey, Henry C. (1972). The Unity of Law, as Exhibited in the Relations of Physical, Social, Mental and Moral Science, Philadelphia: H. C. Baird.

Carlyle, Thomas (1837). *History of the French revolution,* 3 vols, London: Chapman & Hall.

Carlyle, Thomas (1840). *Heroes and hero-worship.* Boston: Estes & Lauriat.

Carlyle, Thomas (1843). *Past and present.* Boston: Estes & Lauriat.

Carlyle, Thomas (1872). *The unity of law, as exhibited in the relations of physical, social, mental, and moral science.* Philadelphia: H. C. Baird.

Churchill, Robert (2005). *Handbook for the study of Eastern literatures: Ancient Japan.* Retrieved on March 4, 2005 from http://mockingbird.creighton.edu/english/worldlit/wldocs/churchill/japan.htm.

Clement, Ambroise (1867). *Essai sur la Science Sociale: Economie politique, morale experimentale, politique theorique.* 2 tomes, Paris: Guillaumin.

Colajanni, Napoleone (1889). *La sociologia criminale.* Catania: Tropea.

Colajanni, Napoleone (1898). *Il Socialismo.* Palermo: R. Sandron.

Collet, Clara E. (1902). *Educated working women.* London: P.S.King & Son.

Combes de Lestrade, Vicomte (1889). *Eléments de Sociologie.* Paris: Alcan.

Comte, Auguste (1830-1842). *Cours de Philosphie Positive.* 6 tomes, Paris: Bachelier.

Comte, Auguste (1844). *Discours sur l'Esprit Positif.* Paris: Carillan-Goeury & Victor Dalmont.

Comte, Auguste (1848). *Discours sur l'Ensemble du Positivisme, Présentation, Notes et Chronologie par Annie Petit.* Paris: Mathias.

Comte, Auguste (1851-1854). *Système de Politique Positive.* 4 tomes, Paris: Carilian-Goeury & Dalmont.

Comte, Auguste (1852). *Catéchisme Positiviste.* Paris: Carilian-Goeury.

Comte, Auguste (1856). *Synthèse Subjective: ou, Système Universal des Conceptions Humaines à l'Etat Normal de l'Humanité.* Paris: Fonds typographique de l'Execution testamentaire d'Auguste Comte.

Comte, Auguste (1868). *Principes de Philosophie Positive.* Paris: J.B. Bailliere.

Comte, Auguste (1870). *Lettres d'Auguste Comte, à M. Valat, 1815-44.* Pierre Laffitte (Ed.), Paris: Dunod.

Comte, Auguste (1877). *Cours de Philosophie Positive,* Emile Littré (intro.), Tome 4.

Comte, Auguste (1883). *Opuscules de Philosophie Sociale. 1819-28,* Paris: Leroux.

Comte, Auguste (1895). *Septe Lettres d'Auguste Comte, à Antoine Etex.* Paris: M. Montenegro Cordeiro.

Condorcet, Marquis de (1822). *Esquisse d'un tableau historique des progrès de l'esprit humain.* Paris: Masson et Fils.

Considérant, Victor P. (1841). *Base de Politique Positive: Manifeste de l'École sociétair.* Paris: Bureaux de la Phalange.

Cossa, Luigi (1893). *An introduction to the study of political economy.* Louis Dyer (tr.), London: Macmillan.

Coste, Adolphe (1899). *Principes d'un Sociologie objective.* Paris: Alcan.

Courcelle-Seneuil, Jean Gustave (1862). *Etudes sur la Science Sociale.* Paris: Guillaumin.

Crafts, Wilbur Fisk (1895). *Practical Christian Sociology.* New York: Funk & Wagnalls.

Crowell, John F. (1898). *The logical process of social development.* New York: Holt.

Cunnigham, D. (2004*). Taiho-Jutsu* [Arrest techniques]: *Law and order in the age of the samurai.* Boston, MA: Turtle.

Cunow, Heinrich (1898). Die ökonomische Grundlagen der Mutterherrschaft, in Die niue Zeit, XVI, I.

Curzon, Emm de (1899). *Frédéric Le Play: sa Méthode, sa Doctrine, son Œuvre, son Esprit).* Poitiers & Paris: Librairie religieuse H. Oudin. *Neue Zeit.* vol. 16, no. 4-8.

Dante, Alighieri (*ca.*1310). *De Monarchia.*

Danz, Heinrich A. A. (1840-1846). *Lehrbuch der Geschichte des römischen Rechts.* 2 Bds., Leipzig: Breitkophf & Hartel.

Dargun, Lothar (1883). Mutterrecht und Raubehe: und ihre Reste im germanischen Recht und Leben, Breslau: W. Koebner.

Dargun, Lothar (1884). *Ursprung und Entwicklungs-Geschichte des Eigenthums,* Stuttgart: Druck von Gebruder Kroner.

Dargun, Lothar (1886). *Sociologische Studien.* [Unidentified book title. This may be *Zür Methodik der sociologischen Rechtslehre,* Freiburg: Mohr. Eds.]

Dargun, Lothar (1892). *Mutterrecht und Vaterrecht,* Leipzig: Duncker & Humblot.

Darwin, Charles R. (1859). *On the origin of species by means of natural selection.* London: J. Murray.

Darwin, Charles R. (1871). *The Descent of Man, and selection in relation to sex.* 2 vols., London: J. Murray.

De Bella (1895). *Corso de sociologia.*

de Coulange, Fustel (1900). *La Cite antique,* Paris: Hachett.

de Coulanges, Fustel (1916). *The ancient city: A study on the religion, laws, and institutions of Greece and Rome.* London: Simpkin, Marshall, Hamilton Kent & Co.

de Coulanges, Fustel (1934). *Histoire des Institutions politiques del'Ancienne France* (5th ed.). Paris: Hachette.

De Greef, Guillaume (1886 & 1889). *Introduction à la Sociologie.* 2 tomes, Bruxelles: Gustave Mayolez.

De Greef, Guillaume (1893). *Les Lois Sociologiques.* Paris: Alcan.

De Greef, Guillaume (1895a). *L'Evolution de Croyance et des Doctrines Politiques.* Bruxelles: Mayolez & Audiarte.

De Greef, Guillaume (1895b). *Le Transformisme Social.* Paris: Alcan.

de Laveleye, Emile (1874). *De la Propriété et de ses Formes Primitives.* Paris: Germer Bailliere.

de Laveleye, Emile (1881a). *Le Socialisme Contemporaine.* Bruxelles: C. Muquardt.

de Laveleye, Emile (1881b). *La Sociologie: Essai de Philosophie Sociologique.* Paris: Germer Bailliere.

de Laveleye, Emile (1891). *La Philosophie du Siècle.* Paris: Alcan.

de Ribbe, Charles (1879). *Les Familles et la Société en France avant la Révolution.* 2 tomes, 4e ed. Tours: Mame.

de Roberty, Eugène (1881). *La Sociologie: Essai de Philosophie Sociologique.* Paris: Germer Bailliere.

de Roberty, Eugène (1891). *La Philosophie du Siècle.* Paris: Alcan.

Diamond, J. (June, 1998). Japanese roots: Just who are the Japanese? Where did they come from, and when? *Discover Magazine* vol. 19 no. 6. Retrieved April 6,

2005, from http://www2.gol.com/users/hsmr/ontent/East%20Asia/Japan/History/roots.html.

Doniger, Wendy (tr.) (1991). *The laws of Manu.* London: Penguin.

Draper, John W. (1864). *History of intellectual development in Europe.* London: Bell & Daldy.

Ducoudray, Gustave (1888). *Histoire Sommaire de la Civilisation ancienne.* Paris: Hachette.

Ducoudray, Gustave (1891). *The history of modern civilization: A handbook based upon M. Gustave Ducoudray's "Histoire sommaire de la Civilisation."* New York: Appleton.

Dunning, William A. (1902). *A history of political theories: Ancient and mediaeval.* New York: Macmillan.

Durkheim, Emile (1893). *De la Division du Travail Social: Etude sur l'Organisation des Sociétés supérieures.* Paris: Alcan.

Durkheim, Emile (1895). *Les Règles de la Méthode Sociologique.* Paris: Alcan.

Ellis, Havelock (1890). *Man and woman: A study of human secondary sexual character.* London: W. Scott.

Ely, Richard T. (1883). *French and German socialism in modern times.* New York: Harper.

E-Museum (2005). Minnesota State University-Mankato. E-museum exhibits (Japan, history, [various time periods]) retreived March 10, 2005, from http://www.mnsu.edu/emuseum/prehistory/japan/japanese_history.html.

Engel, Ernst (1861). *Die Methoden der Volkszahlung, mitbesonderer Berücksichtigungder impreussischen Staate angewandten.* Berlin.

Engels, Friedrich (1886). *Der Ursprung der Familie,* Stuttgart: J.H.W.

Engels, Friedrich (1891). *Die Entwicklung des Sozialismus von der Utopie zur Wissenschaft.* 4 Aufl., Berlin: Verlag der Expedition des "Vorwarts" Berliner Volksblatt.

Escartin, Eduardo Sanz y (1893). *L'Etat et la Reforme Sociale.* Paris: Alcan.

Escartin, Eduardo Sanz y (1896). *El Individuo y la Reforma Social.* Madrid.

Espinas, Alfred Victor (1877). *Des Socéités Animales.* Paris: Alcan.

Eucken, Rudolf C. (1887). Würdigung Comtes und des Positivismus, in Eduard Zeller (Ed.), *Philosophische Aufsätze.* Leipzig.

Fabreguettes, P. (1897-1898). *Societé, Etat, Patrie: Etudes historiques, politiques, philosophiques, sociales et religiesse.* 2 tomes, Paris: Chevalier-Marescq.

Fairbanks, Arthur (1896). *An introduction to sociology.* London: Kegan Paul.

Ferguson, Jan H. (1889). *The philosophy of civilization.* Hague: Martinus Nyhoff.

Ferguson, John (1876). *Primitive marriage: An inquiry into the origin of the form of capture in marriage ceremonies,* 2 vols., London: Bernard Quaritch.

Ferri, Enrico (1892). *Sociologia Criminale.* Torino: Bocca.

Ferri, Enrico (1895a). *Socialismus und moderne Wissenschaft.* Leipzig: H. Wigand.

Ferri, Enrico (1895b). *L'Omicidio-Suicidio: Responnabilita Giuridica.* Torino: Bocca.

Fichte, Johann G. (1794). *Einige Vorlesungen über die Bestimmung desGelehrten.* Jena: C. E. Gabler.

Fiske, John (1874). *Outlines of cosmic philosophy: Based on the doctrine of evolution, with criticisms on the positive philosophy.* London: Macmillan.

Flint, Robert (1874). *The Philosophy of History in France and Germany,* London & Edinburgh: William Blackwood.

Flint, Robert (1893). *History of the Philosophy of History,* London & Edinburgh: William Blackwood.

Fouillée, Alfred J. E. (1880). *La Science Sociale: Contemporaine.* Paris: Hachette.

Fouillée, Alfred J. E. (1889). *L'Avenir de la Metaphysique, fondée sur l'Expérience.* Paris: Alcan.

Fouillée, Alfred J. E. (1893). *La Psychologie des Idées-forces.* 2 tomes, Paris: Alcan.

Fouillée, Alfred J. E. (1895). Un Essai d'Economie sociale par un Americain. *Revue Internationale de Sociologiogie,* Année 3.

Fouillée, Alfred J. E. (1896a). *Mouvement Positiviste: et la Conception sociologique du Monde.* Paris: Alcan.

Fouillée, Alfred J. E. (1896b). *Mouvement Idéaliste et la Réaction contre la Science positive.* Paris: Alcan.

Fournière, Eugéne (1898). *L'Idéalisme Social.* Paris: Alcan.

Funck-Brentano, Théophile (1897). *La Science Sociale: Morale Politique.* Paris: Plon.

Garofalo, Raffaele (1895). *La Superstition Socialiste,* Auguste Dietrich (tr.), Paris: Alcan.

Gaume, Jean (1863). *Geschichte der häuslichen Gesellschaft bei allen alten und neuen Völkern: oder Einfluß des Christentums auf die Familie.* 3 Bds., Regensburg: Manz.

Gentilis, Alberici (1582). *De Legationibus Libri Tres.*

Gentilis, Alberici (1589). *De Jure Belli Libri Commentationes Tres.*

Geyer, August J. (1863). *Geschichte und System der Rechtsphilosophie.* Innsbruck: Wagner'schen Universität.

Giddings, Franklin H. (1896). *Principles of sciology: An analysis of the phenomena of association and of social organization.* New York: Macmillan.

Giddings, Franklin H. (1897). *The theory of socialization: A syllabus of sociological principles for the use of college and university classes.* New York: Macmillan.

Giddings, Franklin H. (1901). *Inductive sociology: A syllabus of methods, analyses and classifications, and provisionally formulated laws.* New York: Macmillan.

Gierke, Otto F. (1880). *Johannes Althusius und die Entwicklung der naturrechtlichen Staatstheorien: zugleich ein Beitrag zur Geschichte der Rechtssystematik.* Breslau: Koebner.

Gierke, Otto F. (1900). *Political theories of the middle age.* Frederic William Maitland (tr. & introd.), Cambridge, U.K.: Cambridge University Press.

Giraud-Teulon, Alexis (1884). *Les Origines du Mariage et de la Famille.* Geneve: A. Cherbuliez.

Gneist, Rudolf von (1879). *Der Rechtsstaat und die Verwaltungsgerichte in Deutschland.* Berlin: Julius Springer.

Gothein, Eberhard (1889). *Die Aufgaben der Kulturgeschichte.* Leipzig: Duncker & Humblot.

Graham, William (1890). *Socialism: New and old.* London: Kegan Paul.

Grosse, Ernst (1896). *Die Formen der Familie und die Formen der Wirthschaft.* Freiburg & Leipzig: Mohr.

Grote, George (1865). *Plato, and the other companions of Sokrates*, 3 vols., London: Murray.

Grotius, Hugo (1604). *Mare Liberum.*

Grotius, Hugo (1625). *De Jure Belli et Pacis.*

Gruber, Hermann (1889). *August Comte, der Begrunder des Positivismus.* Freiburg im Breisgau: Herder.

Guicciardini, Francesco (1527). *Del Reggimento di Firenze.*

Guizot, François Pierre G. (1828). *Histoire generale de la Civilisation en Europe: depuis la Chute de l'Empire Romain jusqu'a la Revolution Française.* Paris: Didier.

Gumplowicz, Ludwig (1885). *Grundriss der Sociologie.* Wien: Manz.

Gumplowicz, Ludwig (1892a). *Sociologie und Politik.* Leipzig: Dunker & Humblot.

Gumplowicz, Ludwig (1892b). *Die sociologische Staatsidee.* Graz: Leuschner & Lubensky.

Gumplowicz, Ludwig (1902). *Das oesterreichische Staatsrecht.* Wien: Manz.

Gunther, Reinhold (1898). *Weib und Sittlichkeit.* Berlin: Duncker.

Haeckel, Ernst H. (1868). *Naturliche Schopfungs-Geschichte: Gemeinverstandliche wissenschaftliche Vortrage über die Entwickelungs-Lehre.* Berlin: Reimer.

Hamilton, Robert S. (1873). *Present status of social science: A review, historical and critical, of the "Progress of thought in social philosophy."* New York: H.L. Hinton.

Harris, George (1896). *Moral evolution.* London: Clarke.

Hartley, David (1749). *Observations on man: His frame, his duty, and his expectation.* 2 vols., London.

Hartmann, Karl R. E. von (1873). *Philosophie des Unbewussten: Versuch einer Weltanschauung.* Berlin: Duncker.

Hegel, Georg Wilhelm (1837). *Vorlesungen über die Philosophie der Geschichte.* Berlin: Dunker & Humblot.

Helion (1894). *Sociologie absolue: les Principes, les lois, les faits, la politique et l'autorité.* Paris: Chamuel.

Hellwald, Friedrich von (1889). *Die Menschliche Familie: nach ihrer Entstehung und naturlichen Entwickelung.* Leipzig: E.Gunther.

Helmholtz, Hermann L. F. von (1873). *Popular lectures on scientific subjects.* Edmund Atkinson (tr.), London: Longmans.

Henderson, Charles R. (1898). *Social elements: Institutions, characters and progress.* New York: Charles Scribner's sons.

Henne-am Rhyn, Otto (1890). *Die Kultur der Vergungenheit: Gegenwart und Zukunft in vergleichen der Darstellung.* 2 Bds., Danzig: Hinstorff.

Herder, Johann G. (1784-1791). *Ideen zur Geschichte der Menschheit.* 4 Bds., Riga & Leipzig: J. F. Hartknoch.

Hildebrand, Bruno (1848). *Die Nationaloekonomie der Gegenwart und Zukunft und andere gesammelte Schriften.* Frankfurt: Literarische Anstalt (J. Rutten).

Hobbes, Thomas (1651). *Leviathan.* London: Green Dragon.

Höffding, Harald (1895-1896). *Geschichte der neueren Philosophie: eine Darstellung der Geschichte der Philosophie von dem Ende der Renaissance bis zu unseren Tagen.* 2 Bds., Leipzig: Reisland.

Honegger, Johann J. (1882-1886). *Allgemeine Kulturgeschichte.* 2 Bds., Leipzig: Weber.

Honjo, E. (1941). Views in taxation on commerce in the closing days of Tokugawa age. *Kyoto University Economic Review, 16,* 1-16. Memoirs of the department of economics in the Imperial University of Kyoto. Retrieved March 21, 2005, from http://www.econ.kyoto-u.ac.jp/review/10000207.pdf.

Hooker, R. (1996). *World civilizations.* Retrieved February 13, 2005, from http://www.wsu.edu/~dee/ANCJAPAN/ANJAPAN1.HTM.

Howland, D. R. (2002). *Translating the west: Language and political reason in nineteenth-century Japan.* Honolulu: University of Hawaii Press.

Hoxlo, E. (1931). The economic development of Japan. *Kyoto University Economic Review, 6,* 1-16. Memoirs of the department of economics in the Imperial University of Kyoto. Retrieved March 21, 2005, from http://www.econ.kyoto-u.ac.jp/review/10000064.pdf.

Humboldt, Alexander von (1845-1858). *Kosmos: Entwurf einer physischen Weltbeschreibung.* 4 Bds., Stuttgart: Cotta.

Huxley, *Social Essays,* (French translation) 1897. [Unidentified book title. It may be included in Huxley, 2001: *Collected Essays,* 9 vols., Bristol; Thömmes, 2001. Eds.]

Huxley, Thomas H. (1891). *Social diseases and worse remedies.* London: Macmillan.

Ibn Khaldun (1986). *The Muqaddimah: An introduction to history. (ca.*1380). 3 vols., Franz Rosenthal (tr.), 2nd ed., London: Routledge.

Ibn Rushd (also known as Averroes) (1179-1180) *Tahafut al-Tahafut* [The Incoherence of the Incoherence]. S Van Den Bergh (tr.), M Hozien (E-text conversion). Retrieved on Dec 30, 2006 from http://www.muslimphilosophy.com/ir/tt/tt-all.htm.

Ibn Tofayl (1782). *Der Naturmensch: oder Geschichte des Hai Ebn Yokdan.* J.C. Eichhom (tr.), Berlin.

Imai, Seikichi & Hayashi, Keikai. (1954). *Tokyo Daigaku Bungakubu Shakaigakka Enkaku 75nen Gaikan* [The 75 Years History of Faculty of Sociology, Department of Letters, University of Tokyo], Tokyo: Tokyo Daigaku Bungakubu Shakaigaku Kenkyushitsu Kaishitsu 50 Shunen Kinen Jigyo Zikko Iinkai.

Imatani, Akira (1993). *Buke to Tennoh* [The samurai and the emperor]. Tokyo: Iwanami.

Ingram, John K. (1888). *A history of political economy.* Edinburgh: Adam & Black.

Ishida, T. (1971). *Japanese society.* New York: Random House.

Izoulet, Jean (1894). *La Cité Moderne: Metaphysique de la Sociologie.* Paris: Alcan.

Izoulet, Jean (1898). *Les Quatre Problemes Sociaux.* Paris: A. Colin.

JAANUS (2005). Japanese architecture and art net users system. Retrieved October 10, 2005 from http://www.aisf.or.jp/~jaanus/deta/k/kangoushuuraku.htm.

Jansen, M. B. (1971). *Sakamoto Ryōma and the Meiji Restoration.* Stanford, CA: Stanford University Press.

Japan-Guide (2005). History. Retreived on January 3, 2006 online from http://www.japan-guide.com/e/e2131.html.

Jevons, William S. (1874a). *Elementary lessons in logic: Deductive and inductive: With copious questions and examples, and a vocabulary of logical terms.* 4th ed., London: Macmillan.

Jevons, William S. (1874b). *The principles of science: A treatise on logic and scientific method.* 2 vols., London: Macmillan.

Jevons, William S. (1883). *Methods of social reform and other papers.* London: Macmillan.

Jhering, Rudolph von (1852-1878). *Geist des römischen Rechts auf verschiedenen Stufen seiner Entwicklung.* 3 Bds., Leipzig: Breitkopf & Hartel.

Jhering, Rudolph von (1874). *Der Kampf ums Recht.* Darmstadt: Wissenschaftliche Buchgesellschaft.

Jhering, Rudolph von (1877-1883). *Der Zweck im Recht.* 2 Bds., Leipzig: Breitkopf & Hartel.

Kada, Tetsuji (1928). *Kinse Shakaigaku Seiritushi* [Formative history of modern sociology], Tokyo: Iwanami Press.

Kant, Immanuel (1884). *Kritik der reinen Vernunft,* herausgegeben von Benno Erdmann. Hamburg & Leipzig: Voss.

Karlowa, Otto (1885-1901). *Römische Rechtsgeschichte.* 3 Bds., Leipzig: Veit & Comp.

Kasahara, Hidehiko (2001). *Rekidai Tennoh soran* [The complete catalog of the Japanese emperors]. Tokyo: Chuoh Koron sha.

Kasahara, Kazuo (Ed.) (1988). *Nihon no rekishi dekigoto jiten* [The encyclopedia of events in Japanese history]. Tokyo: Shuei-sha.

Kato, Hiroyuki (1868). *Rikken Seitai Ryaku* [An outline of constitutionalism]. Tokyo: Kokusanro.

Kato, Hiroyuki (1870). *Shinsei Taii* [A summary of just governance]. Tokyo: Inada Sahei.

Kato, Hiroyuki (1875). *Kokutai Shinron* [The new theory of state constitution]. Tokyo: Inada Sahei.

Kato, Hiroyuki (1882). *Jinken Shinron* [The new theory of human rights]. Tokyo: Maruzen Press.

Kato, Hiroyuki (1893). *Kyosha no Kenri no Kyoso* [The struggle for rights of the powerful]. Tokyo: Tetsugakushoin Press.

Kato, Hiroyuki (1911). *Kirisutokyo no Gaidoku* [The harmful influence of Christianity]. Tokyo: Kinkodo Press.

Kawai, Takao & Takemura, Hideki (1998). *Kindai Nihon Shakaigakusha Shoden* [Brief biographies of modern Japanese sociologists]. Tokyo: Keiso Shobo Press.

Kawamura, N. (1994). *Sociology and society in Japan.* London: Kegan Paul International.

Kawasaki, Kyu-ichi (1982). *Takebe Tongo Hakase Ryakuden* [A biography of doctor Tongo Takebe]. Niigata: Hokuto Press.

Keally, C. T. (1991). A model for the origins of Japanese paleolithic. Paper presented at the 36th International Conference of Orientalists in Tokyo, Japan, May 20, 1991. Retrieved April 10, 2005, from http://www.t-net.ne.jp/~keally/Hoax/icoj91.

Kirkup, Thomas (1887). *Inquiry into socialism*. London & New York: Longmans.

Kirkup, Thomas (1892). *A history of socialism*. London: Black.

Knies, Karl (1853). *Die politische Oekonomie vom Standpunkte der geschichtlichen Methode*. Braunschweig: C. A. Schwetschke und Sohn.

Kohler, Josef (1897). *Zur Urgeschichte der Ehe: Totemismus, Gruppenehe, Mutterrecht*. Stuttgart: Enke.

Kovalevsky, Maksim M. (1890). *Tableau des Origines et de l'Evolution de la Famille et de la Propriété*. Stockholm: Samson & Wallin.

Krohn, (Ed.) (1880). *Beiträge zur Kenntniss und Würdigung der Sociologie*. Jena: Fischer.

Kroopf, S., Engelman, T., Zwick, E., Herskivitz, Cruise, T., & Wagner, P. (Producers) (2003). Field, Solomon, Mulvehill & Ward (Executive Producers) & Zwick, E. (Director). *The Last Samurai* [Motion picture]. Warner Brother Pictures.

Ladd, George T. (1890). *Introduction to philosophy: An Inquiry after a rational system of scientific principles in their relation to ultimate reality*. New York: Scribner.

Lamarck, Jean-Baptiste (1809). *Philosophie Zoologique*. 2 tomes, Paris: Dentu.

Lamprecht, Karl (1896). *Alte und neue Richtungen in der Geschichtswissenschaft*. Berlin: Gaertners & Heyfelder.

Landmann, Max (1896). *Der Souveränitätsbegriff bei den französischen Theoretikern, von Jean Bodin bis auf Jean Jacques Rousseau: ein Beitrag zur Entwickelungsgeshichte de Souveränitätsbegriffes*. Leipzig: Veit.

Lange, Friedrich A. (1866). *Geschichte der Materialismus* und Kritik *seiner Bedeutung in der Gegenwart*. Iserlohn: J. Baedeker.

Langlois, Charles-Victor, & Seignobos, Charles (1898). *Introduction aux Etudes historiques*. Paris: Hachette.

Lazarus, Moritz (1855-1896). *Das Leben der Seele in Monographieen über seine Erscheinungen und Gesetze*. 3 Bds., Berlin: F. Dummler.

Le Bon, Gustave (1894). *Les Lois Psychologiques de l'Evolution des Peuples*. Paris: Alcan.

Le Bon, Gustave (1895). *Psychologie des Foules*. Paris: Alcan.

Le Bon, Gustave (1898). *Psychologie du Socialisme*. Paris: Alcan.

Lecky, William E.H. (1865). *History of the rise and influence of the spirit of rationalism in Europe*. 2 vols., London: Longmans.

Legouvé, Ernst (1864). *Histoire morale des Femmes*. Paris: Didier.

Leibniz, Gottfried W. von (1667). *Nova Methodus discendae docendaeque Jurisprudentiae*.

Le Play, Frédéric (1864). *La Réforme sociale en France: déduite de l'Observation comparée des Peuples européens*. 6e ed., 4 tomes, Paris: Dentu.

Le Play, Frédéric (1874). *L'Organisation de la Famille*. Paris: Bibliothecaire de l'OEuvre Saint-Michel.

Le Play, Frédéric (1876). *La Réforme en Europe et le salut en France: le programme des Unions de la paix sociale*, avec une introduction de M. H. A. Munro Butler Johnstone, . . . par M. F. Le Play. Tours, A. Mame et fils. Les Unions de la paix sociale, publications du comité de la bibliothèque.

Le Play, Frédéric (1881). *La Constitution Essentielle de l'Humanité*. Paris: Dentu.

Leroy-Beaulieu, Paul (1888). *Le Travail des Femmes au 19 Siècle*. Paris: Charpentier.

Letourneau, Charles (1876). *La Biologie*. Paris: Reinwald.

Letourneau, Charles (1887). *L'Evolution de la Morale*. Paris: Delahaye & Lecrosnier.

Letourneau, Charles (1888). *L'Evolution du Mariage et de la Famille*. Paris: Adrien Delahaye & Emile Lecrosnier.

Letourneau, Charles (1889). *L'Evolution de la Propriété*. Paris: Lecrosnier & Babe.

Letourneau, Charles (1891a). *L'Evolution Juridique dans les Diverses Races Humaines*. Paris: Lecrosnier & Babe.

Letourneau, Charles (1891b). *Science et Matérialisme*. Paris: Reinwald.

Letourneau, Charles (1892). *La Sociologie: d'apres l'Ethnographie*. Paris: Reinwald.

Letourneau, Charles (1895a). *L'Evolution de la Guerre*. Paris: L. Bataille

Letourneau, Charles (1895b). *La Guerre dans les Diverses Races Humaines*. Paris: L. Bataille.

Levy-Bruhl, Lucien (1900). *La philosophie d'Auguste Comte*. Paris: Alcan.

Library of Congress Country Studies (1994). *Japan*. Retrieved from http://lcweb2.loc.gov/frd/cs/jptoc.html on March 3, 2005.

Lietz, Hermann (1891). *Die Probleme im Begriff der Gesellschaft bei Auguste Comte im Gesamtzusammenhange seines Systems*. Jena: G. Neuenhahn.

Lilienfeld, Paul von (1873-1881). Gedanken über die Socialwissenschaft der Zukunft, 5 Bds, Mitau:Behre. Vol. 1. Die menschliche Gesellschaft als realer Organismus, 1873; Vol. 2., Die socialenGesetze, 1875; Vol. 3., Die sociale Psychophysik, 1877; Vol. 4., Die sociale Physiologie, 1879; Vol. 5., Die Religion betrachtet vom Standpunkte der real-genetischen Socialwissenschaft, 1881.

Lilienfeld, Paul von (1896). *La Pathologie Sociale*. Paris: Giard & Briere.

Lilienfeld, Paul von (1898). Zur Vertheidigung der organischen Methode in der Sociologie, Berlin: Reimer.

Lindner, Gustav A. (1871). *Ideen zur Psychologie der Gesellschaft, als Grundlage der Sozialwissenschaft*. Wien: Carl Gerold's sohn.

Lippert, Julius (1883-1884). *Allgemeine Geschichte des Priesterthums*. 2 Bds., Berlin: Hofmann.

Lippert, Julius (1884). *Die Geschichte der Familie*. Stuttgart: Enke.

Lippert, Julius (1885-1886). *Die Kulturgeschichte in einzelnen Hauptstucken*. 3 Bds., Leipzig: Freytag.

Lippert, Julius (1886-1887). *Kulturgeschichte der Menschheit in ihrem organischen Aufbau*. 2 Bds., Stuttgart: Enke.

Littré, Paul M. E. (1863). *Auguste Comte et la Philosophie Positive*. Paris: Hachette.

Littré, Paul M. E. (1868). *Principes de Philosophie positive par Auguste Comte.* Paris: J. B. Bailliere.

Locke, John (1689). *The second treatise on civil government.*

Loria, Achille (1900). *Die Soziologie: ihre Aufgabe, ihre Schulen und ihre neuesten Fortschrifte.* Jena: Fischer.

Lorimer, George C. (1886). *Studies in social life: A review of the principles, practices, and problems of society.* London: Sampson Low, Marston, Searle & Rivington.

Lourbet, Jacques (1900). *Le Problème des Sexes.* Paris: Giard & Briere.

Lubbock, John (1870). *On the origin of civilisation.* London: Longmans.

Lubbock, John (1872). *Prehistoric times as illustrated by ancient remains and the manners and customs of modern savages.* New York: Appleton.

Lyell, Charles (1841). *Elements of geology.* London: Murray.

Mackay, Thomas (1896). *Methods of social reform: Essays critical and constructive.* London: Murray.

Mackenzie, John S. (1890). *An introduction to social philosophy.* New York: Macmillan.

Machiavelli, Niccolo (1531). *Discorsi sopra la Prima Deca di Tito Livio.*

Machiavelli, Niccolo (1532). *Il Principe.*

Maine, Henry J.S. (1861). *Ancient law.* London: Dent.

Maine, Henry J.S. (1872). *Village-communities in the east and in the west.* London: Murray.

Maine, Henry J.S. (1875). *Lectures on the early history of institutions.* London: Murray.

Maine, Henry J.S. (1883). *Dissertations on early law and custom.* London: Murray.

Majoranna, Angelo (1891). *I Primi Principii della Sociologia.* Roma: Ermanno Loescher.

Malon, Bénoit (1879). *Histoire du Socialisme.* Lugano: F. Veladini.

Malon, Bénoit (1890). *Le Socialisme Integral.* Paris: Alcan.

Malthus, Thomas R. (1798). *An essay on the principles of population.*

Marsilius de Padova (1328). *Defensor Pacis.*

Martineau, Harriet (1894-1895). *La Philosophie Positive d'Auguste Comte, traduite de l'anglais par Ch. Avezac-Lavigne.* 2 tomes, Paris: L. Bahl.

Masaryk, Tomas G. (1899). *Die philosophischen und sociologischen Grundlagen des Marxismus: Studien zur socialen Frage.* Wien: Konegen.

Mayo-Smith, Richmond (1895). *Statistics and sociology.* New York: Macmillan.

Mayr, Georg von (1877). *Die Gesetzmässigkeit im Gesellschaftsleben: Statistische Studien.* München: Oldenbourg.

McLennan, John F. (1876). *Primitive marriage: an inquiry into the origin of the form of capture in marriage ceremonies.* 2 vols., London: Bernard Quaritch.

Meitzen, August (1886). *Geschichte, Theorie und Technik der Statistik.* Berlin: Hertz.

Menger, Carl (1883). *Untersuchungen über die Mehode der Social wissencshaften und der politischen Oekonomie insbesondere.* Leipzig: Duncker & Humblot.

MetroMuseum (2005). Metropolitan Museum timeline of art history, Jamon Culture retrieved March 18, 2005, from http://www.metmuseum.org/toah/hd/jomo/hd_jomo.htm.

Meyer, Georg (1878). *Lehrbuch des deutschen Staatsrechts*. Leipzig: Ducker & Humblot.

Mill, John Stuart (1843). *A system of logic, ratiocinative and inductive: being a connected view of the principles of evidence, and the methods of scientific investigation*. London: John W. Parker.

Mill, John Stuart (1848). *Political economy: With some of their applications to social philosophy*. London: John W. Parker.

Mill, John Stuart (1870). *The Subjection of Women*, New York: Appleton.

Miyake, Setsurei (1855-1858). *Geschichte und Literatur des Staatswissenschaften*. 3 Bds., Erlangen: Enke.

Miyake, Setsurei (Yujiro) (1891a). *Shin Zen, Bi, Nihonjin* [The Japanese: truth, good, and beauty]. Seikyosha Press.

Miyake, Setsurei (1891b). *Gi, Aku Shu, Nihonjin* [The Japanese: false, evil, and ugly]. Seikyosha Press.

Mohl, Robert von (1855-1858). *Geschichte und Literatur des Staatswissenschaften*, 3 Bds., Erlangen: Enke.

Mommsen, Theodor (1854). *Römische Geschichte*. 5 Bds., Leipzig: Weidmann.

Montesquieu, Charles de (1734). *Considérations sur les Causes de la Grandeur des Romains et de Leur Décadence*.

Montesquieu, Charles de (1748). *De l'Esprit des Lois*.

More, Thomas (1515). *Utopia*.

Morgan, Lewis H. (1871). *Systems of Consanguinity and Affinity*. Washington, DC: *Smithsonian Contributions to Knowledge*. No 218. Reprinted (1997) with introduction by Elizabeth Tooker. Lincoln: Univeristy of Nebraska Press.

Morgan, Lewis H. (1877). *Ancient society: Researches in the lines of human progress from savagery through barbarism to civilization*. Chicago: Charles H. Kerr.

Mucke, Johann R. (1895). *Horde und Familie in ihrer urgeschichtlichen Entwickelung*. Stuttgart: Enke.

Nishio, K. (1999). The Meiji Restoration, more revolutionary than western revolutions. Original Chapter 21: "Seiyou no Kakumei yorimo Kakumeiteki datta Meiji-Ishin," "Kokumin no Rekishi"(Edited by Japanese Society for History Textbook Reform, Fusosha "The history of Japanese people in the world.") Retrieved March 10, 2005, from zttp://www26.tok2.com/home2/nishionitiroku/essays/1999103021.html.

Novicow, Jacque (1886). *La Politique Internationale*. Paris: Alcan.

Novicow, Jacque (1893). *Les Luttes entre Sociétés Humaines et leurs Phases Successives*. [Fights Between Human Societies and Their Successive Phases]. Paris: Alcan.

Novicow, Jacque (1894a). *La Guerre et ses Prétendus Bienfaits.*[War and its Previous Benefits] Paris: A. Hake and Co.

Novicow, Jacque (1894b). *Les Gaspillages des Sociétés Moderne: Contribution à l'étude de la question sociale*. Paris: Alcan.

Novicow, Jacque (1895). *Essai de Notation Sociologique*. [Sociological Test of Notation] Paris: V. Giard & E. Brière.

Novicow, Jacque (1897). *Conscience et Volonté Sociales*. Paris: Giard & Briere.

Oda, S., & Keally, C. T. (1986). A critical look at the paleolithic and lower palaeo-lithic. Research in Miyagi Prefecture, Japan. Published in English in *Jinruigaku Zasshi* 94 (3), 325-361. Retrieved April 10, 2005, from http://www.ao.jpn.org/kuroshio/86criticism.html.

Okano, Tomohiko (2003). *Genji to Nihon kokuoh* [The Minamoto clan and the king of Japan]. Tokyo: Kodan-sha. Publishing.

Osborne, Henry F. (1894). *From Greeks to Darwin: an outline of the development of the evolution idea.* New York: Macmillan.

Owen, Robert (1813). *A new view of society or essays on the principle of the formation of the human character, and the application of the principle to practice.* London: T. Cadell & W. Davies.

Piche, Albert (1892). *De la Place de la Sociologie dans l'Ensembe des Connaissances humaines.* Paris.

Plato, (c 360 BCE) *The Republic* (Dialogues).

Plinius, Gaius Secundus [Pliny the Elder] (c77 CE). *Historia Naturalis.*

Ploss, Hermann, & Bartels, Max (1902). *Das Weib: in der Natur- und Völkerkunde.* Leipzig: Grieben.

Pobedonostzeff, Constantine P. (1897). *Questions Religieuses, Sociales et Politiques.* Paris. (The original title of this book is *Recueil de Moscou*, 1896.)

Poole, Reginald L. (1884). *Illustrations of the history of medieval thought: In the departments of theology and ecclesiastical politics.* London: Williams & Norgate.

Posada, Adolfo (1896). Theories modernes sur les Origines de la Famille, de la société et del'Etat. Frantz de Zeltner (tr.), Paris: Giard & Briere.

Puchta, Georg Friedrich (1844). *Pandekten.* Leipzig: Johann Ambrosius Barth.

Pufendorf, Samuel (1660). *Elementorum Jurisprudentiae Universalis, Libri Duo.*

Pufendorf, Samuel (1672). *De Jure Naturae et Gentium.*

Quételet, Adolphe (1848). *Du Système social et des Lois qui le Regissent.* Paris: Guillaumin.

Quételet, Adolphe (1869). *Physique Sociale ou Essai sur le développement des Facultés de l'Homme.* 2 tomes, Bruxelles: Muquardt.

Rabutaux, Auguste P. (1851). *De la Prostitution en Europe.* Paris: Sere.

Ranke, Leopold von (1881-1888). *Weltgeschichte.* 8 Bds., Leipzig: Duncker & Humblot.

Rappoport, Charles (1896). *Zur Charakteristik der Methode und Hauptrichtungen der Philosophie der Geschichte.* Bern: Siebert.

Ratzenhofer, Gustav (1893a). *Wesen und Zweck der Politik: als Theil der Sociologie und Grundlage der Staatswissenschaften.* Lepzig: Brockhaus.

Ratzenhofer, Gustav (1893b). *Der Zweck der Politik im allgemeinen.* 3 Bds., Leipzig: Brockhaus.

Ratzenhofer, Gustav (1898). *Die Sociologische Erkenntnis: Positive Philosophie des socialen Lebens.* Leipzig: Brockhaus.

Reich, Eduard (1875). *Studien über die Frauen.* Jena: Hermann Costenoble.

Reinhold, Karl L. (1790). *Das Fundament der Elementarphilosophie betreffend.* Jena: Johann Michael Mauke.

Reischauer, E.O. (1970). *Japan: The story of a nation.* New York, NY: Knopf.

Ribot, Paul (1882). *Exposé Critique des Doctrines Sociales de M. Le Play.* Paris: Plon.

Rivier, A. (1893). *La Famille au Droit romain.*

Ricardo, David (1817). *Principle of political economy and taxation.* London: Murray.

Rigolage, Emile (1897). *La Sociologie par Auguste Comte.* Paris: Alcan.

Robertson, John M. (1891). *Modern humanists: sociological studies of Carlyle, Mill, Emerson, Arnold, Ruskin, and Spencer: with an epilogue on social reconstruction and a critique of Carlyle.* London: S. Sonnenschein.

Robinet, Jean François (n.d.). *La Philosophie Positive: Auguste Comte and M. Pierre Laffitte.* Paris: Bailliere.

Rocholl, Rudolf (1893). *Philosophie der Geschichte: Darstellung und Kritik der Versuche zu einem Aufbau derselben.* Göttingen: Vandenhoeck & Ruprecht.

Rogières, Raoul (1884). *Histoire de la Société française au Moyen-age: 987-1483.* 2 tomes, 3e ed., Paris: A. Laisney.

Roscher, Wilhelm G. (1843). *Grundriss zu Vorlesungen über die Staatswirthschaft: Nach geschichtlicher Methode.* Göttingen: Druck & Verlag der Dieterichschen Buchhandlung.

Roscher, Wilhelm G. (1854). *Die Grundlagen der Nationaloekonomie: ein Hand- und Lesebuch fur Geschaftsmanner und Studierende.* Stuttgart: Cotta.

Ross, Edward A. (1901). *Social control: A survey of the foundations of order.* New York: Macmillan.

Rousseau, Jean-Jacques (1754). *Discours sur l'Origine de l'Inégalité parmi les Hommes* [Discourse on the origin and basis of inequality among men].

Rousseau, Jean-Jacques (1755). Discourse on Political Economy.

Rousseau, Jean-Jacques (1762a). *Du Contrat Social, ou Principe de Droit Politique* [The social contract or principles of political right]. Amsterdam: M. M. Rey.

Rousseau, Jean-Jacques (1762b). *Emile, ou de l'Education.* [Émile, on Education]

Rümelin, Gustav (1875-1894). *Reden und Aufsätze.* 3 Bds., Leipzig: Mohr.

Runge, Max (1896). *Das Weib in seiner geschlechtlichen Eigenart.* Berlin: Springer.

Sako, Teruhito. (1999). Takebe, Tongo no shakai-shinnkaron wo sai-hyoka suru. [Reevaluating the social evolution theory of Tongo Takebe.] Paper presented at the 72nd Annual meeting of the Japan Sociological Society. Tokyo, Japan.

Santamaria de Paredes, Vincente (1896). *El Concepto de Organismo Social.* Madrid.

Sargant, William L. (1860). *Robert Owen and his social philosophy.* London: Smith Elder.

Savigny, Friedrich K. von (1815-1834). *Geschichte des römischen Rechts im Mittelalter.* 7 Bds., Heidelberg: Mohr.

Say, Jean-Baptiste (1803). *Traité d'Economie Politique: ou simple Exposition.* Paris: Crapelet.

Schäffle, Albert E. (1875-1878). *Bau und Leben des socialen Körpers.* 4 Bds., Tübingen: Laupp.

Schirokauer, C. (1993). *A brief history of Japanese civilization.* Fort Worth, TX: Harcourt Brace & Company.

Schlegel, Friedrich von (1829). *Philosophie der Geschichte.* 2 Bds., Wien: C. Schaumburg.

Schlosser, Friedrich C. (1844-1857). *Schlosser's Weltgeschichte, für das deutsche Volk.* 19 Bds., Frankfurt: Franz Varrentrapp.

Schmidt-Warneck, Fedor (1889). *Die Sociologie im Umrisse ihrer Grundpricipe.* Braunschweig: Selbstverlag des Verfassers.

Schmoller, Gustav (1888). *Zur Litteraturgeschichte der Staats- und Socialwissenschaften.* Leipzig: Duncker & Humblot.

Seckendorf, Veit Ludwig von (1685). *Der Christenstaat.*

Shimizu, Ikutaro (1935). *Shakai to Kojin: Shakaigaku Seiritsushi* [Society and individual: The formative history of sociology]. Tokyo: Tohkohshoin Press.

Shimizu, Ikutaro (1936). *Shakai to Kojin: Shakaigaku Seiritsushi* [Society and Individual: A Study on the Formative History of Sociology], Toko Shoin Press, 1936.

Shimizu, Ikutaro (1937). *Ryugen Higo* [Rumors]. Tokyo: Nihonhyoronsha Press.

Shimizu, Ikutaro (1972). *Rinrigaku Noto* [Notes on ethics]. Tokyo: Iwanami Press.

Simcox, Edith Jemima (1894). *Primitive Civilizations; or, Outlines of the History of Ownership in archaic Communities,* 2 vols., London: Sonnenschein, New York: Macmillan.

Simmel, Georg (1890). *Über sociale Differenzierung: Sociologische und psychologische Untersuchungen.* Leipzig: Duncker & Humblot.

Simmel, Georg (1892). *Die Probleme der Geschichtsphilosophie: eine erkenntnistheoretische Studie.* Leipzig: Duncker & Humblot.

Simmel, Georg (1895). The problem of sociology. *Annals of the American Academy of Political and Social Science.* 6, 3, 52-63.

Small, Albion W., & Vincent, George E. (1894). *An introduction to the study of society.* New York: Appleton.

Smith, Adam (1776). *An inquiry into the nature and causes of the wealth of nations.* Dublin: Whitestone.

Sommer, Hugo (1885). *Die positive Philosophie: August Comte's.* Berlin: Carl Hab.

Spencer, Herbert (1851). *Social statics.* London: J. Chapman.

Spencer, Herbert (1862). *First principles.* London: Williams & Norgate.

Spencer, Herbert (1864). *The sciences: Reasons for dissenting from the philosophy of M. Comte. Published in Essays: Scientific, Political, and Speculative* -Vol II. London: Williams & Norgate. Reprinted (1968) Berkeley: Glendessary.

Spencer, Herbert (1864-1867). *The principles of biology.* 2 vols., London: Williams & Norgate.

Spencer, Herbert (1873). *Study of sociology.* London: King.

Spencer, Herbert (1876-1896). *The principles of sociology.* 3 vols., London: Williams & Norgate.

Ssuma Ch'ien, Shin Chi (1961). *Records of the grand historian of China* (ca. BCE 90). Burton Watson (tr.), 2 vols., New York: Columbia University Press. (originally written around BCE 90).

Stahl, Friedrich J. (1846-1847). *Geschichte der Rechtsphilosophie.* 3 Bds., Heidelberg: Mohr.

Stammhammer, Joseph (1893-1906). *Bibliographie des Socialismus und Communismus.* 3 Bds., Jena: Fischer.

Stammhammer, Joseph (1896-1912). *Bibliographie der Social-Politk.* 2 Bds., Jena: Fischer.

Starcke, Carl N. (1888). *Die primitive Familie in ihrer Entstehung und Entwickelung.* Leipzig: Brockhaus.

Stein, Lorenz von (1852-1856). *System der Staatswissenschaft,* 2 Bds., Stuttgart & Tübingen: Cotta.

Stein, Lorenz von (1856). *Die Gesellschaftslehre.* Stuttgart: Cotta.

Stein, Lorenz von (1876). *Gegenwart und Zukunft der Rechts- und Staatswissenschaft Deutschlands.* Stuttgart: Cotta.

Stein, Ludwig von (1842). *Der Socialismus und Communismus des heutigen Frankreichs: ein Beitrag zur Zeitgeschichte.* Leipzig: Wigand.

Stein, Ludwig von (1850). *Der Begriff der Gesellschaft und die sociale Geschichte der Französischen Revolution bis zum Jahre 1830.* 3 Bds., Leipzig: Wigand.

Stein, Ludwig von (1897). *Die soziale Frage im lichte der Philosophie: Vorlesungen über Sozialphilosophie und ihre Geschichte.* Stuttgart: Enke.

Stein, Ludwig von (1898). *Wesen und Aufgabe der Sociologie: eine Kritik der organischen Methode in der Sociologie.* Berlin: Reimer.

Steiner, Jesse Frederick (1936). The Development and Present Status of Sociology in Japanese Universities. *The American Journal of Sociology, 41,* 707-722.

Steinthal, Heymann (1864). *Philologie, Geschichte und Psychologie in ihren gegenseitigen Beziehungen.* Berlin: F. Dummler.

Steinthal, Heymann (1871). *Einleitung in die Psychologie und Sprachwissenschaft.* Berlin: F. Dummler.

Steinthal, Heymann (1885). *Allgemeine Ethik.* Berlin: G. Reimer.

Stewart, Balfour (1873). *The conservation of energy.* New York: Appleton.

Stintzing, Roderich von (1880-1910). *Geschichte der deutschen Rechtswissenschaf.* 4 Bds., München: R. Oldenbourg. [Takebe listed this as Stintzing: *Deutsche Rechtsgeschichte.* We believe that the reference above is the correct reference Eds.]

Stuckenberg, John H. W. (1898). *Introduction to the study of sociology.* New York: Armstrong.

Sully, James (1877). *Pessimism: A history and a criticism.* London: King.

Tait, P. G. (1876). *Lectures on some recent advances in physical science with a special lecture on force.* Second edition revised. Macmillan: London.

Takata, Yasuma (1922). *Shakaigaku Gairon* [Introduction to sociology]. Tokyo: Iwanami Press.

Takata, Yasuma (1925). *Kaikyu oyobi Daisanshikan* [Class system and the third view of history]. Tokyo: Kaizosha Press.

Takata, Yasuma (1940). *Seiryokuron* [A theory of powers]. Tokyo: Tokyodaigaku Keizaigakubu.

Takebe, Tongo (1897). *Riku Shozan* [Lu Hsiang-shan]. Tokyo: Tetsugakushoin Press.

Takebe, Tongo (1898). *Tetsugaku Taikan* [Overview of philosophy]. Tokyo: Kinkodo Press.

Takebe, Tongo (1902). *Seiyu Manpitsu* [Essays on the study-abroad in west Europe]. Reprinted Tokyo:Yumani Shobo Press.

Takebe, Tongo (1903). *Rekishi-kenkyu no Seishin wo* Ronjite Rekishi-tetsugaku to *Bunmei-shi ni Oyobu* [Of historical study, philosophy of history, and civilizational history]. *Shigaku Zasshi* [History Journal] May, Meiji 36.

Takebe, Tongo (1904). *Shakaigaku Josetsu* [General sociology, vol. 1, prolegomenon of sociology]. Tokyo: Kinkodo Press.

Takebe, Tongo (1905). *Shakai Rigaku* [General sociology, vol. 2, social logic]. Tokyo: Kinkodo Press.

Takebe, Tongo (1909). *Shakai Seigaku* [General sociology, vol. 3, social statics]. Tokyo: Kinkodo Press.

Takebe, Tongo (1918). *Shakai Dogaku* [General sociology, vol. 4, social dynamics]. Tokyo: Kinkodo Press.

Takemitsu, Makoto (1999). *Han to Nippon-jin: Gendai ni ikiru "okuni-gara"* [Feudal states and the Japanese: The provincial characteristics that are still alive today]. Tokyo: PHP Kenkyu sho.

Takeuchi, S. A. (2003). Was the chonin class in edo period allowed to wear/carry swords? Retrieved March 20, 2005, from http://www2.una.edu/Takeuchi/ DrT_ Jpn_Culture_files/Nihon_to_files/Chonin_sword.htm.

Takinami, Sadako (2004). *Josei Tennoh.* [The female emperors of Japan]. Tokyo: Shuei-sha.

Tarde, Jean-Gabriel (1890a). *Les Lois de l'Imitation: Etude Sociologique.* Paris: Alcan.

Tarde, Jean-Gabriel (1890b). *La Philosophie Pénale.* Lyon: A. Storck.

Tarde, Jean-Gabriel (1895a). *La Logique Sociale.* Paris: Alcan.

Tarde, Jean-Gabriel (1895b). *Essais et Mélanges Sociologiques.* Paris: A. Maloine.

Tarde, Jean-Gabriel (1898a). *Les Lois Sociales: Esquisse d'une Sociologie.* Paris: Alcan.

Tarde, Jean-Gabriel (1898b). *Ecrits de Psychologie Sociale.* Paris: Giard & Briere.

Tarde, Jean-Gabriel (1899). *Les Transformations de Pouvoir.* Paris: Alcan.

Tcheko (1884). *Essai de Sociologie: Science de l'Organisation de la Société Humanitairement Heureuse.* (French tr.) Paris: A. Ghio.

Thomson, William [Lord Kelvin] (1891-1894). *Popular lectures and addresses.* London: Macmillan.

Thomson, William [Lord Kelvin] & Tait, Peter G. (1872). *Treatise on natural philosophy.* 2 vols., Cambridge: Cambridge University Press.

Tillier, Louis (1898). *Le Mariage, sa Genèse, son Evolution.* Paris: Société de Editions Scientifiques.

Toda, Teizo (1926). *Kazoku no Kenkyu* [Study of family]. Kyoto: Kobundo Press.

Toda, Teizo (1933). *Shakai Chosa* [Social survey]. Tokyo: Jichosha Press.

Toda, Teizo (1934). *Kazoku to Kon-in* [Marriage and family]. Tokyo: Chubunkan Press.

Tönnies, Ferdinand (1887). *Gemeinschaft und Gesellschaft: Abhandlung des Communismus und des Socialismus als empirischer Culturformen.* Leipzig: Fues's Verlag.

Tönnies, Ferdinand (1894). Neuere Philosophie der Geschichte: Hegel, Marx, Comte. *Archiv für Geschichte der Philosophie.* Bd 7, pp. 486-515.

Toyama, Masakazu (1880). *Minken Benwaku* [The arguments for people's rights]. Tokyo: Toyama Masakazu.

Toyama, Masakazu (1886). *Engeki Kairyoron Shiko* [A plan of reformation of theaters]. Tokyo: Maruzen Press.

Toyama, Masakazu (1890). *Nihon Kaiga no Mirai* [The future of Japanese paintings]. Tokyo. (Privately published.)

Toyama, Masakazu (1895a). *Nihon Chishiki Dotokushi* [The history of Japanese intellect and morals]. Tokyo: Maruzen Press.

Toyama, Masakazu (1895b). *Shintaishi Kashu* [The collection of new style poems]. Tokyo: Dainihontosho Press.

Treitschke, Heinrich G. (1859). *Die Gesellschaftswissenschaft: ein kritischer Versuch.* Leipzig: S. Hirzel.

Treitschke, Heinrich G. (1897-1898). *Politik: vorlesungen gehalten an der Universität zu Berlin.* 2 Bds., Leipzig: Hirzel.

Tylor, Edward B. (1873). *Primitive culture: Researches into the development of mythology, philosophy, religion, language, art, and custom.* 2 vols., London: Murray.

Tyndall, John (1863). *Heat: A mode of motion.* London: Longman

Ueberweg, Friedrich (1857). *System der Logik und Geschichte der logischen Lehren.* Bonn: Adolph Marcus.

Ueberweg, Friedrich (1872). *A history of philosophy: From Thales to the present time.* Geo. S. Morris (tr. from the 4th German edition), with additions by Noah Porter, London: Hodder & Stoughton.

Vadala-Papale, Giuseppe (1882). *Darwinismo Naturale e Darwinismo Sociale.* Torino: E. Loescher.

Vandervelde, Emile, Demoor, Jean, & Massart, Jean (1897). *L'Evolution Régressive en Biologie et en Sociologie.* Paris: Alcan.

Vanni, Icilio (1888). *Prime Linee di un Programma Critico di Sociologia.* Perugia: V. Santucci.

Vico, Giovanni Battista (1720). *Il Diritto Universale* [Universal Rights] translated by Giorgio Pinton and Margaret Diehl. Amsterdam and Atlanta: Editions Rodopi B.V., 2000.

Vignes, Maurice (1897). *La Science Sociale: D'àpres les Principes de Le Play et de ses Continuateurs.* Paris: Giard et Brière.

Waentig, Heinrich (1894). *Auguste Comte und seine Bedeutung für die Entwicklung der Socialwissenschaft.* Leipzig: Duncker & Humblot.

Wagner, Adolf H. G. (1892-1893). *Grundlegung der politischen Oekonomie.* 3 Aufl., Leipzig: Winter.

Wallace, Alfred Russel (1864). The Origin of Human Races and the Antiquity of Man Deduced From the Theory of "Natural Selection" *Journal of the Anthropological Society of London* 2: clviii-clxx (followed by an account of related discussion on pp. clxx-clxxxvii). Paper read at the ASL meeting of 1 March 1864.

Wallace, Alfred Russel (1870). *Contributions to the Theory of Natural Selection. A Series of Essays.* Macmillan & Co., London & New York.

Walter, Ferdinand (1853). *Deutsche Rechtsgeschichte* (2nd ed.) Bonn: Adolph Marcus.

Ward, Lester F. (1883). *Dynamic sociology or applied social science, as based upon statical sociology and the less complex sciences.* 2 vols., New York: Appleton.

Ward, Lester F. (1893). *The psychic factors of civilization.* Boston: Ginn.

Ward, Lester F. (1898). *Outlines of sociology.* London & New York: Macmillan.

Ward, Lester F. (1903). *Pure sociology: A treatise on the origin and spontaneous development of society.* New York: Macmillan.

Warschauer, Otto (1892). *Geschichte des Socialismus und neueren Kommunismus.* Leipzig: Gustav Fock.

Wasserrab, Karl (1900). *Sozialwissenschaft und sociale Frage.* Leipzig: Duncker & Humblot.

Watanabe, Shujiro (1893). *Sekai ni okeru Nihon-jin* [The Japanese within the world]. Tokyo: Keiaizasshisha Press.

Weber, Max (1904). *The protestant ethic and the spirit of capitalism.* Talcott Parson (1930), (tr). New York: Charles Scribner's Sons.

Weber, Max (1915-1920). *Die Wirtschaftsethik der Weltreligionen: Konfuzianismus und Taoismus.* Schriften. [Economic ethics in world religions: Confucianism and taoism]. Reprinted (1989) Tübingen: J.C.B.Mohr.

Weitzel, Johannes (1832-1833). *Geschichte der Staatswissenschaft.* 2 Bds., Stuttgart & Tübingen: Cotta.

Westermarck, Edward (1893). *Geschichte der menschlichen Ehe.* Berlin: Costenoble.

Worms, René (1895a). Les Etudes Récents de Sociologie, *Revue Internationale de Sociologiogie*, Année 3.

Worms, René (1895b). *Organisme et Société.* Paris: Giard & Briere.

Worms, René (1896a). *De Natura et Methodo Sociologiae.* Paris: Giard & Briere.

Worms, René (1896b). *La Science et l'Art en Economie Politique.* Paris: Giard & Briere.

Worms, René (1903-1907). *Philosophie des Sciences Sociales*, 3 tomes, Paris: Giard & Briere.

Wundt, Wilhelm M. (1896). *Grundriss der Psychologie.* Leipzig: Engelmann.

Wundt, Wilhelm M. (1900-1911). *Volkerpsychologie: eine Untersuchung der Entwicklungsgesetze von Sprache, Mythus und Sitte.* 10 Bds., Leipzig: Engelmann, Stuttgart: Kroner.

Yamasa Institute (2005). *Japanese history online* [various periods]. Retrieved March 7, 2005, from http://www.japan-101.com/history/history_period_yayoi.htm

Yawata, Kazuo. (2004). *Edo 300 han saigo no hanshu.* [The last daimyo lords of the 300 States in the Edo period.] Tokyo, Japan: Kohbun Sha.

Yokota, Fuyuhiko (2002). *Nippon no rekishi 16: Tenka taihei* [Japanese history vol. 16, The period of peaceful society]. Tokyo: Kodan-sha Publishing.

Yoneda, Shotaro (1919-1920). *Bankin Shakaishiso no Kenkyu* [The study of current social thoughts]. 3 vols., Kyoto: Kobundo Press.

Yoneda, Shotaro (1920-1921). *Gendai Shakaimondai no Shakaigakuteki Kohsatsu* [Sociological inquiry on modern social problems]. 2 vols., Kyoto: Kobundo Press.

Yoneda, Shotaro (1924). *Rekishitetsugaku no Shomondai* [The issues of the philosophy of history]. Kyoto: Kobundo Press.

Yoneda, Shotaro (1927). *Shakaigaku no Gainen no Hihan oyobi Juritsu* [A critical observation on the sociological concepts: To establish sociology], *Nihon Shakaigakuin Nenpo* [Annals of Japan Sociological Association], *1*, .4-5.Yawata, Kazuo (2004). *Edo 300 han saigo no hanshu* [The last daimyō lords of the 300 states in the Edo period]. Tokyo: Kohbun Sha.

Yoshida, Shoin (1868). *Tokugawa Seikyo-ko* [Reflection on Tokugawa politics].

Index

Page numbers followed by the letter "f" indicate figures.